PATENT SHOCK SERIES ®

GREEN FIELDS PATENTING

BUILDING PATENT PORTFOLIOS

ROBERT D. FISH, ESQ.

Printed in the United States of America
ISBN 979-8-9876415-0-7
January 2023

To Julie and Sky, for their
unending patience and support.

Additional thanks to Dave Walston for his
incredible drawings, and to many individuals
at Fish IP Law, LLP for their ideas and
inspiration.

Table of Contents

PREFACE

Technical people tend to expect patents to protect inventions. My companion book, White Space Patenting, focuses on that goal, but with a twist. Instead of limiting guidance to the mechanics of filing applications, the focus is on writing patent applications that broadly claim underlying ideas, as opposed to mere embodiments of those ideas.

Business people tend to be much more interested in markets, i.e., to what extent patents provide barriers to entry against competitors. In this book the focus is on using patents to dominate a marketplace. To do that one needs to claim more than just the white space of an underlying idea. One needs to look over the horizon, to patent not only what the invention is, but what the invention could become. One needs to put road blocks in the paths of competitors (or at least toll booths).

A preliminary focus of Green Fields Patenting is therefore to facilitate innovation within an organization. Chapter I identifies three steps to that process, namely: (a) identifying barriers to innovation that exist within the organization; (b) figuring out how to remove those barriers; and (c) devising suitable metrics to measure the company's progress. This involves identifying offensive and defensive choke points, and filing applications to address those choke points with respect to current and contemplated technologies.

Chapter II focuses on building a portfolio, one that matches the patent strategy to the business strategy. This entails many considerations, including strategic goals, how many patent applications to file, numbers and types of patent claims.

Chapter III addresses strategic considerations in using the different types of patent applications (provisionals, utilities and PCT applications) to build a dominating portfolio.

Chapter IV discusses ways of speeding up prosecution, including description of Prioritized Examination, which can reduce time to first office action from 18 months or more, to as little as 3 -4 months.

Chapter V discusses issues of confidentiality; when applications are published, and how to file submarine applications.

Chapter VI discusses costs. Since even the most innovative efforts can be scuttled by an out-of-control patenting process, a company needs to understand how bad decisions can push patenting costs through the roof, and what to do about it.

Chapter VII discusses the major patent valuation models, including the willing buyer/seller, marginal profit, and cost/replacement models. Chapter V also provides guidance on appropriate royalty rates, and suggests strategies for resolving disparate valuations determined by opposite parties during negotiations.

Chapter VIII provides real-world suggestions on assignments, licenses, employment contracts and non-disclosure agreements.

Chapter IX discusses infringement issues. The first section provides examples and pointers on drafting opinion letters. The balance of Chapter VII addresses steps that one can take to proactively protect oneself, whether a patent holder or an alleged infringer.

Note that there is a detailed index and a table of authorities. For ease of reading, claim text is marked out in blue frames, and specification text is marked out in green frames.

Chapter I - Facilitating Innovation

Green Fields Patenting℠ begins with identifying and removing whatever barriers lie in the way of innovation. That involves putting in place a culture of innovation, implementing a strategy for capturing the innovative ideas, and using the right metrics for measuring success of the program.[1]

A)   Identifying Barriers To Innovation

Barriers to innovation can arise from many different things, including financial and other resource limitations. Obviously, if a company is having financial difficulties, and doesn't have needed laboratory or other facilities, it is likely to lose key players and will have a markedly reduced ability to innovate. On the other hand, it is often more about culture than finances. There are stories every day about minimally funded companies that innovate far ahead of their more well-heeled competitors. In our[2] experience, the most critical circumstance militating against innovation is not a lack of money or other resources, but the company culture.

(1)   Short-Sighted Company Goals

One major aspect of a company's culture is its goals. In a highly innovative company, the goal is *market dominance*. Such companies appreciate that an innovative culture is critical to reaching that goal, and is willing to trade off short term revenue for long term gains in the marketplace. Among other things, innovative companies appreciate that a significant percentage of time needs to be devoted to reading papers and attending talks, building trust and camaraderie within work groups, and pursuing other activities that don't directly or immediately relate to solving short-term problems. In a highly innovative company, the intellectual property (IP) efforts reflect those goals, with strategies and metrics focusing on the long-term and indirect benefits of a strong patent portfolio.

In contrast, the goal is often just a *comfortable market share*, even if that share is relatively small. Their intellectual property efforts are generally quite restricted as well, focusing mostly on direct licensing revenue. Their IP metrics tend to also be short-sighted, possibly focusing on nothing more than the number of invention disclosures the number of patents. Often such companies have a long history in the marketplace, with a cash cow that has brought in money for many years. Or they might have a strong reputation that could be relied upon to bring in new business. In any event, management sees little need to invest many resources on innovation, and the employees respond accordingly.

(2)   Closed Innovation Environments

Many companies kill the innovative spirit in their employees by the very structure of the office. They tend to physically isolate workers from one another, and especially from management. Innovative ideas are typically vetted in closed patent review committees, where they likely cannot benefit from ideas that might arise from crowd sourcing. Where new ideas do float to the top, they tend to be disseminated only in didactic instructional meetings, rather than being brainstormed across the company.

1   Green Fields Patenting℠ and Blue Sky Patenting℠ are service marks of Fish IP Law, LLP, for legal services in the field of intellectual property, as described herein.
2   Fish IP Law, LLP, 19900 MacArthur Blvd. Suite 810, Irvine CA 92612; www.fishiplaw.com; 949-943-8300.

The situation tends to be exacerbated where a company is split into business units. Individuals tend to interact only within their own business units, often devolving into "group think" rather than gaining the vibrancy of cross-fertilized ideas.

(3)   Excessive Focus On Individual Goals

Another cultural aspect that impacts innovation is how employees see their relationship to the company. In a highly innovative company, the personal goals of the employees tend to become conflated with *helping the*

team achieve success. Thus, an employee might say "I'm here to achieve great things with my friends." One engineer we knew years ago, who had a major role in a NASA contractor, would often say, "I'm here to put a man on the moon." Interestingly, the receptionist in that same company would also say, "I'm here to put a man on the moon." They share a common goal.

Less innovative companies interfere with innovation by focusing overmuch on individual goals. In a moderately innovative company, an employee might say that he is at the company because he loves his job, and wants to see the company succeed. He has the right approach, but he doesn't feel the excitement of being on a team.

In a minimally innovative company, employees are even further self-oriented. They might be staying at the company primarily because of the pay, or the medical benefits. Either way, an excessive focus on the individual tends to produce employees who leave the creativity to others, or worse, leave the company with great ideas, and then start a competing company.

(4)   Rejecting All But The Very Best Ideas

Yet another cultural aspect is how a company handles new ideas. Highly innovative companies focus on where an idea *could* take the company. They think "blue sky," "over-the-horizon," "green fields." In such companies, innovators recognize that *all ideas are valuable seeds*, even those that never sprout. Management has a similar attitude, wanting to see a full spectrum of ideas, including the home runs, the base hits, and even the strike outs. Far-out ideas are not summarily dismissed, but are welcomed as ways of exploring new vistas. Supporting innovation might well mean filing patent applications that don't necessarily have big commercial value.

In contrast, more moderately innovative companies tend to filter out all but the most promising new ideas. They support only the best of the innovators, and wind up excluding others from the process. Moderately innovative companies do look for the "white space" surrounding core ideas, but they never seem to reach the critical mass where the whole company is excited about the process of innovation.

Minimally innovative companies tend to put up the greatest barriers to feting new ideas. In those companies, management is mostly concerned about the bottom line for the next financial reporting period, and sees time spent innovating as time that could have been spent bringing in revenue. Unless an innovator comes up with a "game changer," he/she is usually sidetracked to merely writing up the idea and submitting it to a committee.

(5)   Inadequate Versus Formulaic Rewards

It has been said that "whatever you feed will grow", and that is certainly true in the world of innovation. Highly innovative companies find many ways to reward inventiveness, from bonuses and stock options, to recognition within the company or profession, or perhaps freedom to pursue additional interesting ideas.

Less innovative companies tend to focus only on formulaic rewards, which are sometime worse than nothing at all. Consider, for example, the following comic strips from the Patent Beast.™[3]

Patent Beast

© FISH 2007

Panel 1: I PUT FIVE YEARS OF WORK INTO THAT INVENTION.

Panel 2: HERE, YOU GET A NICE PLAQUE.

Panel 3: OH, AND ONE OTHER THING.......

Panel 4: ...THE PATENT ATTORNEY NEEDS YOU TO WRITE A 20 PAGE DISCLOSURE.....

Companies sometimes falter in their compensation schemes even where they have the best of intentions. For example, a company that gives a substantial bonus to inventors for submitting patentable ideas might find the program backfires if the bonus is shared among the named inventors, as opposed to all the collaborators. Doing that is almost guaranteed to reduce collaboration.

(6) Isolating The IP Team From The Rest Of The Company

Still another cultural aspect that can be a huge barrier to innovation is a tendency to isolate the patent counsel. Highly innovative companies include patent counsel in the R&D and other strategy meetings. If they have inside counsel, those individuals likely report directly to the CEO or CTO.

In moderately and minimally innovative companies, the IP counsel tend to be hidden under the general counsel's umbrella. In the worst cases, IP counsel are regarded as highly paid scriveners, who merely fluff out disclosures given to them by the inventors.

B) Removing The Barriers

If your company is not as innovative as you think it could be, what can you do about it?

How Can Management Facilitate Innovation?

- Find and develop innovation champions
- Create an open innovation environment
- Mine ideas with enthusiasm
- Include the IP team in R&D
- Reward innovation appropriately
- Allocate sufficient resources
- Develop an innovation pipeline

(1)   Find and Develop Innovation Champions

To some extent, it is unlikely that any one person can make major overnight changes in a company's culture all by himself. That ship is just too difficult to turn. Consider, for example, a typical engineering company, where the focus is on finding solutions to everyday problems. In this company the engineers are busy, day in and day out, but most of their work is not patentable. The solutions are either too narrowly tailored, or they are merely technical improvements that are probably best kept as trade secrets.

One possible starting point is to identify innovation champions, i.e., those who are most interested in taking part in a program of innovation. Champions can reside anywhere in the organizational chart, and can have any level of experience. Indeed, innovation champions may or may not be the ones who are themselves the most innovative. What is key is that they are leaders. They should be individuals who are both "addicted to innovation" and have the personality and communication skills to get other excited as well.

If the company is divided into business units, there should be at least one champion for each of the business units. Ideally, the champions meet at least once a month with individual innovators, and then get together regularly with other champions (perhaps by phone) to share ideas and brainstorm new ones.

It is also important to realize that most people are just not innovative, and pushing them to innovate will frustrate everyone involved. It's fairly common that perhaps only 2-3% of the engineers and scientists will be truly innovative, with the rest being much better at pursuing ideas generated by others. Innovation-focused management will find ways to develop rapport among those 2-3%, whether it be through titles, workshops, or whatever.

(2)   Create an Open Innovation Environment

Management can also encourage innovation by implementing physical environments that encourage cross-fertilization of ideas. If the architecture permits, this can mean combined work areas, or good sized meeting rooms with lots of white boards. Many highly innovative companies have an "open floor" architectural structure, with glass walls so everyone can see what each other is doing.

On an interpersonal level, creating an open innovation environment means encouraging *ad hoc* groups to form and dissolve, as some ideas gain momentum and others are tossed aside. At the very least, a company should be able to establish semi-annual meetings where innovators present their ideas to a disparate group of other co-workers.

One strategy that has been very successful in our experience is to develop ideas in stages. For example, a company having many offices around the world might identify a problem that needs to be solved, and send out a memo inviting those with potential solutions to attend a conference call. On that first call each of the attendees might take a maximum of five minutes to present a brief sketch of one or two solutions. It is important that all ideas are welcomed, even "bad" ideas that are easily shot down.

A second call can be convened a week later, with attendees commenting on each other's proposed solutions. That delay allows ideas to develop in a collaborative manner, and allows individuals to contribute even though they might not have had any of the originally presented ideas.

Following that second call, decisions are made to pursue one or more of the ideas, and assignments are given out to individual participants, with yet a third call a few weeks down the road to review progress.

The information technology (IT) group can help as well, by providing a secure server into which individuals can load a synopsis of their ideas. Ideally, others in the company will regularly review the new ideas, adding their own perspectives. Even if those additions seem minimal, they can be quite useful in broadening the original idea, and helping find ways to implement what might otherwise be merely an ephemeral concept.

(3)   Mine New Ideas With Enthusiasm

In highly innovative companies, thought leaders tend to be charismatic. They have a passion for innovation, and that passion eventually invigorates everyone in the company. In such companies, management recognizes that triggering epiphanies can be a repeatable process. There is an expectation that individuals come up with new ideas on a regular basis, not every few years, or only as a result of millions of dollars of R&D. Innovation is best *bubbling up* from the innovators, not being *extracted* from them in meetings.

Another key factor is that in highly innovative companies, management tends to be comfortable in allowing, and even encouraging, innovators to explore paths that have no clear endpoint. "Only those who see the invisible can accomplish the impossible."

(4)   Include The IP Team In Research & Development

One of the very best ways to foster innovation is to hire creative, green-fields-focused patent counsel, and then have them actively participate in research and development (R&D) efforts. IP counsel can reside inside or outside the company, but either way it can be helpful to have them involved in management decisions relating to technology.

First, patent counsel can be a great link between technical and non-technical people. Although some companies grow their management from the ranks of the engineers, programmers or other technical people, others raise management from the sales ranks or from business colleges. In that latter case there can be a huge disconnect between innovation and management, which can be bridged by patent attorneys and agents. But doing so might mean that the patent counsel be included in budgeting and other strategy meetings.

Second, patent counsel can go a long way towards keeping the company out of hot water. A current fear among many technology companies is that they will be sued by their competitors or trolls for patent infringement. To address that fear properly, a company can do well to engage the IP team in periodic right-to-practice searches, and then in strategy meetings to find ways to circumvent possible infringement. At Fish IP Law we even have a name, TROLL-B-GONE™, for our service of keeping trolls at bay[4]

A third area where patent counsel can add value is in brainstorming. When attorneys and agents from our office meet with inventors to discuss their technologies, we almost invariably suggest ideas that were not previously contemplated by the inventors. Sometimes it's the insight accrued from conducting right-to-practice searches, and sometimes it's the very *lack* of formal training in a specific field that allows patent counsel to provide useful insights.

4   TROLL-B-GONE and the no-trolls logo are trademarks of Fish IP Law, LLP, PC.

Brainstorming meetings seem to be most effective when they include at most five or 6 people, and at least one of those people is involved in marketing or sales. Otherwise the group can find itself focusing on very clever inventions that are impractical, or not market relevant. It is also important to keep the meetings relatively short – no more than four hours, with a follow-up meeting a week or two later where some of the original ideas are matured, and others are discarded.

A fourth area where intimate involvement of patent counsel can pay off is in selling the benefits of innovation to investors. Many investors fail to appreciate that the return on investment (ROI) of a properly designed patenting program can be huge. And patent counsel is often in a good position to point that out. Whereas it might take many millions of dollars to get a new product on the market, the cost of protecting the marketplace for that product might only be in the tens of thousands of dollars.

(5)   Reward Innovation In Appropriate Ways

As discussed above, innovation needs to be rewarded. And this doesn't necessarily mean cash. In a highly innovative company, innovators are rewarded by internal motivations as much or more than external rewards. Ideally, innovators innovate because that's who they are; it's in their blood. Not only is the process exciting, but they have a strong feeling of contribution to the team, and enjoy a high level of respect from their peers.

Strong extrinsic motivators can also work, including management treating the innovators as mentors within the company, and giving them additional time and resources to innovate. Obviously, it helps if innovators can see monetary or monetizable rewards resulting from their innovations. But it's not necessary.

In a moderately innovative company, innovators tend to be rewarded monetarily, such as with a bonus paid for each disclosure submitted, application filed, or patent issued. But management can make a huge mistake by focusing overmuch on external rewards. For one thing, the company's success, or even the success of a given product line or product, is usually dependent upon so many factors that it is almost impossible to attribute the right amount of reward to a given innovator. For another thing, innovators who are rewarded mostly with cash and/or stock may correctly surmise that their best interests are met by creating value in one company, and then moving on to another company to repeat the process. In addition, there is often a very long lag time between innovation and external reward. Being creative today for an unspecified potential reward a decade from now may not be terribly motivating.

In a minimally innovative company, innovators are either not rewarded at all, or are rewarded only with formal recognition. While recognition at annual company dinner might be sufficient reward for past innovation, it might not be sufficient to encourage creativity in the future.

Companies should note that some countries require that inventors receive at least some royalty from their inventions. Two regions that come to mind are China and BeneLux (Belgium, the Netherlands and Luxembourg).

Ryerson University in Toronto, Canada has an extremely inventor-friendly patent policy. It is the inventor's In that program inventors can opt to pay for their own patents. However, if Ryerson helps out financially with the patent costs, then Ryerson is entitled to a percentage of revenue generated from the patent. Ryerson also provides startup funds, typically in the $200K to $300K for minority ownership in the company.

(6)   Allocate Sufficient Resources

Innovators need several different types of resources to be creative, with time being possibly the most important of all. Yes, there are individuals who can work 12 hour days, and then work creatively at home in the evenings and weekends. But for most people, that just isn't realistic. With relatively long commute times, family responsibilities and so forth, most people are just too tired to keep that up for very long, regardless of the motivation. And even if they do, their work product suffers. The proof is that innovators often make their best advances during or just after a vacation. Several of the most innovative companies on the planet encourage innovators to allocate 5 - 10% of their time on outlier projects.

A corollary is that innovation can be severely handicapped by work overloaded. If work is so hectic that employees are forever craving down time, then the 5 - 10% of time allocated to new ideas will be spent recuperating, not really innovating.

Providing adequate research or physical resources is also important. We once saw a very sad situation where a pharmaceutical company spent millions of dollars developing a drug, only to discover that a competitor had previously filed a patent application on the same compound. Practically the entire development effort could have been obviated with an STN (Scientific and Technical Information Network) chemical database search, but the company was too cheap to approve the expense. Not only was the entire investment lost, there was also a significant opportunity cost by not working on other projects.

In another instance a researcher we know made adult stem cell discoveries that should have won him a Nobel prize. But the company he worked for didn't have the physical or monetary resources to conduct relatively simple experiments to prove the idea. As a result, that company's leading position in the field steadily evaporated.

Adequate resources also need to be allocated to protecting intellectual property. As discussed elsewhere in the book, this entails securing patents not only (1) on the company's own inventions, but also (2) on technologies that competitors might use, and (3) on technologies that the marketplace might not even want for several years. What is the cost of all that? Possibly 5 - 10% of the engineering budget.

Finally, providing adequate resources often means focusing on the long-term. Yes, a company's innovation efforts need to pay off. But in the short term, that is often not practical. Innovation doesn't fall neatly into monthly or even yearly time frames.

(7)   Develop An Innovation Pipeline

Green Fields Patenting℠ (and Blue Sky Patenting ℠) require not only covering the white space within the current marketplace, but figuring out how to address opportunities that the future may bring. One way of doing that is to understand how technology evolves. The trick is appreciating that most technologies evolve according to similar principles. In mechanical and electromechanical fields, for example, technologies tend evolve along the following lines:

- Few to many

- Lower dimensions to higher dimensions

- Lower frequency to higher frequency

- Standalone system to feedback

- Stationary to mobile

- Generalized to specialized

- Single systems to overlapping systems

Consider the process of cleaning teeth. The first tooth cleaner device was undoubtedly a person's own finger, moving at a rate of about one hertz. The device has only a single element, operates at low frequency, has no feedback, has a generalized function, and has no cooperation with other systems.

TOOTHBRUSH EVOLUTION
(FEW TO MANY)
(LOWER DIMENSIONS TO HIGHER DIMENSIONS)

Without knowing anything else about cleaning teeth, one could use the first two principles of technology evolution to predict that the first major development in tooth cleaning would be to go from few to many, and from lower dimensions to higher dimensions. In fact, that is exactly what happened.

Instead of a finger or a stick, people began using brushes, which of course have many "fingers" arranged in a two dimensional array. Can one go to a third dimension? Yes, by using bristles of different lengths, which is now commonplace on toothbrushes.

Advances along the third principle (moving from lower frequencies to higher frequencies) should also have been easy to predict. Since a hand operated toothbrush can only move at a few hertz, the next invention had to be some sort of motorized toothbrush movement. We saw that in early electric toothbrushes that rotated back and forth, at frequencies of dozens or hundreds of hertz. The next step, of course, was to go to higher frequencies, which meant sonic toothbrushes operating in the kilohertz range.

And then what? At ever higher sonic frequencies the marginal effects on tooth cleaning start to vanish. A clever inventor would have realized, however, that in order to get even higher frequencies one must start using light waves. Indeed, that is also what happened. There are now toothbrushes in which laser light emanates from the ends of the bristles, using coherent radiation from the lasers to whiten teeth and repair gums.

TOOTHBRUSH EVOLUTION
(STATIONARY TO MOBILE)
(LOWER FREQUENCY TO HIGHER FREQUENCY)

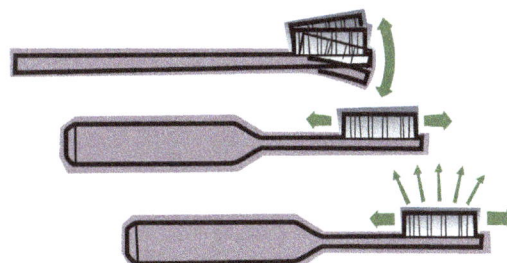

The fourth principle of mechanical evolution is to incorporate feedback. In fact, the newest toothbrushes do just that, having bristles that change color when they need to be replaced. Toothbrushes of the future will undoubtedly have feedback in some other manner, such as interacting with a little display to keep track of when they were last used, and for how long. In 2003 I predicted that toothbrushes would be developed that beep or play music after a certain amount of use, or perhaps non-use - calling the child or errant adult to his tooth cleaning responsibilities. Any supermarket now sells just such devices!

What about the fifth principle, mobility? Toothbrushes are inherently mobile, and are readily carried about in a purse or suitcase. But *parts* of a toothbrush can be made mobile relative to other parts. We have already seen toothbrushes that come apart, or have a handle that flexes in some manner.

Looking at the sixth and seventh principles, we can expect that toothbrushes of the future will become more and more specialized. We already have different toothbrushes for children, for adults, for those with sensitive gums, and so forth. The Phillips HX 9332 electric toothbrush has a USB port for charging, and might in the future store frequency of use and other data.

Toothbrushes of the future will also have overlapping systems. There are already mechanical toothbrushes on the market that have a combination of rotating and reciprocating parts. Perhaps newer toothbrushes will combine rotating or reciprocating parts with sonic vibration, or perhaps diodes for producing laser at a frequency that breaks up plaque. The point is that all of these invention evolution concepts should have been vetted during brainstorming sessions of engineers and other inventors before the first word of a patent application is drafted.

Of course, other fields have their own, analogous principles of evolution. In the field of electronics, for example, one finds that inventions tend to evolve from include synchronous to asynchronous, sequential to concurrent processing, and continuously processed to interrupt driven.

One example that illustrates the point is the evolution of glucose testing meters. In 1980 glucose meters were stand-alone devices that did nothing other than provide a readout of a color on a test strip. Subsequent developments have seen glucose meters evolve in many different ways, which often closely followed along the principles of technology evolution discussed above. For example:

- Few to many - modern lancets and test strips are packaged in cartridges, rather than individually;

- Lower dimensions to higher dimensions - The readouts on modern units are two dimensional displays, rather than what was effectively a one dimensional glucose reading;

- Lower frequency to higher frequency - modern glucose meters use cell phone and WiFi signals to report data to doctors and pharmacies;

- Standalone system to feedback - modern glucose meters provide audible reminders to users as to when they should be testing their blood sugar, and when the reading is dangerously low or high;

- Stationary to mobile - modern glucose meters have mechanically movable parts that advance the lancets and test strips;

- Generalized to specialized - modern glucose meters maintain an historical record of a particular person's readings, and can instruct the user to re-do a test, or contact his/her physician;

- Single systems to overlapping systems - the latest glucose testing units record caloric (food) intake and even act as a voice recorder;

- Synchronous to asynchronous - instead of requiring a user to write down his/her readings at the time of the test, modern glucose meters store the data for automatic later delivery to a physician or database;

- Sequential to concurrent processing - instead of needing two or three test strips to run two or three tests, modern systems can run multiple tests simultaneously;

- Continuously processed to interrupt driven - modern systems can change the reminder schedule depending on prior test results.

The bottom line here is that one can significantly facilitate innovation by training employees in principles of technology evolution. That, along with the right corporate culture, resources, and focus, can make innovation a repeatable process.

(8)   Capture Inventions With Invention Disclosure Forms

There are definitely pros and cons to having an inventor complete an invention disclosure form. One side of the coin is that such forms can be useful tools for employers, helping to reduce the likelihood that an employee will invent something at work, leave the company, and then later claim that the invention was made after the inventor left the company.

The flip side of the coin is that invention disclosure forms can be used by opposing counsel against the inventor at trial, as evidence that the inventor conceived of less than that claimed in the issued patent. Basically, the problem is that inventors tend to be sloppy in their descriptions, and tend to state things in disclosure statements in an unnecessarily limiting manner. Among other things, inventors tend to use language that confuses preferred embodiments with the inventions.

One of the worst propensities of inventors in drafting invention disclosure forms is that they tend to pepper their writings with the word "invention." What the inventor probably means to say is "preferred embodiment," which is almost *never* the same thing as the invention. Preferred embodiments are merely examples of the invention. The invention is "whatever can be claimed by the inventor and allowed by the patent office," and is almost always much broader than the preferred embodiments.

Patent Beast   © FISH 2007

I DRAFTED A PATENT APPLICATION ON MY INVENTION.

THESE CLAIMS ARE ALL DIRECTED TO YOUR PREFERRED EMBODIMENT....

....WHAT WE WANT TO CLAIM IS THE WHITE SPACE.

NO, I WANT TO PATENT MY INVENTION.

Patent Beast © FISH 2007

HERE IS MY INVENTION!

THAT'S NOT THE INVENTION, IT'S JUST...

... AN EMBODIMENT OF ASPECTS OF YOUR INVENTION.

WHATEVER....

Inventors also need to avoid unalloyed use of the word "is." For most purposes the word is much too definitive, and needs to be employed with softening terms such as "preferably" or "advantageously." For example, inventors often write that a component is made of a particular material. But when challenged, an inventor will almost always allow that the component could be made of any number of other materials. What an inventor should say is that the component is preferably made from a particular material, or that the component "can" be made of a particular material.

Inventors also get themselves in trouble using the term "consists of." In patent law the term "consists of" is another term of art, and is usually interpreted as meaning that the *only* components in the item being described are the listed components. Thus, if an inventor states that a radio consists of a receiver, an amplifier, and a speaker, he can be held to the interpretation that the radio contains no housing, display, dials, or battery. More properly, the inventor should say that the radio "includes" or "comprises" a receiver, an amplifier, and a speaker.

Still another problem is that inventors typically fail to list all the various options that they have conceptualized. Attorneys can make considerable hay from that failure at trial, arguing that a patent claim is invalid because it claims a scope greater than that appreciated by the inventor at the time of filing. A subset of this problem is that inventors often fail to list choices that they think are sub-optimal. A new type of serration for a knife might only be described with respect to steel or other metal containing knives. But if the concept can advantageously be applied to plastic knives, then the attorney should include a reference to plastic knives. In the chemical world, this problem often manifests by inventors failing to disclose compounds that they have conceptualized, but are possible to synthesize only with great difficulty. Such embodiments should still be described.

If a disclosure form is needed, we recommend using something along the lines of that set forth at Appendix G - Invention Disclosure Form. One significant feature of this particular form is that it is directed to the "preferred embodiments" rather than to "the invention." That language at least arguably reduces the damage done by sloppy wording on the part of the inventor in completing the form. Another significant feature is that the form uses the indefinite format, "at least as early as..." when defining the dates of conception and reduction to practice. Yet another significant feature is that the recommended form includes a signature line for a witness. An un-witnessed form is potentially much less useful than a witnessed form. Note that the witness needs to be someone who understands the technology; otherwise the witness is of limited value later on in testifying that all the material on the form was there when he/she signed it.

Inventors should complete an invention disclosure form in a manner that "sells" the invention, rather than merely identifies it. How will a patent claiming the invention protect a marketplace from encroachment from competitors? Why is this invention likely to make money for the company? Calculations are very helpful along those lines, demonstrating for example that use of the invention would save the company a million dollars a year in energy costs. The disclosure should also identify relevant prior art, and explain why the invention is not merely an obvious variant of the prior art. Finally, the invention disclosure form should be written in bare technical and financial terms. It should avoid legalese, and should certainly avoid statements of opinion.

(9)   Information Gathering Discussions

The lazy man's way of drafting a patent application is to have the inventor draft a lengthy disclosure, and then beef up the disclosure with a few claims. That's a bad strategy.

The better practice is for the patent attorney to (a) discuss preferred embodiments with the inventors, and then (b) brainstorm alternative embodiments.

One strategy we have employed successfully with research companies is to gather together several researchers in a room for a morning or afternoon. We start the meeting by identifying problems in a field of interest, and then take suggestions on what is needed in that field. It is usually helpful to have a marketing person in the room, and engage the researchers in a tête-à-tête with the marketing person. The goal is to stimulate thought on what would provide the company with a competitive advantage, and then work backwards to figure how those goals can be accomplished through intellectual property protection.

> **Brainstorming is a really important step in securing broad patent protection**

Although the problems raised at a brainstorming meeting may be difficult to solve, and the solutions proffered of questionable practicality, it is important to be broad-minded. At Fish IP Law, LLP, we generally try to classify the "inventions" in some manner, and then figure out how to generalize the classes. We then go back to the office, run patentability searches on the classes of solutions, and begin drafting claims. If the claims seem broadly patentable, and useful to the company, we then circle back and work with the inventors to run experiments that provide examples that support the broad claims. A good brainstorming meeting can often produce half a dozen or more patentable inventions.

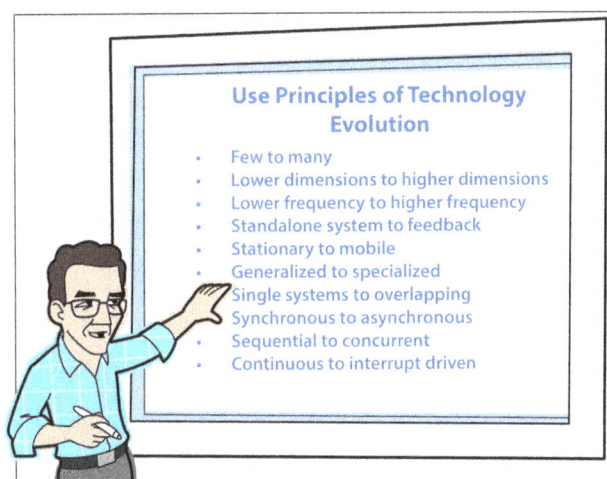

Use Principles of Technology Evolution
- Few to many
- Lower dimensions to higher dimensions
- Lower frequency to higher frequency
- Standalone system to feedback
- Stationary to mobile
- Generalized to specialized
- Single systems to overlapping
- Synchronous to asynchronous
- Sequential to concurrent
- Continuous to interrupt driven

C)   Measuring Progress

In our experience, companies are only willing to expend the time and resources needed to develop an innovation culture *if* they can measure the progress, and compare the benefits with the costs. One needs to make sure that Green Fields patenting doesn't become Black Hole patenting!

This is a difficult task because different metrics work for different companies. We can, however, offer the following general guidance.

(1)   Revenue- and Market-Related Metrics

One of the easiest things to track is revenue derived from out-licensing or assigning portions of a patent portfolio. It may well take five years or more to see those results, but eventually they should be visible. In companies that rarely out-license or assign, changes in revenue might still be tracked by looking to funding from a parent company, government programs, non-profit contributors, and so forth.

In still other instances revenue can be tracked indirectly, for example, by allocating contribution of a patent portfolio to landing a contract. In a large engineering construction company a patent portfolio covering a proprietary process might be viewed as having had a 5% contribution to landing a contract with a hundred million dollar profit. For that sale alone, the portfolio should be seen as having at least a five million dollar value.

Other indirect metrics relate to activities of competitors. If a company's patents can scuttle a multimillion-dollar R&D effort of a competitor, then those patents should be allocated some value related to the damage done to that competitor. Similarly, a value can be placed on an innovative portfolio if it requires a competitor to travel an expensive R&D path, rather than a simpler one it could have taken without those patents being in place.

Growth of a patent portfolio can sometimes be correlated with increased market share, or in some instances with keeping a competitor out of a segment of the marketplace altogether. For example, Adobe™ has so many patents relating to its PDF format that it is essentially impossible for a competitor to enter the marketplace with a competing product. In those instances, a value can be placed on maintaining a monopolistic or oligopolistic position, and of course correspondingly monopolistic or oligopolistic profits.

There may also be an aspect of market validation. Even if one's market share does not perceptively increase as a patent portfolio builds, that portfolio may still be allocated a value if the salespeople have an easier time selling a patented product, for example by granting less discounts.

Still further, a growing patent portfolio can be valued as having a cross-licensing or other defensive value. One strategy along those lines is to file patent applications that fence in a competitor's technology, even though the company securing the patents has absolutely no intention of ever producing products or using methods covered by those patents. Then, if the competitor sues for patent infringement, or on some other basis, the otherwise superfluous patents can be used as currency to cross-license to avoid or end litigation. We have seen several instances where a company eventually spent millions of dollars buying or licensing a patent to end a litigation, but had been unwilling to spend even a hundred thousand dollars in earlier years to build a defensive portfolio that could have precluded the litigation. Such short-sighted strategy can be very costly.

(2)   Platform-Related Metrics

Platform-related metrics commonly measure the number of invention disclosures, applications and/or issuances. Those numbers can be filtered by business units or perhaps individual innovators, and in either of those cases the numbers can be compared against manpower or other resources used to create the innovations. Thus, at a most simplistic level, a company could say that their 20 scientists created 20 patentable inventions over some period of time.

More sophisticated metrics are also available, and can be of greater value. For example, where a company has implemented an electronic meeting room (forum) for innovators to share their ideas, exemplary metrics can include the number of invention postings to the forum, the number of people viewing a given post, the amount of time spent on a post, and perhaps some sort of peer rating given to a post. Depending on how the "meeting room" is arranged, it should also be possible to determine which posts tend to be generative of other ideas. After all, the goal of the forum is not to fill up a database, but to light fires in the minds of the innovators.

(3)   Velocity-Related Metrics

Velocity-related metrics include measurements such as how fast an innovation gets from the drawing board to a patent committee, how fast it gets out of committee to the patent attorney, how fast a patent application is filed, and how fast it gets allowed. Such metrics do not address the amount or quality of innovation, but they can be of significance in identifying bottlenecks in the patenting process. Is the patent committee or patent attorney too slow? Are the applications so long and detailed that they are taking months to get on file? These latter issues are especially significant now that the United States is following the rest of the planet to a "first-to-file" patenting system.

Looking at velocities also helps management measure the strategic creativeness of its patent counsel. Do the company's patent applications languish for years and years in the patent office, or does the patent counsel use clever strategies to get matters examined and issued quickly? One useful strategy is to keep track of which technology classes have the fastest or slowest resolution rates. By drafting claims to a fast technology class, we have often been able to get patents issued years before those stuck in slow, overburdened classes.

Caution must be used, however, when tracking velocity of prosecution through the patent office. If there is too much emphasis on speed, one could easily end up with quickly prosecuted patents that have claims with little or no commercial significance. Patents are like real property in that no two properties are alike. The value for real property depends in large degree on where the property is located and how big it is. In the IP world, that translates into whether the claims address the commercially relevant choke points, and whether the choke-holds are strong or weak.

(4)   Cost-Related Metrics

On the expense side of the equation, a company should try to measure how much innovation is costing. There are, of course, direct costs such as personnel, lab space, and so forth. But there are also indirect costs, including the costs of enforcing the company's portfolio. Litigating a patent infringement case through trial is now running at least a million dollars on each side, and where large litigation firms are used, the figure can easily run into the multiple millions.

One also needs to keep in mind balancing the depth and breadth of the portfolio against the prosecution and maintenance costs. It might be better to invest in a few strong patents than a basket of many weak patents.

There is also the issue of foreign vs domestic filings. As discussed in CHAPTER III - I) (1), foreign patenting costs are horrendous. Not only does it cost a lot to get foreign patents issued, but the annual maintenance fees can add up very quickly. And once foreign patents are issued, it may well be that no one in the company is ever willing to take personal responsibility for allowing them to lapse.

Chapter II - Building A Portfolio

Tactics are not the same thing as strategies. A tactic is knowing how to take the hill. A strategy is knowing which hill to take. In this chapter we focus mostly on strategy.

A)   Strategic Patenting Is All About Choke Points

The most basic thing to understand about patenting strategy is the concept of choke points. In the diagram below, the army on the left is attacking the army on the right.

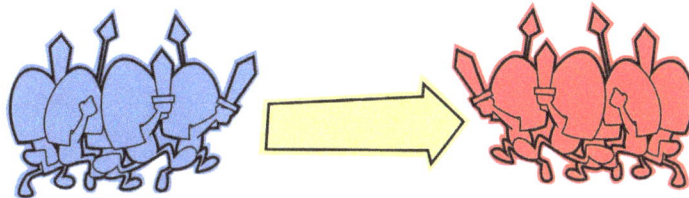

Whom do we expect to win? We can't tell. It depends on which side has more troops, which side has better weapons, training, strategy, and so forth.

What we do know is that even in today's world, a mountain range can make all the difference. If there is only one path through the mountain, then even a small number of troops from the army on the right can hold off a huge number of troops on the left. The passage through the mountain is a choke point, and in the world of intellectual property, the thing blocking that choke point is a patent.

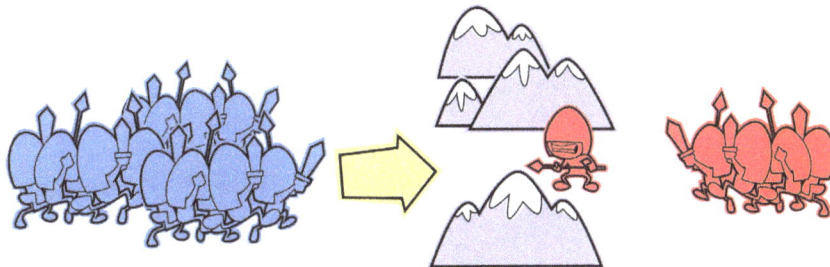

Now, what happens when there are many passages through the mountain range? The choke points only work if one can block all of the passages, or at least those that the other side knows about, and can readily cross over. In that case one needs multiple patents to be effective.

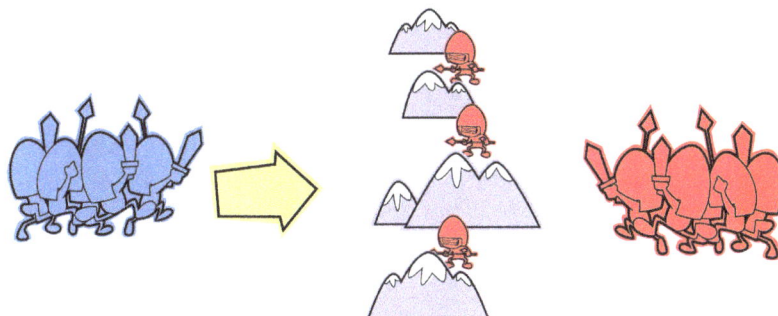

If the defending side cannot block all those passages, then the next best thing is to fall back to another mountain range where there are fewer passages. The same principal applies to the patent world. If one can't block a competitor's cell phone by focusing on use of a touch screen, for example, one might have to focus on phone apps, or handling of social networking, or some other feature.

To be effective, we need to block off all the possible choke points – (1) with respect to our clients' own products, (2) with respect to competitors' products, and (3) with respect to what the market might want years hence. That's why Green Fields and Blue Sky Patenting really is patenting the future!

B)   Block Off Your Own Product / Services

The most rudimentary task of patent counsel is to secure patents (through invention, purchase, exclusive license, and so forth) that place barriers around *one's own* products and services. In the drawing below this is shown diagrammatically by blocking passageways through the mountains.

There are basically two strategies for blocking those passageways. One strategy is to obtain lots and lots of patents, with lots and lots of claims. Some of the largest corporations use that strategy, and it works very well for them. Given IBM's 50,000+ patents, for example, it is essentially impossible to manufacture a commercially viable computer that completely escapes infringement. Another benefit is that a huge portfolio can provide a company with currency to counter lawsuits initiated by competitors. Instead of battling it out in the courts, IBM and other very large corporations can use their enormous patent portfolios as barter in cross-licensing deals.

For most companies, of course, a many-patents strategy is just not realistic. IBM is said to have 50 full time patent engineers, whose job it is to dispense and guide the work that is being done by their outside patent counsel. Most companies can't possibly do anything even close.

A second, and more realistic strategy in most instances, is to secure a handful of patents that circumscribe the current and near-term offerings of the company. A realistic budget for filing two or three new applications a year, and prosecuting pending applications is probably $100,000 a year. As we'll see in CHAPTER VI, those numbers apply to U.S. filings and prosecution only. Foreign filings can multiply that number tenfold.

C) Patent Around Your Competitors' Products And Services

The flip side of the coin to patenting one's own products and services is to block off those of one's competitors. In most cases a company cannot use patents to stop competitors from doing what they were already doing. But it can try to block them from *expanding* their offerings. In other words, defensive patenting. This is depicted in the drawing below.

Here the company at the top of the drawing is claiming features and embodiments that it has absolutely no desire to ever manufacture. The only purpose is to lay a wet blanket over future aspirations of its competitors at the bottom of the drawing. Where a competitor has a core product, for example, the strategy might be to patent *uses* of that core product. Where a competitor's product is expensive to manufacture, another strategy might be to patent less expensive ways of manufacturing the competitor's product. Where the core product could have spin-offs, a good strategy is to patent those spin-off products.

Patenting around the iPhone™ is a good example. Yes, Apple™ has numerous patents on its iPhone, but others have patented cases for the iPhone, wall mounts, battery packs, and so on *ad nauseum*. In fact, a database search done in 2022 revealed more than 26,000 patents and applications that mention the iPhone, the vast majority of which are not owned by Apple. The results of all that patenting, of course, are billion dollar verdicts and multibillion-dollar asset purchases.

Interestingly, the cost of such defensive patenting need not be terribly great. One mostly needs to appreciate how the product line could evolve, as discussed in CHAPTER I B) (7), and then get those applications on file before the competitor does.

D)   Protect What You Believe The Market Will Want In Five Or Ten Years

Fencing off one's own products and services, and those of the competitors, is a necessary but often *insufficient* step to dominate a marketplace through a patent portfolio. One must also focus on what the market might want years in the future. In the diagram below, the company expects the marketplace will be in the green area, off to the right, several years hence.

If the desired features are *possible* with today's technology, but *impractical* at this point in time, one can still file patent applications today that claim those features. Indeed, that may be the best time to patent something. Someday, technology will advance to the point where the features are commercially practical, and then it will be extremely valuable to have obtained patents on those features.

To some extent, this Patenting The Future™ strategy is the *least expensive* thing to do. If one can conceptualize the future, and figure out even a few of the major choke points, it may only take five or six patents to block out a whole new technology field.

Examples are easy to come by. In the late 1990s, a visionary could readily have patented cell phones (a) with touch screens and (b) that communicated by cellular technology as well as local hotspots. The electronics to do so was entirely possible, but not anywhere near practical. *That was the time* to file the patent applications on those features.

E) Block The Competitors From Migrating To Your Vision Of The Future

Continuing along with the diagrams, one can appreciate that the competitors will also eventually see where the market is headed. And they will respond by trying to migrate in that direction. They will likely do so by modifying their own platforms, but regardless they will move in that direction.

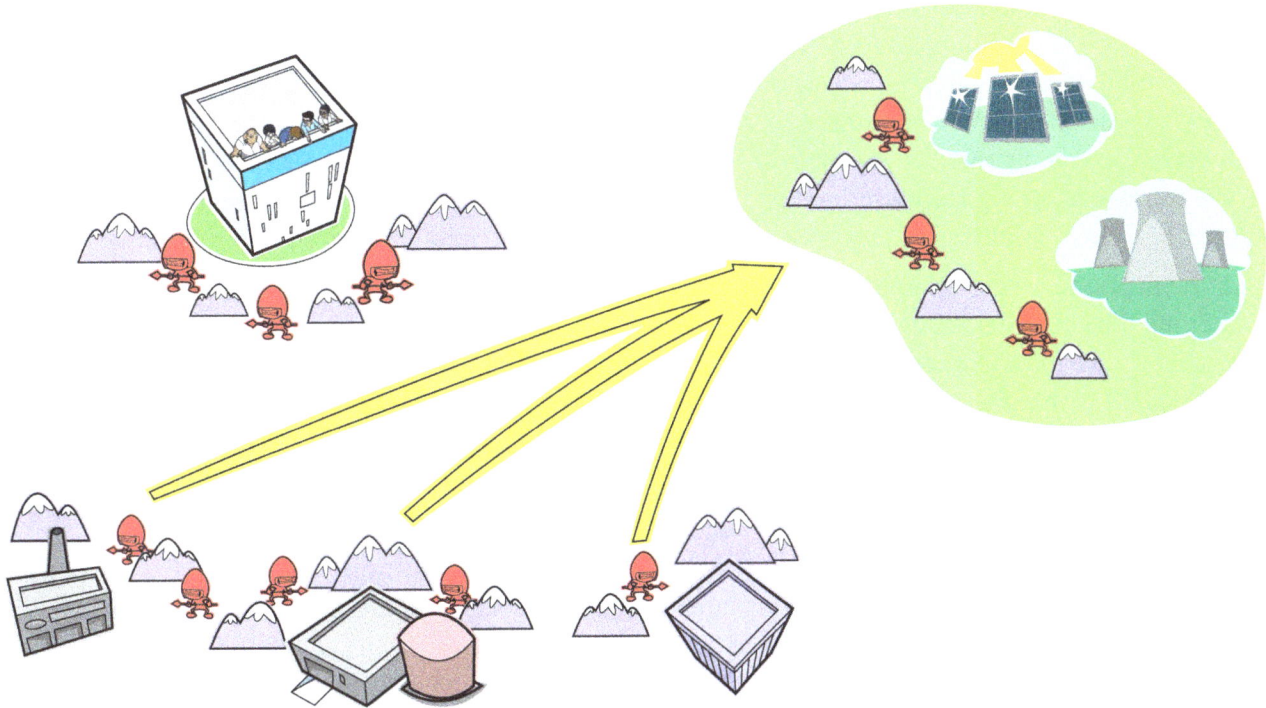

Patenting the Future for this scenario means looking over the horizon, and putting patents and applications in place that block how a competitor would likely move in a new direction.

F) Using Multiple Types Of Claims

Now that you have a conceptual idea of "what" you are trying to do, the question becomes "how" should you do it. The answer is that you need to build a "patent thicket", using a web of overlapping claims.

Yes, one can theoretically secure a monopoly with only a single claim. But more realistically solid patent protection is dependent on having numerous claims, and often numerous claims in numerous patents. One reason is that different claims have different scopes, and a thicket of claims are less likely to be circumvented than a single claim. Another reason is that a thicket of claims appears to a competitor to be a more formidable obstacle, and serve more of a deterrence function.

Almost any given subject matter can be claimed using both structure (apparatus/device/composition) claims and method claims. For example a new type of screw that can be used with fiberglass sheets can be claimed (1) based on the structure of the screw and/or (2) as a method of using a screw with fiberglass. A new drug can be claimed (1) as having a given chemical structure and/or (2) as use of the drug to treat a given disease. Using both types of claims can often increase the protection by expanding the scope of the covered subject matter.

One should not, however, include both types of claims in a patent application without weighing the potential benefits against the marginal costs incurred by prosecuting additional claims. For example, if the method claims are just rewordings of the apparatus claims, they add little or nothing to the scope of protection. A method claim that recites producing light by providing a light bulb having the new type of filament adds little or nothing to a structure claim directed to a light bulb having the new type of filament.

A better approach uses structure claims to protect a unique combination of structural elements, which would apply regardless of how the claimed apparatus/device/composition/software would be used. Correspondingly, the method claims should be used to protect a combination of steps that is unique regardless of what apparatus/device/composition/software is utilized to perform the steps. In the light bulb example, a method claim could significantly add to the scope of protection by focusing on a benefit of the new filament. Thus, an applicant might advantageously claim a method of reducing energy costs, by providing a light bulb having a filament that produces light at an efficiency greater than x. Such a claim would be applicable to any light bulb having an efficiency at least as high as bulbs having the inventive filament, regardless of the nature of the filament. A useful method claim might also focus on a method of reducing the frequency of light bulb changes.

It might be useful to include claims written in an "improvement" format. For example, instead of claiming a screw having a head, a shaft with particular thread, and a point, it is often useful to claim an improved screw having a head, a shaft, and a point, in which the improvement comprises a particular thread on the shaft. The potential benefit is that the claim clearly focuses the patent drafter on the inventive feature. The benefit can be enhanced by claiming the inventive element as part of a larger structure. Thus, the inventive screw can be claimed as an improved boat having a fiberglass component, wherein the improvement comprises a screw of a particular type that affixes at least one item to the fiberglass component.

One downside of filing both structure and method claims in the same application is that the Patent Office tends to issue restriction requirements, forcing the applicant to either prosecute the structure and method claims in different applications, or abandon one type of claim or the other. When patents used to be granted for 17 years from the issue date, restriction requirements were a wonderful way of keeping patents pending for decades. (Wonderful for the patent holders, that is!) But now that all patents with filing dates after June 7, 2010 are granted for 20 years[5] from the earliest claimed U.S. priority date (not counting provisionals, PCT or foreign national applications), there can be a significant unrewarded expense in filing lots and lots of claims that will never be prosecuted[6].

That detriment can be mitigated to some extent by filing combination structure and method claims. Thus, it is entirely possible to file a structure claim to a particular device as claim 1, and then have claim 10 comprise a method of using the device of claim 1. Claim 10 is thus dependent on claim 1, and is often not subjected to a restriction requirement. This strategy is often used in claiming pharmaceuticals, where a treatment claim is dependent upon a chemical composition claim. See for example:

---

5 For patent applications filed on or after May 29, 2000, the 20 year period is extended by one day for every delay on the part of the patent office, and begins accruing after 3 years of prosecution, subject to numerous exceptions. 35 USC §154; American Inventors Protection Act of 1999 (Pub. L. No. 106-113, § 4405, 113 Stat. at 1501A-560). The term of a patent may also be extended under a separate section of the Patent Statute for up to 5 years for patents on products involving human drugs, medical devices, food additives, and color additives subject to regulation under the Federal Food, Drug, and Cosmetic Act (21 USC §§301–399f). 35 USC §156(f)(1)–(2).

6 Incidentally, the Patently-O blog reported that 64% of patents have an average of 8 months longer term under the new 20-year term than they would have been entitled under the older 17-years-from-issuance system. The exception is Biochemistry and Organic Chemistry technologies, that have an average 11–month shorter term under the new system.

> 11. A **method of treating** hyperlipidemia, hypercholesteremia, hyperglycemia, insulin resistance or type II diabetes in which insulin resistance is an underlying pathophysiological mechanism comprising administering a **compound of formula (I) as defined in claim 1** to a patient in need thereof.

The strategy can, of course, be applied to other technologies as well:

> 5. The method of claim 1, wherein said passive device is selected from the group consisting of: a watch, a pen, a telephone, a frame, a wallet, and a beeper.

The reverse is also possible, where a structure claim is dependent upon a method claim. For example:

> 21. An outer plate of an automobile containing a concave portion, *manufactured in accordance with the method of claim 18*.

Of course it is extremely common for a dependent method claim to recite an additional limitation on a physical element utilized in the method. That form of claiming is technically defective because the added element is not a step. But most patent examiners are currently letting applicants get away with such claiming.

> 14. A method as in claim 1 wherein *the member is selected from* a pillar, a radiator support beam and a door.
>
> 7. The method of claim 2 wherein the insulating layer of the printing member is a ladder polymer.
>
> 43. The method of claim 42, wherein the non-aqueous, water miscible *solvent is selected from the group consisting of* acetonitrile, dimethylsulfoxide, glyme, methylpyrrolidone, ethanol, triacetin and mixtures of these.

Software claims are a special case. They often recite a processor programmed to accomplish a series of steps, and thereby effectively use method language in a structure claim.

> 2. A variable length encoded frame decoding hybrid buffer, comprising: ... *a processor programmed to*: (i) provide first and second buffers in memory...; (ii) fill the first [and second] buffer with encoded bits....
>
> 25. A network access device comprising *a processor programmed with computer-executable instructions that perform the steps of:* (1) receiving a unicast data packet; (2) determining whether the unicast data packet contains a tunneled multicast data packet....

G)   Chip Away At The Tree

Sometimes it just isn't possible to secure the proper scope of protection in a single patent. In such cases it is *entirely reasonable* to file multiple applications to cover different aspects of the technology. The following claims all cover different aspects of using voids to produce electronic materials having extremely low electrical conductivity:

1. *A low dielectric constant structural layer* having increased mechanical strength and having a plurality of voids comprising:

a substrate layer;

a low dielectric structural layer...; and

an infiltrating layer comprising an infiltrating material having a volatile component and a reinforcing component juxtaposing the structural layer and coating at least some of the plurality of voids.

1. *A method of fabricating* a nanoporous material, comprising:

providing a first polymeric strand;

crosslinking the first and second polymeric strands...; and

providing an energy to at least partially degrade the thermolabile portion.

1. A dielectric material comprising:

an amalgamation layer having a nanoporous aerogel and a blending material, said nanoporous aerogel having a plurality of pores and said blending material further comprising a reinforcing component and a volatile component.

1. A low dielectric constant material, comprising:

[first and second backbones, at least one of which has a thermosetting monomer having the formula:

wherein G is a cage structure....

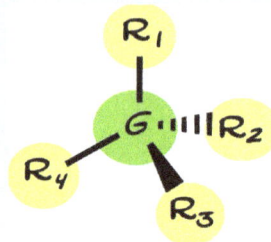

In other instances new patents are filed to extend a franchise on a commercially successful product. This can be done in any field, by adding a new little twist to the product, which might be a new method of use, and so forth. This form of "patent extension" is especially common in the pharmaceutical field, where profits from a single product can range in the billions of dollars per year. Schering-Plough, for example, secured an initial patent[7] for loratadine, which is the active ingredient in its wildly popular Claritin™ product. With patent expiration looming the company then secured a formulation patent[8] for a combination of loratadine and pseudoephedrine (CLARITIN-D 24 Hour™) that expired in 2012 after 23 years.

(1) Multiple Terminologies

A person drafting a patent application can more or less use whatever language they like in drafting patent claims. Thus, a door knob could be called a "door knob" or a "door opener". One useful strategy for drafting independent claims is a to refer to the same physical element or step using different terms. That way if one of the terms is somehow deeded to be indefinite, or one of the claims is invalidated at trial as being anticipated or obvious over the prior art, there is still an opportunity to save the other claim because of the difference in language. In the following example[9] the writer alternatively refers to his inventive sole assembly as being part of an article of "footwear" and a "shoe".

> 1. A sole assembly for *an article of footwear* comprising: a sole having a heel region and a ball region; a first multi-turn wave spring disposed within the sole....
>
> 11. *A spring cushioned shoe* comprising an upper support member for receiving a human foot and a sole assembly in accordance with claim 6.

In another example claiming a beach chair holder for a bicycle[10], the writer variously refers to the chair as "an object having a tubular portion" and "a beach chair". This makes sense because it eliminates argument (at least as to some of the claims) as to what constitutes a beach chair. The writer also cleverly refers to the bicycle as both "a wheeled vehicle" and "a bicycle".

> 1. An apparatus for retaining *an object having a tubular portion on a wheeled vehicle*, comprising: a metal plate..., a cylindrical clamp... fastened to a first member of a locking device....
>
> 15. A method of transporting *a beach chair on a bicycle*; comprising the steps of: removing a nut from a treaded member ....

Similarly, in a patent for a guitar body[11], the writer variously refers to a guitar as "stringed instrument" and "a guitar".

> 1. *A body for a stringed instrument* comprising: a bottom wall having a peripheral edge; a sidewall having a top edge....
>
> 8. *A guitar* comprising: a body having a soundboard and a bottom wall, said soundboard and said bottom wall interconnected in spaced....

---

7   U.S. 4804666 (Feb. 1989) "Antiallergic_6,11-dihydro-11-(4-piperidylidene)-5H-benzo(5, 6)cyclohepta(1,2-B)pyridines".
8   U.S. 5314697 (May 1994) "Stable extended release oral dosage composition comprising loratadine and pseudoephedrine".
9   U.S. 6886274 (May 2005) "Spring cushioned shoe".
10   U.S. 6749096 (June 2004) "Beach chair holder for bicycle".
11   U.S. 6894209 (May 2005) "Guitar having a partially sloped sounding board".

In other cases it can be useful to refer to ordinary objects in an unusual manner, and thereby cause the reader to believe that the inventor devised something more novel than he really did. A 1989 patent[12] appears to have taken this approach, referring to water as "condensed steam".

(2) Don't Let The Patent Office Write The Claims

Inventors who prosecute their own patents often seek the patent examiner's assistance in revising the claims. That's usually a bad idea. Yes, it is true that the vast majority of inventors don't have a clue how to write a good claim, and the examiner's claims will be better by a long shot than those drafted by the inventor. But allowing the patent examiner to draft the claims is akin to letting a fox guard the hen house. The examiner will invariably draft claims that are narrower than necessary, and are likely to be of little or no commercial value because they leave a door wide open for the competition to enter. This is not to disparage the examiners. Inventors and patent counsel should certainly take advantage of an examiner's willingness to discuss possible claim language. However, examiners simply do not have the same level of interest as an inventor in securing broad claims.

(3) U.S. vs "Japanese" Styles

In contrast to the U.S. practice of filing a relatively small number of patent applications on a core technology, the typical Japanese practice is to file many applications for minor variations or improvements. The Japanese approach is commonly (and perhaps a bit derisively) referred to as "flooding".[13] Actually, the Japanese strategy makes perfect sense in some circumstances, such as for a competitor that did not invent the core technology. By filing dozens or even hundreds of patents claiming minor variations, a competitor is able to force the inventor of the core technology into cross-licensing, which in this case means exchanging rights to minimally inventive improvements for rights to the core technology.

The strategy also makes good sense when a company is trying to lock up a marketplace for a core technology that is already in the public domain. For example, although many different types of flying toys are known (balsa wood and plastic airplanes, flying tubes, darts and so forth). However, a company wishing to dominate the market for flying toys could still implement a strategy of claiming flying toys that include materials having certain desirable characteristics, or that have a given weighting, or that fly a given distance. The strategy would require a fairly sizable number of claims, but at the end of the day the company could come to dominate the market.

It is also important to appreciate that flooding can be accomplished without filing quite so many applications. The basic principle is to create a field of land mines all around a given core technology. That can be done by figuring out what sets of characteristics future products will likely have, and then claim those combinations now.

(4) U.S. vs "European" Styles

There are considerable differences between U.S. and European styles of claiming. These are briefly summarized below, and discussed in much greater detail in the third *Patent Shock* book, *Patent Magic: Tips and Tricks*.

---

12   U.S. 5711950 (Jan. 1998) "Process for preparing microclustered water".

13   Excellent article can be found at Wolfson, Jeffrey A., "Patent Flooding in the Japanese Patent Office: Methods for Reducing Patent Flooding and Obtaining Effective Patent Protection", *The George Washington Journal of International Law and Economics*, Volume 27, Numbers 2 & 3, 1993-1994.

Probably the most important difference is that the USPTO is much more lenient than the EPO in the amount of detail needed in the disclosure to support claims that cover multiple combinations. For example, claims that recite a combination having one component from list 1, another component from list 2, and a third component from list 3, will likely not fly in EPO practice, unless the specification includes a working example for that permutation. Along the same lines, specified ranges in an EPO application are *not* considered to include all values within the range, even though the Specification includes a catch-all phrase expressly stating that intermediate values are contemplated.

There are potential workarounds, including the use of multiple-multiple dependent claims. But there are numerous tricks to drafting such claims, and our recommendation is to run the proposed U.S. application by an EPO attorney for guidance, *before* filing the application in the U.S. At the very least the EPO attorney can give some sort of guidance as to how broadly the invention can be claimed in EPO practice.

H) Using Claims To Lay A Wet Blanket Over The Competition

In addition to inventing things and patenting them in a novel space, a good patentee tries hard to prevent the competition from expanding beyond the spaces the competition already control. This might have nothing to do with inventing anything useful, or adding any value to society, but is simply directed towards stifling the competition. One powerful way to accomplish that task is to (a) map the competitive landscape in a given field, (b) try to determine where the technology is headed in that field, and then (c) secure patents that prevent competitors from advancing in that direction.

(1) Mapping The Competitive Landscape

The mapping step is straightforward. One reviews recent patents and published applications for each of the top ten or fifteen players in the field, and prepares a table that includes very short (5-10 word) summaries of each matter. In the field of ink cartridges, for example, during the first 10 months of 2005, Brother™ has at least 17 patents and applications, Canon™ has at least 6, and Hewlett-Packard™ has at least 17. A table summarizing a sampling of those patents and applications is set forth below:

Competitor	Patent / Appl. Number	Issue/Publ. Date	Subject Matter
Brother™	2005/0025521	2005/02/03	Cartridge guiding grooves
Brother	2005/0031359	20050210	Cartridge detection gear
Brother	2005/0068369	20050331	Colored ink cartridges with differential insertion positions
Canon™	6866374	20050315	Absorber for waste ink
Canon	6915094	2005070	Unit for rotatably holding developing-agent-containing cartridges
Hewlett Packard™	2005/0030336	20050210	Cap and actuator mechanism for interfacing with nozzle
Hewlett Packard	6840603	20050111	Inkjet cartridge re-filler station having particular fluidic connections

(2) Determining Where The Technology Is Headed

Using the information in the table, one then speculates about where technology in the field is headed. In this particular example one might surmise that technology is headed towards ever more sophisticated techniques for preventing generics from providing replacement cartridges, and towards greater complexity in number and type of cartridges. The key is to focus on possibilities rather than practicalities. Since the intent is to secure blocking patents rather than create new technology, it is of little consequence whether the subject matter of those hypothetical patents has any immediate application.

(3) Securing Patents That Prevent Competitors From Advancing In That Direction.

The final step is to secure patents that prevent competitors from advancing in whatever directions one thinks technology may be headed. For example, it's clear from the mapping step that dozens of different physical interfaces have been used to prevent generics from providing replacement cartridges. But we also know that physical interfaces can usually be defeated, and that in any event generics can always find a way to refill genuine cartridges. A better strategy would be to follow advances in security of automobiles and other areas, by replacing or supplementing physical constrains with electronic constraints. In the field of desktop printers, this would mean electronically interrogating a printer cartridge to obtain a serial number or other access code, and using the obtained information to limit use of the cartridge. Sample claims that place a heavy wet blanket over the competition in this regard might read:

A method of using a printer cartridge that contains a consumable medium, comprising:
electronically interrogating the cartridge to obtain information other than amount of remaining medium; and
using that information to restrict access to the cartridge.

2. The method of claim 1, further comprising using the information to limit functioning of the car-tridge to a specific computer.

3. The method of claim 1, further comprising using the information to limit functioning of the cartridge to a time period.

4. The method of claim 1, further comprising using the information to limit functioning of the cartridge to a quantity of ink dispensed.

5. The method of claim 1, further comprising using the information to ascertain a characteristic of the medium.

6. The method of claim 5, wherein the characteristic comprises a color.

7. The method of claim 5, wherein the characteristic comprises a chemical composition.

One might use the same approach to block the competition from advancing technology with respect to using multiple different cartridges. This could become especially important as ink jet printers are used with different types of inks, and with media than can print electronic circuits, and so forth.

Keying off Canon's idea for interchangeable reader and printer cartridges, one should probably also secure claims that prevent competitors from interfacing interactively with the paper. For example, one might claim the following:

> 1. A method of using a printer cartridge that contains a consumable medium, comprising:
>
> electronically interrogating the cartridge to obtain information other than amount of remaining medium; and
>
> using that information to restrict access to the cartridge.

(4) Graph Of Patent Concept Map

There are innumerable strategies for graphing an invention space. The trick is to visualize the space at an appropriate level of abstraction. Patent drafters often prepare figures that show the interrelation of claims in a patent or application along the lines of that set forth below. In this particular example claims 2, 5, and 6 are directly dependent on claim 1. Claims 3 and 4 are indirectly dependent on claim 1, and directly dependent on claim 2. Claim 9 is multiply dependent on claims 5 and 8.

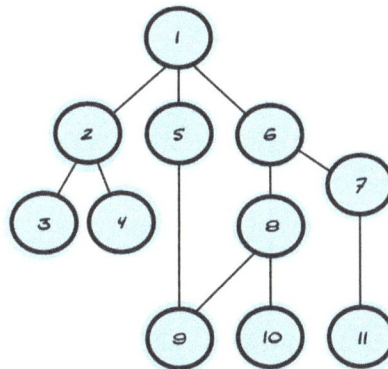

It is also possible to graph individual elements in a set of claims, although such graphing can become unwieldy on paper for more than five or ten elements.

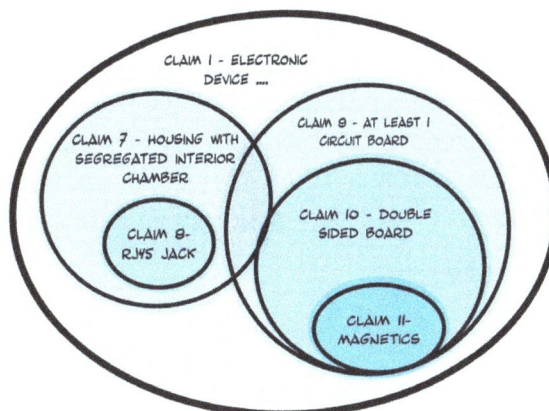

For more complicated spaces one can use a branched tree structure space, which can conveniently graph hierarchies of information sets. Thus, the center could represent the core technology of an invention, and the various trunks and branches represent collections of prior art patents and other references.

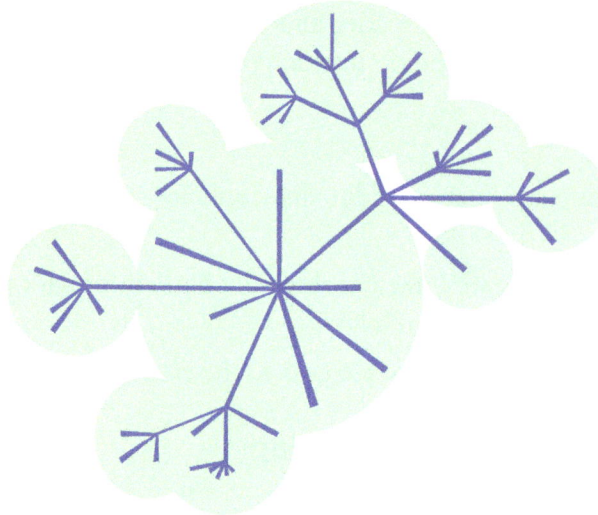

Fascinating examples of moving concept maps can be found at Network Analysis And Visualization web site.[14] Some of these maps allow users to expand and contract any portion of the structure merely by "pulling" on elements with a mouse. Lexis TotalPatent[15] and TT Consultants'[16] AI search engines con construct such information spaces automatically.

I)   Filing Considerations

(1) Size Of Applicant

The USPTO lists their fees with respect to large entities. Many fees are reduced by 50% for small entities, and some are reduced by 75% for micro entities. The entity status is determined on an application by application basis, and can change over time. An applicant is required to keep the USPTO apprised of the current entity status, and failure to pay the correct fee can result in invalidation of a patent or application.

In general, a small entity is a person or organization having less than 500 employees, and not having assigned, or having an obligation to assign the application or patent to a large entity. Universities and non-profits can also be considered small entities. The details are a bit more complicated than that, and can be found at 37 C.F.R. § 1.27 and 13 C.F.R. § 121.801 through 121.805.

The category of micro entities was introduced in the America Invents Act of 2011. To qualify as a micro entity, the applicant must (1) qualify as a small entity; (2) must not have been named as an inventor on more than 4 prior U.S. utility[17] applications (not including those assigned to or required to be assigned to the inventor's previous employer; (3) must not have a gross income greater than 3x median household income; and (4) must not have assigned, or be obligated to assign, the application to an entity having a gross income greater than

14   http://networkviz.sourceforge.net
15   https://www.lexisnexisip.com/
16   https://ttconsultants.com/
17   The USPTO currently "prefers the terminology "non-provisional utility" application in place of "utility". But in fact they are used interchangeably even on the PTO's website and, in this book, whenever "utility application" is used, it can be understood as "non-provisional utility application" as well.

3x median household income. As of Jan 2023, the 3X income threshold is $212,352. The main exception is university employees obligated to assign or license the application to the university. The patent office's final rules for micro entities took effect March 19, 2013.[18]

(2) Filing Costs

Patent prosecution can be <u>very</u> expensive, and the costs grow exponentially with divisionals and foreign filings. Please don't let the tail wag the dog. Find out how to proceed cost-effectively in CHAPTER VI.

(3) File Early

Priority of invention in the US is currently determined on a "first-to-file" basis, i.e. race to the patent office. The United States had a first-to-invent system, but converted to a "first-to-file" system on March 16, 2013 with the America Invents Act[19] (AIA). While many individuals and small companies were adamantly opposed to that change, it does simplify the law, and does substantially harmonize U.S. patent law with other countries. Among other things, moving to a first-to-file system eliminates all manner of confusion for new filings with respect to conception,[20] reduction to practice,[21] diligence,[22] and other issues.

Patent Beast © FISH 2010

THE U.S. USES A FIRST-TO-FILE SYSTEM FOR ESTABLISHING PRIORITY.

BUT MY DIVORCE ATTORNEY TOLD ME I SHOULD...

... WAIT TO FILE UNTIL AFTER MY DIVORCE WAS FINALIZED.

WOW. THAT'S WRONG ON SO MANY LEVELS.

Perhaps surprisingly, the change in law does not completely eliminate issues relating to priority, since one still has to analyze priority in terms of overlapping claims. If Joe invents a new mechanism for stabilizing the plasma in a plasma blowtorch, and Peter invents a new power supply that is useful for Joe's blowtorch, the priority is clear because there are two distinct inventions. Joe has an invention and Peter has an invention, and each is entitled to his own patent. In more complicated instances we'll just have to see how the case law plays out. The first-to-file system also leaves an opening for parties to argue priority in very limited circumstances, where an inventor discloses an invention, and another person files on <u>substantially identical</u> subject matter

---

18 www.uspto.gov/aia_implementation/77fr75019.pdf.

19 Leahy-Smith America Invents Act, Pub. L. No. 112-29, 125 Stat. 284 (2011).

20 See 35 U.S.C. § 102(g) (in determining priority "there shall be considered... the reasonable diligence of one who was first to conceive and last to reduce to practice, from a time prior to conception by the other"); *Coleman v, Dines*, 754 F.2d 353 (Fed. Cir. 1985); *Sewall v. Walters*, 21 F.3d 411 (Fed. Cir. 1994) ("Conception exists when a definite and permanent idea of an operative invention, including every feature of the subject matter sought to be patented, is known . . . . Conception is completed when one of ordinary skill in the art could construct the apparatus without unduly extensive research or experimentation".)

21 *Medichem, S.A. v. Rolabo, S.L.*, 2006 U.S. App. LEXIS 2653 at 28 (Fed Cir. Feb. 3 2006).

22 *Mahurkar v. C.R. Bard, Inc.*, 79 F.3d 1572, 1578 (Fed. Cir. 1996) (a party that is first to conceive but second to reduce to practice "must demonstrate reasonable diligence toward reduction to practice");

before the inventor files an application.[23] The act also maintains a one-year grace period for disclosures made by the inventor or another who obtained the inventive subject matter from the inventor.

The critical point, is that <u>now more than ever</u>, an inventor should get his/her application on file as soon as possible. If funds are tight, or various technical aspects are still being worked out, filing early might mean filing one or more provisional applications, and then tying them all together when filing a utility application. This is possible because a utility application can claim priority to any number of provisionals (provisional patent applications) filed within one year of the utility application filing date.

If an inventor is worried about disclosing the idea when the application gets published at 18 months, then the application can be filed with a request for non-publication. The goal is to draw a line in the sand, by just getting something on file.

(4) Experimental Use Exception

Companies sometimes want to hold off on filing patent applications because an invention is "not quite completed". Big mistake.

First, some inventors never get around to completing their inventions. There is always some new experiment to run or some new improvement to consider, and the patent applications never get filed.

Second, while those experiments and improvements are in the works, competitors are filing their own patent applications. Under the past, first-to-invent laws, there might have been some small justification for delaying, because one could argue that a first inventor filing later should prevail over a second inventor filing first. But under the first-to-file provisions of the AIA, it's a race to the patent office. Whoever gets to the patent office first wins.

Third, provisional applications are inexpensive to file ($120 for a small entity), and have incredibly lax substantive requirements. One can submit a provisional with only a few paragraphs and a drawing figure or two, and can be filed with or without claims. One can even submit multiple provisional applications on various aspects and improvements, and then tie them all together with a formal (utility or PCT) application within a year of the first filed provisional. And if one or more of the applications isn't up to snuff, or would be better left as trade secret, the utility can be filed without claiming priority to those applications.

Fourth, it isn't clear how the experimental use exception will be treated under the AIA. Under the old law, an inventor could prevent "on sale" and "public use" activities from barring the issuance of a patent if those activities were in furtherance of experimentation. The exception was always relatively narrow, and was

23   www.uspto.gov/news/pr/2012/12-44.jsp.

limited to situations where the experimentation was necessary to determine whether the invention would actually work.[24] More recent decisions have further defined experimental use as perfecting or completing an invention to the point of finding that it will work for its intended purposes, and thus ends with actual reduction to practice.[25] Similarly, there was no experimental use exception where the purpose of sales was to determine marketability of product,[26] and where the inventor failed to retain control over invention during the testing.[27] Thus, even if the old interpretations survive under the AIA, the experimental use defense is likely to be narrow, and could be limited to situations where the experimental activity is not otherwise public.

Fifth, under old § 102, and presumably under new § 102, the experimental use exception to the on-sale bar of 35 U.S.C. §102(b) does not apply to design patents.[28]

J) Patent Trolls

(1) What Are Trolls?

Patent trolls (also called "Patent Assertion Entities" and "Non-Practicing Entities") are companies or individuals that aggressively enforce patent rights against others, often in technology spaces that they have no intention of commercializing themselves. Patent trolls are usually viewed as "pirates" or "sharks" that extort money from bona-fide industry players. Even the Federal Trade Commission has gotten into the act, assessing their impact on innovation and competition.[29]

The questions for patent holders are usually (a) how do they get away with their trolling, and (b) what can be done to stop them?

Trolls succeed where the benefits of enforcing patents greatly outweigh the costs. Highly successful trolls[30] only purchase patents that are thought to have high commercial value, and they usually pay nothing upfront to the patent holders. That means trolls don't invest in research and development. And they certainly don't waste money pursuing technologies that the market sidestepped, or that could only secure narrow patent protection.

Accordingly, when trolls do litigate, they have huge advantages. First, the larger trolls are extremely well funded, through industry consortia, Wall Street, and/or venture capitalists. When a troll comes knocking at a target company's door, that target better take notice. Second, since trolls only litigate patents that appear to have great commercial value, their judgments tend to be huge, in the tens or hundreds of millions of dollars.[31] Third, a troll's downside is negligible. Trolls typically use contingency attorneys so that they have very limited

---

24   *Elizabeth v American Nicholson Pavement Co.* (1878) 97 US 126, 24 L Ed 1000 (use of experimental road pavement on a privately operated toll road for several years before the critical date of a patent was excused from both the public use and on-sale bars).

25   *RCA Corp. v Data Gen. Corp.* 887 F2d 1056, 1061(Fed Cir 1989), *abrogated on other grounds in Pfaff v Wells Electronics, Inc.* (1998) 525 US 55, 142 L Ed 2d 261, 119 S Ct 304.

26   *Dippin' Dots, Inc. v Mosey* 476 F3d 1337, 1344 (Fed Cir 2007), *cert denied* (2007) 552 US 948.

27   *Atlanta Attachment Co. v Leggett & Platt, Inc.* 516 F3d 1361, 1366 (Fed Cir 2008).

28   *Continental Plastic Containers v Owens Brockway Plastic Prods., Inc.* (Fed Cir 1998) 141 F3d 1073.

29   https://www.ftc.gov/news-events/news/press-releases/2013/09/ftc-seeks-examine-patent-assertion-entities-their-impact-in-novation-competition

30   Top tier trolls include Acacia Research Corporation, Intellectual Ventures, Millennium IP, Cygnus Telecommunications Technology; General Patent Corp International, Plutus IP, Papst Licensing GmbH, F&G Research, Ronald A Katz Technology Licensing, and Catch Curve.

31   It's a sure bet, for example, that Acacia made a bundle licensing 74 smartphone patents to Microsoft in 2010.

outgoing expenses. They typically even sue through shell companies that make no products, and therefore can't be countersued for infringement. If a trolls win, it gets rich. But if it loses, it likely doesn't even have to pay the defendant's costs because the shell company simply goes bankrupt. Acacia Research, for example, has filed hundreds of patent lawsuits since 2003, under more than 35 different company names.[32]

Trolls also have economies of scale. The more successful trolls have numerous employees that specialize in prior art searching, they have strong industry-knowledgeable contacts that can provide valuable insight as to the practicability of competing technologies, and they have licensing specialists that know how to approach infringers to secure the greatest licensing fees.

Trolls have yet another advantage in that licensing and suing is their main business, so they get very good at it. They tend to use the same litigation counsel, sue the same large companies, and they even litigate in the same courtrooms over and over. All of that makes them very efficient predators. In some cases the troll's patent portfolios are so extensive that just the threat of a lawsuit causes potential defendants to settle. In short, trolls are formidable players. They are the bane of existence for many chief legal counsel.

(2) Fighting The Trolls

It seems the go-to strategy among larger companies for fighting against patent trolls is a scorched-earth policy; deny everything and never negotiate.

The idea is that giving in to the trolls in any manner, will merely encourage more trolls.

---

32   See   http://techrights.org/files/trolltracker/20080528155008/

(3) How To Turn The Tables On Patent Trolls

On the other hand… it is fascinating that patent trolls are regarded so negatively. The inventors whose patents are litigated by the trolls might well be forward thinking individuals who obtained patent protection on impractical ideas, and then waited around for the market to catch up. In a sense that is little different from someone who buys farmland at the outskirts of town, and then waits for the town to grow up around the property. Indeed, it's a bit strange that people who do that in real estate are admired as visionaries, and those who do so with intellectual property are derogated as trolls.

In some sense patent troll companies are merely commercial arbitragers, equalizing the value between what the inventions are really worth, and what industry players are willing to pay for them. Once one appreciates this perspective, it becomes fairly obvious what to do about the trolls.

1) Green Fields Patenting. For more than two hundred years, inventors, their companies, and their attorneys have been drafting patent applications to cover *inventions*. That's the wrong approach. At the very least they should be covering the white space, i.e., the *ideas* underlying the inventions. And more than that, companies should be hiring visionary inventors to look over the horizon, and claim what the ideas could become. If management follows the ideas in our companion book, *White Space Patenting*, and adopts the steps in this book to turn their companies into innovation engines, there shouldn't be much opportunity for trolls. The bridge will be too high for trolls to drag anyone down.

2) Reward Innovative Thinking. In many companies the compensation of upper management has gone up many fold in the last decade, but compensation of innovators has gone up only slightly. That may work for companies whose bread and butter is selling commodities, but it might not work so well in the long run for technology companies. Moreover, as insurance companies and others have found out in recent years, (having been hit with their own patent infringement suits), it may not even work for "non-technology" companies. The fact is that the Internet has leveled the playing field so that even minimally funded innovators can research, create and patent ideas that have far-reaching application and value. If companies don't adequately reward innovation, some innovators *will* leave the company, secure the patents on their own, and work with trolls to sue their previous employers.

3) <u>Be Realistic About the Value Of Patents</u>. When an inventor approaches a major corporation with a patent for sale or license, that inventor needs to be taken seriously. It's not enough to dismiss the inventor as having insufficient resources to enforce the patent, or to dismiss the idea because the market might be years away. The inventor may get troll backing in a few years, and the patent that could have been purchased or licensed for a few hundred thousand dollars might wind up costing the company tens of millions of dollars down the road. That's the lesson Research in Motion discovered to their great detriment in the Blackberry™ litigation.[33]

4) <u>Work With Innovative Patent Counsel.</u> Most industry leaders have a bevy of patent counsel that they have used for years, if not decades. That cozy relationship might not be in the company's best interest. From our perspective, many patent counsel have no clue about strategy. Of course, they will say they do white space patenting. But they patent from an invention-centered approach, not a market-centered approach. They ask "what is the invention?" not "what do you want to stop the competitors from doing?" And even if they do true white space patenting, they almost never do Green Fields Patenting, i.e., brainstorm over-the-horizon ideas. Nor do they typically assist the company in building a culture of innovation.

5) <u>Cooperate With Competitors</u>. Just as trolls have economies of scale in litigating patents, industry players can have economies of scale in fighting back. When one industry player is sued, it should get together with others in the same field in a joint defense agreement, to search for invalidating prior art, and to retain litigation counsel. The divide and conquer approach of patent trolls won't work as well if the industry players stick together.

The bottom line is that companies need to out-troll the trolls. Indeed, it has been observed that many of the ideas in this book actually turn industry players into trolls

---

33   *NTP, Inc. v. Research In Motion, Ltd.,* 418 F.3d 1282 (Fed. Cir. 2005).

Chapter III - Filing The Right Type Of Application

In building a dominating patent portfolio, one needs to consider not only which subject matters should be claimed, but also what types of applications to file. The key types of U.S. applications are provisionals, utilities, and Patent Cooperation Treaty (PCT) applications.[34] Most portfolios will include a combination of these.

A) Provisional Applications

Provisional patent applications are inexpensive placeholders. They are official patent applications, and an inventor having a provisional application on file can truthfully say his disclosed invention is "patent pending." Provisionals are, however, never examined by the patent office. And unless a provisional is claimed as a priority filing in a formal application (utility or PCT application), it dies at its one-year anniversary.

As of January 2023, the Patent Office charges only $120 for a small entity (generally less than 500 employees) to file a provisional patent application, and $300 for a large entity (generally 500 employees or more).[35] The fees are even less for micro entities under the America Invents Act. More information about these different entity types can be found at the USPTO's pages on Entity Status[36]. Filing a provisional application though our office, including preliminary searching, brainstorming, drafting and filing, generally costs about $3,500.

Provisionals can be extremely short, sometimes running as little as a single paragraph or two. It is not necessary to include the usual sections such as background, brief description of the drawings, and so forth. The only requirements are that the application disclose sufficient information that one skilled in the art would understand how to make and use the invention (enablement), that the application include the best way that the inventor knows how to practice the invention as of the filing date (best mode),[37] and that a reader would appreciate that the inventor was in possession of the claimed invention (written description).

One great use of a provisional is to record a PowerPoint or other presentation that an inventor is about to make to a potential investor. Filing the entire presentation as a provisional draws a line in the sand that establishes the inventor's possession of the subject matter of the presentation as of the filing date. In many ways, that is much more powerful protection than getting everyone at the meeting to sign a non-disclosure agreement.

Another advantage of filing a provisional application is that its contents remain secret at the patent office – at least until the provisional is incorporated into a utility application, and then a formal application claiming priority to the provisional is published. That lack of publication can be a significant benefit to an applicant because it allows the applicant to establish a priority date without revealing the invention to the competitors.

In 2021 the patent office received about 650,000 applications, up from about 300,000 ten years earlier. About 50% of provisionals are used as priority applications in a utility or PCT, with the others dying on the vine, or perhaps being re-filed as new provisionals.[38] Viewed from another perspective, about 35 - 40% of utility

---

34 There are other types of patent applications, including for example design applications for the ornamental appearance of objects, and plant applications for non-sexually propagated plants (e.g. roses). But those are of relatively little concern for most technology companies.

35 USPTO fees as of Jan 2023 can be found at https://www.uspto.gov/learning-and-resources/fees-and-payment/uspto-fee-schedule

36   https://www.uspto.gov/patents/apply/applying-online/entity-status-fee-purposes

37 Under the America Invents Act of 2011, the best mode requirement continues to exist during prosecution, but failure to include best mode is no longer a defense to infringement during litigation.

38 See PatentlyO.com, Jan. 2, 2013.

applications claim priority to at least one provisional application. The graph below shows the number of patent application filings in the United States from FY 2000 to FY 2021[39].

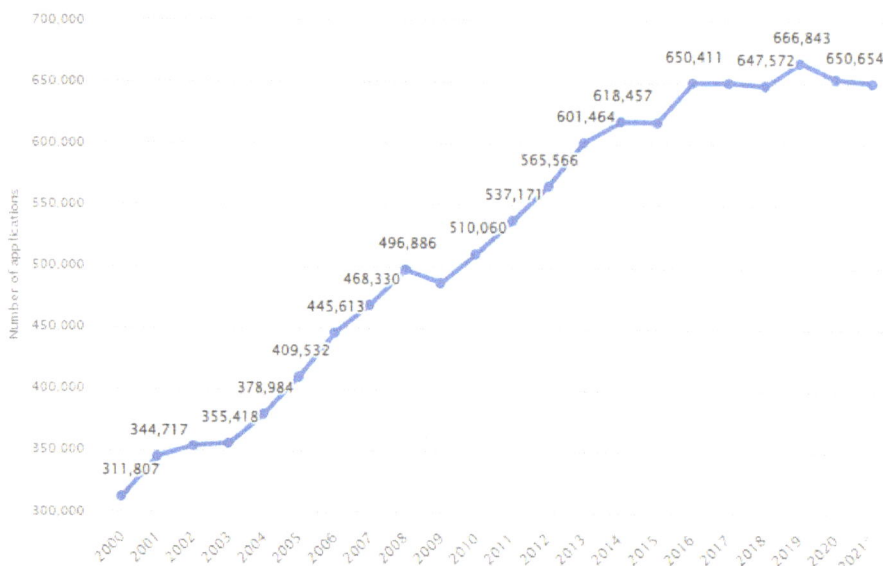

A formal application (utility or PCT) can claim priority to any number of provisionals. Our office once filed a utility application claiming priority to 11 provisionals. Every time the inventor devised an improvement to his idea, we filed a new provisional. Within one year of the earliest provisional, we filed a utility application that included all of the various improvements.

The U.S. patent office allows filing of provisionals without claims. Indeed many or possibly even most provisionals are filed without claims. The ability to file without claims reduces the cost of the application considerably, and may be advantageous when the person drafting the application doesn't really doesn't know what is inventive. There is a danger, however, in that provisional applications without claims are not recognized by some foreign patent offices (including the European Patent Office, EPO) for priority purposes. Thus, if an inventor files a provisional patent application without claims in January, and starts selling his product in February, he might very well lose his right to secure foreign patents in some jurisdictions.

There is another danger as well, in that filing a provisional without claims could well mean that the disclosure of the provisional is insufficient to support claims in a later-filed formal application. Writing claims tends to focus the writer's mind on what is patentable, and at the very least helps satisfy the written description requirement.

Appendix A – Sample Provisional Patent Application provides an example of a perfectly adequate provisional application. This particular example includes a short description of the background, a description of the general subject matter, a few claims and a simplistic figure. Although there are no specific formatting requirements, the paragraphs in this example are numbered using the format [xxxx] where "xxxx" is the paragraph number. This format is preferred, although one could alternatively use the older, line number format.

---

39   https://www.statista.com/statistics/256554/number-of-patent-application-filings-in-the-us/#:~:text=Number%20of%20patent%20application%20filings%20in%20the%20U.S.%20FY%202000%2DFY%202021&text=In%20the%20fiscal%20year%20of,653%2C311%20patent%20applications%20were%20filed

B)   Utility Applications

Non-provisional utility patents applications are what people generally mean when they say they have "an application on file." A non-provisional utility application is a formal application, which *will* be examined by the patent office, as long as all the formalities are satisfied.

Filing a non-provisional utility application through our office generally runs about $8,000 to $12,000, which includes searching, brainstorming, drafting, and filing. In some fields such as software and pharmaceuticals, the complexity of the applicant can push the charges even higher.[40] The details of drafting and filing a utility application can be found in our companion book, *White Space Patenting*.

The patent office has made valiant efforts to reduce the delay in examination of new non-provisional utility patent applications. As of December 2022, there are about 716,000 total applications waiting to be examined, with an average wait time of about 16.4 months . Of course, the backlog in some groups (e.g., software and business methods) is longer.[41]

Patents Pendency Data December 2022

First Office Action Pendency

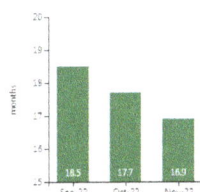

First Office Action pendency is the average number of months from the patent application filing date to the date a First Office Action is mailed by the USPTO. The term "pendency" refers to the fact that the application is pending or awaiting a decision. This measure of First Office Action Pendency includes the time until a first action by the USPTO, as well as any time awaiting a reply from an applicant to submit all parts of their application. The first action pendency number displayed, measured in months, is the average for all applications that have a First Office Action mailed over a three-month (one quarter) period.

ᴵᵃˡ View the last two years chart   View comparison by technology center   Show/hide chart data

Traditional Total Pendency

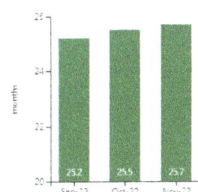

This is the measure of total pendency as traditionally measured. Historically, pendency has been measured as the average number of months from the patent application filing date to the date the application has reached final disposition (e.g., issued as a patent or abandoned, which is called a "disposal". This pendency includes the time periods awaiting action by the USPTO, as well as any time awaiting reply from an applicant.

The Traditional Total Pendency pendency number displayed, measured in months, is the average for all applications--excluding applications in which an RCE has been filed--which are "disposed" over a three-month period.

ᴵᵃˡ View the last two years chart   View comparison by technology center   Show/hide chart data

One can speed up that process in several ways, including: (1) filing an application with a Petition to Make Special, (2) filing an application with a request for Prioritized Examination, (3) using the Patent Prosecution Highway countries; (4) using a PCT First filing strategy, and (5) filing with a petition for Accelerated Examination.

The Patent Office has experimented with other programs from time to time, but they have mostly fallen by the wayside either because they were abused, or were not very popular. For example, the Patent Office canceled

---

40   There are some savings if the applicant is a micro entity, but those are minor compared with the patent attorney / agent fees. USPTO fees can be found at https://www.uspto.gov/learning-and-resources/fees-and-payment/uspto-fee-schedule

41   Current patent office statistics can be found on the USPTO's performance dashboard, https://www.uspto.gov/dashboard/patents/

the Green Technology Pilot Program[42] in 2012, after only 3,500 applications were accorded special status over a three year test period.

If an inventor expects to make significant improvements to an invention during the next six months or so, he/she might do well to file a provisional application to begin with, and then wait for the new subject matter to file the non-provisional utility application. But note that this strategy effectively gives the applicant two priority dates, one as of the provisional filing for whatever subject matter is disclosed in the provisional application, and a second priority date for the new subject matter added in the non-provisional utility application.

Utility or PCT applications usually take about two to three weeks or so to prepare. The drafting itself probably only requires 10 or 15 hours, but it takes time to search for prior art, and to brainstorm the claims. Sometimes there is a further delay because the search involves foreign publications that must be secured and translated.

C)   Size Of Applicant

As discussed above, the USPTO lists their fees with respect to large entities, small entities, and micro entities. In many categories small entities get a 50% reduction in fee, and micro entities get a 75% reduction.[43] The entity status is determined on an application-by-application basis, and can change over time. An applicant is required to keep the USPTO apprised of the current entity status, and failure to pay the correct fee can result in invalidation of a patent or application.

In general, a small entity is a person or organization having less than 500 employees, and not having assigned, or having an obligation to assign the application or patent to a large entity. Universities and non-profits can also be considered small entities. The details are more complicated than that, and can be found at 37 C.F.R. § 1.27[44] and 13 C.F.R. 121.801[45] through 121.805.

The category of micro entities was introduced in the America Invents Act of 2011. To qualify as a micro entity, the applicant must (1) qualify as a small entity; (2) must not have been named as an inventor on more than 4 prior U.S. utility applications (not including those assigned to or required to be assigned to the inventor's previous employer; (3) must not have a gross income greater than 3x median household income; and (4) must not have assigned, or be obligated to assign, the application to an entity having a gross income greater than 3x median household income. The main exception is university employees obligated to assign or license the application to the university. The patent office's final rules for micro entities took effect in 2013.[46]

D)   Fitting Provisionals Into The Portfolio

Assuming an applicant is contemplating filing a provisional application, how should that filing fit into the overall patenting strategy? There are several important ways to use provisional applications, and not all of them are completely obvious.

The normal use of a provisional application is as a precursor to a non-provisional utility application. In the diagram below, a single provisional application is filed at 0 months, and expires at 12 months (depicted by the break at the end of the time line). As already discussed, the provisional application can be very simple and inexpensive, or it can be drafted as a complete formal application and merely filed as a provisional application

42   https://www.uspto.gov/patents/initiatives/green-technology-pilot-program-closed
43   https://www.uspto.gov/learning-and-resources/fees-and-payment/uspto-fee-schedule
44   https://www.govinfo.gov/app/details/CFR-2011-title37-vol1/CFR-2011-title37-vol1-sec1-27/summary
45   https://www.govinfo.gov/app/details/CFR-2002-title13-vol1/CFR-2002-title13-vol1-sec121-801
46   www.uspto.gov/aia_implementation/77fr75019.pdf.

to delay filing the formal application. Of course the drawback is that the patent office tries to get out the first office action at about 18 months after the U.S. application is filed. Delaying filing of the non-provisional utility application by filing provisionals first, pushes back the date when the clock starts ticking for the office action.

In any event, before the end of the 12 months the applicant files a non-provisional utility application claiming priority to the provisional application. In this particular diagram the patent attorney/applicant filed at about eight months into the twelve month period. If the inventor is unlikely to develop any new subject matter, and especially if the provisional application is relatively thin, it is desirable to file well before the 12 months is up.

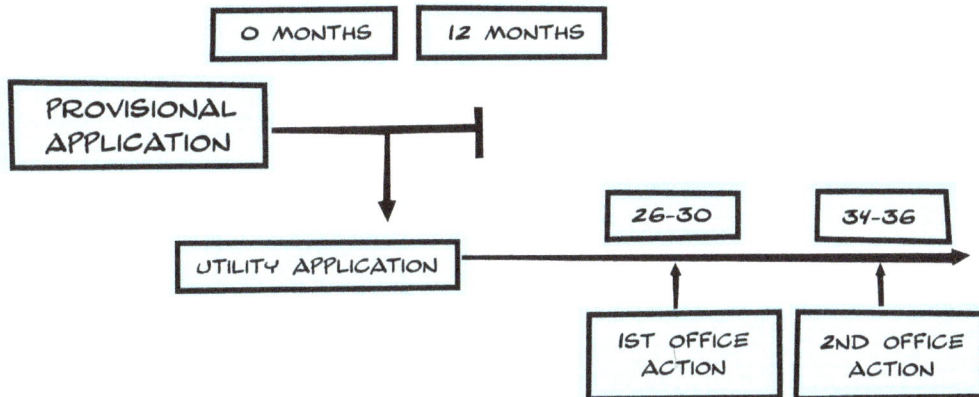

This "normal" strategy works very well for circumstances in which there is only one invention, and the inventor/applicant has a clear understanding of what the invention is at the time the application is filed.

We have also used single provisionals to file multiple inventions. The most common occurrence is to write up a few pages of description that disclose the various inventions, and then pull out various parts as needed when it comes time to write and file the formal applications.

From time to time we have also written several full-blown non-provisional utility application or PCT applications, but then for various reasons the inventor decided not to spend the money right away to file each of those applications. In those instances we simply collected all the various applications together, and filed the entire collection as a single provisional. Then, before the one-year deadline, we separately filed each of the applications, with each one claiming priority to the provisional. The total cost was about the same as filing them a year earlier, but the filing cost was delayed by a year. This is diagrammed in the figure below.

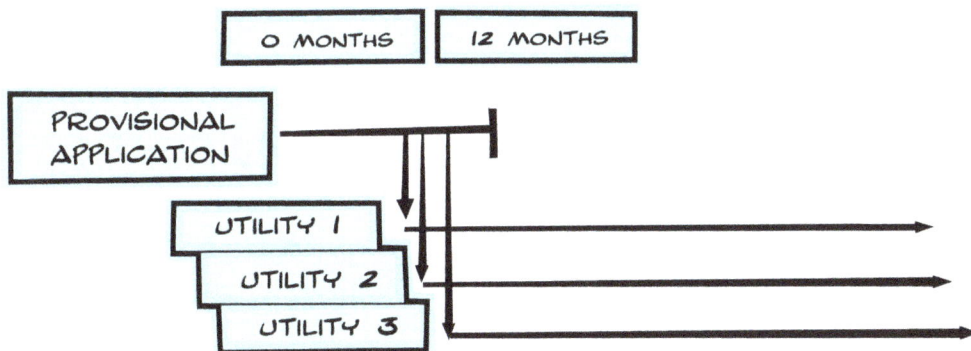

Provisionals are also extremely useful where an inventor expects to develop some new wrinkles on his invention after filing of a first application. An applicant can't file a second provisional application claiming priority to an earlier provisional application, but he can serially file multiple provisionals, and then file a formal application that claims priority to any combination of applications filed within the previous 12 months. In the following diagram, the utility application claims priority to five different provisionals. Filing of such "serial provisionals" can be extremely cost-effective.

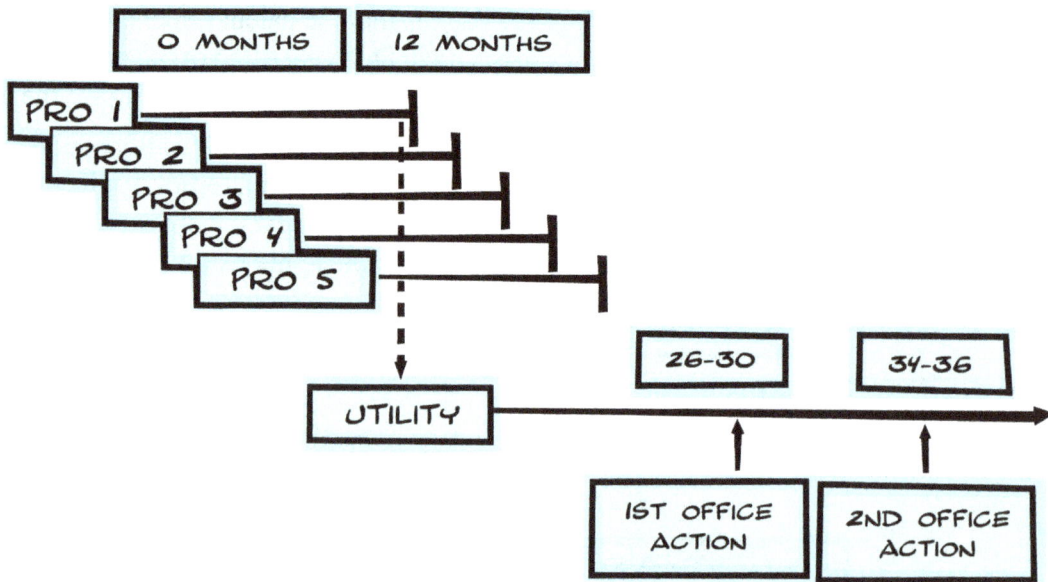

E) Using Provisionals With CIP Applications

Another use of a provisional application is to provide an inexpensive priority date for a CIP (Continuation In Part) application. For example, if an applicant files a utility application with disclosure to several embodiments of an invention, and subsequently wants to claim another embodiment, the inventor could file the new material in a provisional, and then file the CIP application claiming priority to both the utility application and the provisional application. The CIP application would then have two priority dates, one for the material disclosed in the utility application, and one for the new material disclosed in the CIP application.

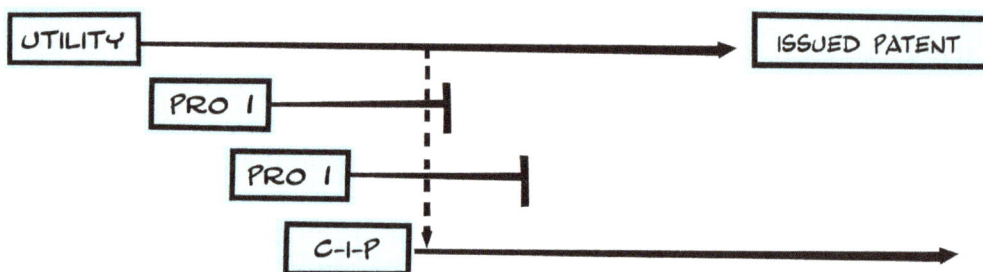

F) Filing Precautionary Provisionals For PCT Applications

The main drawback of waiting to file a non-provisional utility application as a priority document for a PCT application is "intervening development" of the subject matter. Since a PCT application can only claim priority back 12 months, the inventor is left with the devil's choice of either filing the PCT with priority to the utility (and omitting disclosure to the improvements), or waiting to file the PCT with the new disclosure, (but then losing priority).

One solution is to re-file the utility as a precautionary provisional part way through the one-year window following filing of the utility. The utility is unaffected, and will continue down the road of prosecution. But filing of the provisional establishes a new one-year window in which to file the PCT application. That extra time can be significant. If the applicant files the precautionary provisional close to the end of the original one-year window, then the PCT application need not be filed until almost two years after the filing of the utility. By that point the PCT application can claim priority to the provisional, and include disclosure as to any inventions made during the prior two years. Thus, even though the applicant fails to capture the filing date of the utility in the PCT application, prosecution of the utility continues unabated, and the PCT is able to claim at least some priority back to the subject matter of the utility (which was re-filed as the provisional).

G) Foreign Filing Issues Regarding Provisionals

Provisional applications can be filed in much of Europe and Japan, as well as in Australia, Canada, India, Ireland, New Zealand and most other current and former members of the British Commonwealth. Surprisingly, provisional applications cannot currently be filed in the United Kingdom, where the idea of provisional applications originated. The organization that administers PCT applications, the World International Property Organization (WIPO), publishes a very good article on provisional applications.[47]

One major caution here – one should generally file at least one omnibus patent claim in a provisional application if there is any substantial chance of filing foreign counterpart applications. The reason is that several foreign patent offices (including EPO) will only allow priority claims to the provisional to the extent that the claims in the formal application fall within the scope of the claims of the provisional. Hence, one should file at least one claim in the provisional that is extraordinarily broad, even if the filer knows that there is no chance of ever having that claim issued.

A second caution is that most foreign patent offices (including EPO) will only recognize a claim through the PCT back to the earliest application in a family. Consider the case where an applicant files a provisional application in February, a non-provisional in January of the following year, and then a PCT application a few months later. In U.S. practice, the PCT application could properly claim priority back to the utility, but not the provisional because the provisional was more than a year before the PCT Chapter I filing. Thus, a second utility filed as a U.S. national phase to the PCT application would claim priority back to the first U.S. utility. Not so in the EPO and most or all other Paris Convention countries. In EPO, for example, one could claim priority back through the PCT to the first U.S. utility,[48] but EPO would refuse to recognize the priority claim because the utility was not the first application in the family.[49]

A third caution is that the U.S. Patent Office requires an English translation of any foreign-language provisional application that is used as a priority document for a non-provisional application. Some countries, including Brazil, Chile, China, the Czech Republic, Denmark, Hungary, Norway, Netherlands, Sweden, Taiwan, and the United States do allow an applicant to file an application in a foreign language on a provisional basis, and then follow up with a translated application. Such informal filings are sometimes loosely referred to as "provisional" filings, but they are not provisional applications.

A fourth caution is that provisional applications should usually incorporate other patents and/or applications by reference. That practice goes a long way towards satisfying the enablement requirement.

---

47   https://www.wipo.int/pct/en/faqs/faqs.html
48   Under Art. 87 (4) EPC.
49   T 0952/93, OJ EPO 1993, reasons point 4.2.

H) PCT Applications

As noted above, the PCT (Patent Cooperation Treaty) is administered by WIPO (the World Intellectual Property Organization).[50] The PCT has more than 180 member states[51] (countries). A good summary of the types of patent protection available in the member states is available online.[52] The two-letter country codes used by WIPO are also listed on-line.[53] PCT applications *are* examined, and the examining office does issue a search report / written opinion summarizing its findings. PCT filing offers numerous benefits, but most applicants use the PCT merely to extend the deadlines for foreign filing.

The PCT has several receiving offices around the globe, including one in the U.S. for U.S. applicants, one in Europe for European applicants, one in Japan for Japanese applicants, and so forth. But most countries don't have their own PCT receiving office, and a provision has been made for a citizen or subject of any PCT country to file in the main PCT office in Geneva, the so-called International Bureau (IB).

The various PCT receiving offices are responsible for conducting their own patentability searches. Thus, the U.S. patent office, which is the PCT receiving office in the United States, generally conducts patentability searches for PCT applications filed with that office. Regardless of which receiving office is selected by the applicant, the search is supposed to be an "international type" search, and is supposed to be quite thorough.

Some attorneys believe that the European Patent Office (EPO), which conducts patentability searches for the International Bureau, does a better job of searching than the U.S. patent office. Since a U.S. resident can file in the IB, the question is whether or not that is a good idea.

In the past, that was generally a bad idea. The International Bureau applies EPO laws and standards, and is thus unnecessarily restrictive relative to U.S. practice. For example, the IB office routinely rejects "methods of doing business" claims, and is very hard on computer software claims. The IB is also quite insistent on limiting the scope of the claims to the scope of the examples set forth in the specification. We have also found that the EPO examiners are less receptive than the U.S. patent examiners to informally talk through the claims issues.

There are other advantages of filing in the US. One is that the PCT considers the application to be filed on the day it is mailed using the Express Mail procedure or received electronically. The IB takes just the opposite approach, and only considers the application to be filed on the day it is actually received in Geneva. An applicant can fax file the application, but the applicant takes the risk that the fax doesn't go through correctly. In any event, filing directly with the IB reduces the filing window because Geneva is six to nine hours ahead of most cities in the United States, and the application is not considered received *until the fax actually goes through*.

For technologies other than Internet-related software and business methods, and methods of treating humans, the best strategy may well be a hybrid choice – filing the PCT application with the U.S. Receiving Office (US/RO), but designating that the search be done by the EPO. In many ways that strategy provides the best of both worlds.

We have also had very good success designating the Korean patent office (KIPO) as the searching authority. KIPO does a particularly good job of searching for prior art filed in Eastern languages, including Korean, Chinese, and Japanese. KIPO is also more accommodating on searching multiple claims where the USPTO and EB would need additional funds because of supposed disunity. Unfortunately, KIPO will not conduct searches

---

50   www.wipo.int.
51   https://www.wipo.int/members/en/
52   https://www.wipo.int/members/en/
53   https://www.wipo.int/export/sites/www/pct/guide/en/gdvol1/annexes/annexk/ax_k.pdf

in the areas of business methods, games, methods of treating human or animals, diagnostics practiced on humans or animals, or computer programs.

Since 2013, one can file a PCT naming the assignees as applicants, and then amend the national stage to include the inventor names. The PCT does not have to be filed with the names of the inventors.[54]

I)   Foreign Patent Applications

(1)   Costs of Securing Foreign Patents

The most salient fact about foreign patent filings is that they are expensive -- many times more expensive that U.S. filings. Foreign patents are also generally more expensive to enforce, and damages may be severely limited. In a prominent Japanese case, for example, a lower court approved an award of 60 billion Yen, but that amount was reduced during appeal to a mere 1-2% of the original award.[55]

As a general rule of thumb, it costs about $3,500 - $8,000 per country or region to get a foreign patent application on file, and at least that much again for each country by the time the patent issues. It gets even worse down the road, because most of the foreign countries have maintenance fees of about $600 - $800 per year. Note that these are annual maintenance fees, rather than the 3.5, 7, and 12 year payments due in the US. The long and the short of it is that securing foreign patents will likely set an applicant back at least $15,000 - $20,000 per country, and about $30,000 per country over the life of the patent.

Costs are at the lower end in Canada, Australia, and New Zealand, in large measure because filing and prosecution can be done in English. Canada is also advantageous for many applicants because the Canadian patent office distinguishes between large and small entities, thereby reducing fees for many applicants by 50%. The Japanese Patent Office (JPO) distinguishes among different entity sizes as well. Mexico doesn't distinguish small entities, but Mexico does allow 50% reduction of fees if the applicant is an individual inventor. One would expect that charges would also be low in the EPO, where applications can also be filed and prosecuted in English. But filings in the EPO tend to run quite high, $7,500 minimum to place an application on file and request examination.

(2)   Where To File

Filing costs, of course, are not the only factor in deciding where to file. It is probably not worth filing in many countries because: (a) their populations don't have a lot of money; (b) they don't have a reliable legal system; and/or (c) they have a cultural history of turning a blind eye to infringement. Countries that come to mind are China, India, Russia and Indonesia.

Obviously, the game plan is different for different technologies. In petroleum processing, for example, companies often file in Venezuela, Norway, and several of the Middle Eastern countries. In electronic chip manufacturing, companies often choose to file in China and Taiwan. In general, we recommend the following filing schedule based upon the likely budget. Note that the dollar figures shown in the table reflect the estimated costs of securing a patent, not just filing it.

---

54   H.R. 6621, signed into law on January 2, 2013, repealed, 35 U.S.C. § 373.
55   *Shuji Nakamura v. Nichia Chemical Industries* (private communication).

Country	Countries	Countries	Countries	Countries
USA	USA W. Europe	USA W. Europe Japan	USA W. Europe Japan China Canada Mexico	USA W. Europe Japan China Canada Mexico Korea India Brazil Taiwan
$15,000	$75,000	$90,000	$120,000	$150,000

It is critical to appreciate that filing costs in regional filings, such as the EPO (European Patent Office) must still be followed up with national phase validation in the various countries (referred to as "states"). Thus, even after spending perhaps $15,000 to secure grant of an EPO patent, that patent must be validated (within six months) in specific EPO countries to be effective. Typical costs for validating a PCT patent in selected European Countries are as follows:

Country (State)	Estimated Validation
AT (Austria)	$4,000
BE (Belgium)	$1,500
CH (Switzerland)	$1,300
DE (Germany)	$3,200
DK (Denmark)	$4,500
ES (Spain)	$3,800
FR (France)	$3,000
GB (Great Britain)	$320
GR (Greece)	$3,200
IE (Ireland)	$1,000
IT (Italy)	$3,000
LU (Luxembourg)	$850
MC (Monaco)	$850
NL (Netherlands)	$4,200
PT (Portugal)	$4,300
SE (Sweden)	$6,500

Note that these costs are estimates only, and include official out-of-pocket fees, translation fees, and attorneys' fees. Under the London Agreement of 2008, some countries do not require translation. There are services that will perform the validation at relatively low cost, but we can't vouch for their accuracy in translation.

Starting in spring 2023, the EPO will begin a new program where validation takes place in all EPO countries unless the patentee opts out of the program.[56]

(3)   Utility Model Applications

Utility model patents (also known as "petty patents" or "innovation patents") can be granted in many countries[57] for inventions with reduced novelty and nonobviousness requirements. They are generally very easy to get because they have little or no substantive examination. The idea is that the patent office will merely handle the paperwork and address technical sufficiency of the application. If litigation ever arises, the courts address the issues of anticipation, obviousness, and so forth.

One downside is that *validity* of a utility model is determined during litigation, which is expensive, and where there is no chance of amending the claims. Another downside is that utility model patents usually expire in only 7-14 years, versus instead of extending for 20 years for non-provisional utility patents.

In practice, an applicant usually files a utility model patent application because: (a) the invention has a short life cycle; (b) the applicant wants to get some form of patent protection right away; and/or (c) the invention is of an incremental character that might not satisfy the nonobviousness standard for a utility patent. Outside China, it is relatively common to file both utility and utility model applications on the same invention. Since utility model applications are not examined, they often issue in 6-9 months after filing.

Utility model applications are especially advantageous in countries such as China, where competitors might well file a patent application on a technology that they learned of, but didn't invent. We've even seen cases where a company's own factory filed a patent application on one of their customer's technology as a defense against the customer taking their business to another factory. Patents resulting from such shenanigans can be attacked, but at a high cost, and in a process that might take several years. The only realistic defense against such unscrupulous competitors and vendors is to get one's own utility model on file, and issued as soon as possible.

Utility model applications are available in several other countries, including notably Germany. Given the dominance of the German economy in Europe, it is often very advantageous to be able to claim that one has a patent already issued in Germany, with others to follow. Utility model patents are not available in the United States.

(4)   Delaying Examination

When filing national phase applications it is often possible to pay only the filing fees, and delay examination fees for several months to several years. Of course this trick provides a cash flow advantage, and also possibly an expense benefit. It may well be that by the time the examination fees are due, the company has discovered that any allowable claims are not worth the cost of prosecution, at least not in the foreign countries.

---

56   https://www.unified-patent-court.org/en/registry/opt-out
57   See listing at https://en.wikipedia.org/wiki/Utility_model

Requesting examination can be delayed until 36 months after the priority date in China, Japan, and Korea, and 48 months after the priority date in EPO. In the EPO, a request for examination must be filed when filing the EPO application.

Chapter IV - Speeding Up The Patenting Process

A) Petitions To Make Special

Years ago there were many different categories of petitions to make special. Now there are basically only four categories: (1) Patent Prosecution Highway, (2) Green Technology Pilot Program, (3) inventors in poor health; and (4) inventors being at least 65 years old.

Petitions to make special don't always work as advertised. In mechanical and chemical fields they often get an application examined in only a few months. But in other cases (such as business methods inventions), the patent office has taken several years just to consider the petition to make special!

At least the process is easy, and inexpensive. One simply files the petition along with the new application filing papers.

B) Prioritized Examination (Track 1)

As discussed in CHAPTER III - B), the patent office is heavily backlogged. In business methods groups (including computer software) the office can be several years backlogged in taking even the first substantive look at a patent application.

Probably the best way of circumventing that delay is filing an application with a request for Prioritized Examination (PE). Basically, one files the same non-provisional utility application one normally files, but pays an extra fee[58] to get the application placed at the top of the stack. Prioritized Examination applications are limited to 4 independent claims, 30 total claims, and must be filed with formal drawings and signed declarations. Requests for prioritized examination must be filed at the time of filing the application and must be accompanied by the filing, publication and prioritized examination fees.[59] An excellent listing of FAQs is available on-line[60], as well as Track 1 statistics[61].

Prioritized Examinations are a creature of the America Invents Act of 2011. The statute requires that the subject matter be for products, processes or technologies "that are important to the national economy or national competitiveness", but the patent office has interpreted this to include substantially all subject matters.

The most obvious motivation for filing a PE application is to shorten the time to the first substantive office action. After about the first year of the program, the patent office appears to be getting first office actions out the door on PE applications in about 60 days[62] and final disposition in under six months. Compared with three to five years or more for an ordinary application, that's just incredible! Such an early substantive office action can be absolutely critical in securing funding from investors, and for informing the use of available funds. In many instances it makes no sense to pursue research and development, let alone marketing, manufacturing and distribution, if the product is not broadly patentable.

---

58 As of Jan 2023, the fees are $840 for micro entities, $1,680 for small entities, and $4,200 for large entities. See https://www.uspto.gov/learning-and-resources/fees-and-payment/uspto-fee-schedule

59 https://www.govinfo.gov/app/details/CFR-2018-title37-vol1/CFR-2018-title37-vol1-sec1-102

60 https://www.uspto.gov/help/patent-help

61 https://www.uspto.gov/dashboard/patents/track-one.html

62 1.9 months days as of December 2022; see https://www.uspto.gov/dashboard/patents/track-one.html

In other instances the motivation lies in getting a patent issued so that the patent holder can go after infringers. The good news here is that a PE application can often result in a utility patent being issued within 8 - 12 months from the filing date.

> **Prioritized examination can receive 1st office action in two months**

Another motivation is that in the long run it may actually be less expensive to proceed with prioritized examination than with an ordinary utility application. The reason is that the marginal costs of filing a PE application pale in comparison to the R&D costs of developing a new prototype or product. We all too often see a startup spending next to nothing on patents, and tens of millions of dollars on a new product -- only to be dominated in the market by a "me too" competitor. In some cases the cost for filing a PE application would have only been 1/100th the cost of developing the technology! By filing an application with prioritized examination, a company can very quickly learn what is or is not patentable, and possibly save millions of dollars in either eliminated or redirected R&D costs. And if a patent issues rapidly from the program, the company can possibly squelch R&D and marketing efforts of competitors before they even get off the ground.

Other motivations for pursuing PE applications exist beyond speed and funding. One tactical reason for pursing PE applications is to bolster one's defensive posture. Should a competitor assert its intellectual property, a prioritized patent application (or a rapidly issued patent) can often be used as currency in a cross licensing deal to prevent a law suit.

Yet another benefit of filing PE applications is that they can be used to accelerate foreign filings. In many cases, accelerated examination applications can be allowed in much less than one year. Once claims in the PE application have been allowed, a corresponding application can be filed directly with international patent offices without going through PCT. Such international filings can sometimes be fast-tracked via the patent prosecution highway program. At the time of this writing, the USPTO has patent prosecution highway agreements with Japan, the United Kingdom, Canada, Korea, Australia, Europe, Denmark, Singapore, and Germany.

C) Patent Prosecution Highways

Kudos must certainly be extended to the past USPTO director Jon W. Dudas. Under his leadership, the Patent Office began to focus on the Patent Office as a business rather than a government agency. Much more needs to be accomplished, but at least the Office started experimenting with all sorts of creative ideas for making its "products" (patents and patent prosecution) align with the needs of its "customers" (inventors, companies and patent practitioners).

One effort in this direction resulted in the so-called Patent Prosecution Highways (PPH).[63] Through a series of bilateral agreements, the USPTO fast tracks examination of any claim in a U.S. application for which a corresponding claim was allowed in any of more than 25 national or regional patent offices, which as of August 2022 including Australia, Austria, Canada, Chile, Denmark, EPO, Estonia, Finland, Germany, Hungary, Iceland, Israel, Japan, Korea, New Zealand, Norway, Peru, Poland, Portugal, Singapore, Spain, Sweden, and the United Kingdom.[64] The process works for both national stage applications, and in many bases PCT applications.

---

63   https://www.uspto.gov/patents/basics/international-protection/patent-prosecution-highway-pph-fast-track
64   As of March 11, 2022, interactions with Russia's IP office have been suspended due to Russia's invasion of Ukraine.

Patent Prosecution Highways are not difficult to use. The USPTO even has materials to explain the benefits and details of the process.[65]

In practice, the real benefit often lies in filing relatively narrow claims in a foreign country that issues office actions quickly, and has low filings fees. Obviously, it does little good to a U.S. applicant to file a foreign application for the sole purpose of riding the patent prosecution highway if the U.S. patent office substantively examines the non-provisional application *before* the foreign patent office does, or if the costs are high. Thus, one needs to take into account not only filing fees, but also translation and foreign associate fees.

D) PCT First Filing Strategy

A non-provisional utility application patent application is normally the first filing that an inventor makes. Starting at month zero, it takes about 18 months before the patent office comes back to the applicant with a first substantive office action. Yes, sometimes the patent office works faster, especially in technology groups that have a light workload. At the other extreme, office actions in computer software and business methods can take at least 2-3 years before the patent office issues its first office action!

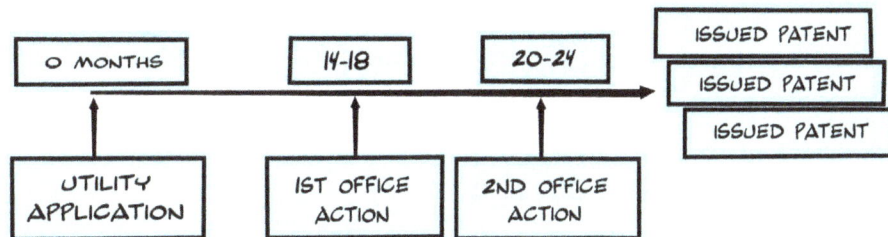

The first office action is almost always a rejection, which is proper. If someone offers to sell his car for $30,000 and the potential purchaser immediately pulls out his checkbook to write the check, the first thing that should go through the mind of the seller is that he offered to sell the car at too low a price. The same is true of the patent office. If the office accepts all the claims on the first go-round, the patent attorney should seriously consider whether the allowed claims are too narrow.

Assuming that the first office action is a rejection of at least some of the claims, the patent attorney then argues back and forth with the patent examiner. That process usually takes about six months to a year, and may go on to several years if a second, third office or subsequent office action is issued. Assuming all goes well, the patent can issue in about two to four years (or more in software and business methods). Divisional applications, can issue in about the same time if the applications are prosecuted in parallel, or much later if the applications are prosecuted consecutively.

Foreign filing foreign application must be done within one year of the earliest claimed priority date of the U.S. application. On average, getting a foreign application on file costs about $3,500 per country in English speaking countries, and about $5,000 to $8,000 per country or region in non-English speaking countries. So the costs can add up pretty quickly.

Filing a PCT application extends the foreign deadline from one year after filing of the priority application, to 30 months in most countries or regions. The deadline is 31 months in the European Patent Office, and up to 42 months in Canada with payment of penalty fees. A complete listing of the deadlines can be found on the Internet.[66]

---

65   https://www.uspto.gov/patents/basics/international-protection/patent-prosecution-highway-pph-fast-track
66   www.wipo.int

The PCT application must be filed by the one-year anniversary of the earliest claimed U.S. application, which could be a provisional, a utility, or even another PCT application.

One benefit of PCT filings is that the arguing (prosecution) period is shortened. The PCT is supposed to issue a combination search report and written opinion by the 16th month after the earliest claimed priority date. There is no longer any formal provision by which the PCT is required to argue back and forth with the applicant or applicant's attorney, but when such arguing does take place, it is also highly compressed. The process is depicted below.

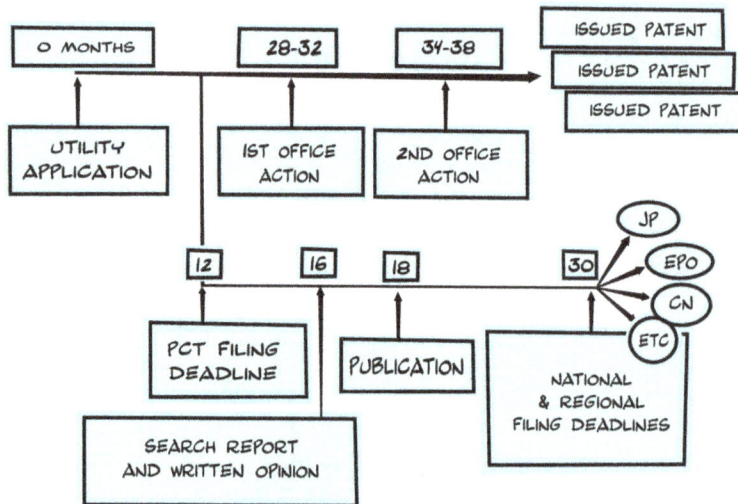

The problem, of course, is that since a PCT application must be filed within one year of the earliest filed U.S. application, the U.S. patent office will generally not have issued the first office action (search report) by the deadline to file the PCT application. Thus, when the PCT filing deadline rolls around, the attorney/applicant doesn't know whether it is worthwhile to file foreign applications.

There is a better way. It is perfectly legal to file the PCT application first, which in effect treats the United States as a foreign country for national phase filing at 30 months. In many cases the PCT examiners will issue that search report/written opinion in about three and a half to four months! That is a huge advantage when trying to raise money from the marketplace in the early life of a company. Investors are understandably skeptical about what an inventor says about patentability, and even what a patent attorney says about patentability. But here we have a way to secure a search report from one of the patent offices, in a matter of months instead of years.

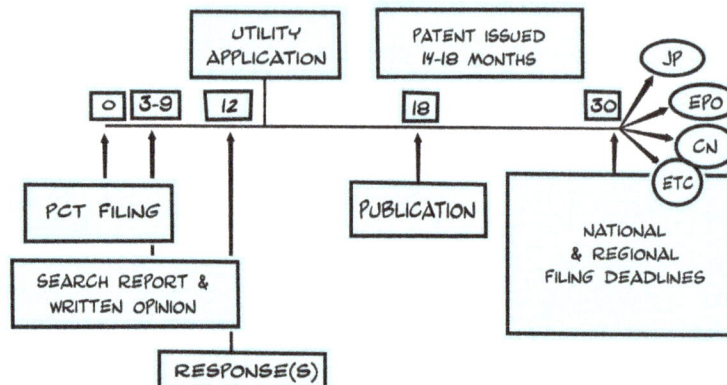

There are other advantages as well. If the examiner does respond quickly with the combination search report/written opinion, and the applicant pays the Chapter II fee of about $900 when he files the response to the search report/written opinion), then the entire process of arguing back and forth with the examiner can be completed near the end of the first year. The attorney/applicant can then file the U.S. national phase off the PCT application, having the benefit of the all the references and arguments used against the applicant during the PCT prosecution.

Now it is true that some examining groups (e.g. the Internet and software groups) re-examine everything at the utility / national phase stage, even if all claims were deemed allowable at the PCT stage. But other times the utility sails through without further examination. Indeed, when filing the U.S. national phase on an application with all claims allowed, it is possible to be allowed for less than $1,000, because the patent office is not contemplating an additional search. If all goes well, the U.S. patent can *issue* within the same year and a half period that would be required just to get the search report under the normal filing procedure.

Yet another advantage of filing PCT first is that the PCT deals with divisionals differently from the U.S. patent office. Instead of issuing a "restriction requirement" to split the application into multiple parts, the PCT issues disunity rejections that can usually be resolved by filing an extra $2,080 fee for each separate "invention." Upon filing national or regional applications at 30 months (or longer in some countries or regions), the various countries (including the US) often keep all the claims together rather than issuing restriction requirements - especially if all claims were deemed allowable by the time the preliminary examination report was issued. If the application is being protected in many countries, keeping multiple independent claims together at the national phase can save many thousands of dollars.

There is even a further advantage in filing PCT first, namely simplification of the U.S. prosecution. Amendment of claims during U.S. prosecution gives rise to "file wrapper estoppel," which precludes the applicant from later arguing that the issued claims cover subject matter that was given up during prosecution. For awhile the law was even stronger, precluding application of the doctrine of equivalents (which broadens the scope of patent claims beyond their literal meaning) for any claim that was amended in any manner. The complete bar of the so-called *Festo* doctrine was overturned by the U.S. Supreme Court, but there are fears that it may yet rise again. In any event, handling many or all of the objections and rejections during the PCT phase of prosecution means that there is often much less amending of claims during the U.S. national phase.

Filing PCT first also opens up a very interesting strategy for using provisional applications - something that could be called "patent judo" since one uses the examiner's own arguments against him. As shown below, one can prepare and file a PCT application, and then file it again on the same day as a provisional application. If the patent examiner comes back with a terrible search report, the attorney may well wish that he could start all over again with a new application.

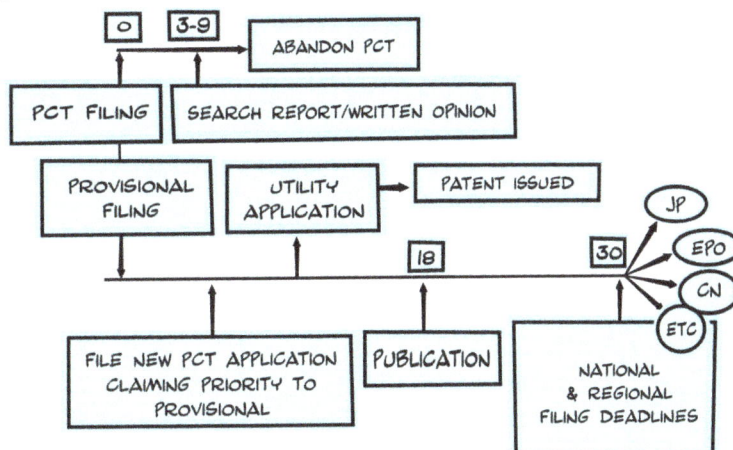

By filing PCT first, an applicant can do just that. All one needs to do is abandon the previously filed PCT application, and draft a new PCT application taking into account all the prior art that the examiner found. The applicant then files that new PCT application, claiming priority to the provisional filing. Assuming the examiner took his best shot at the previously filed claims, the new PCT application can be written to overcome the examiner's best arguments. Voila! The claims might be deemed allowable right away. Of course one can do the same thing by filing an initial non-provisional utility application in place of the provisional.

E)   Accelerated Examination (AE)

For many years the Patent Office has been under intense pressure from applicants to speed up patent prosecution times. The demand has been especially acute in the software and business methods fields, where first office actions are currently being issued perhaps 2 – 3 years after filing.

On August 25, 2006 the Patent Office instituted the Accelerated Exchanged program ("AE" for short). The process never gained widespread acceptance, and there are several reasons for that lack of acceptance, including high cost and effort on the part of the patent attorneys and agents handling the filings. Nevertheless, the AE process works well, and for several years was one of only a few quick paths through the most heavily trafficked examining groups.

> **Accelerated examination has many benefits, but likely adds $12,000 to the cost of filing**

Perhaps the greatest benefit is that the very rigorous hoops that the Patent Office forces patent practitioners to jump through in filing AE applications means that the filed claims are likely to have been well researched prior to filing. For a really crucial new technology, where the applicant wants the claims to be right from the start, and to secure a patent quickly, a PE application may still be the way to go.

In addition, the Patent Office seems to assign experienced examiners to AE applications. Having experience on the other side of the case makes the prosecution go forward much more smoothly and professionally. We would be shocked if an accelerated examination examiner rejected a dependent claim on a completely invalid objection, such as where the parent claim was allowed but its dependent claim rejection as being obvious (something that did happen in a non-accelerated case). Still further, the accelerated examination examiners are required to contact the patent practitioner to try to work out the claims. This is a far cry from many other situations, where the examiners condescend to speak with the practitioners, and require all communications to be in writing.

The fact that office actions must be responded to within a shortened statutory period of only one month can also be a big plus. Accelerated examination cases necessarily move forward quickly, so that both applicants and examiners have the arguments fresh in their minds.

Chapter V - Hiding And Publishing Applications

A) Submarine Applications

In the bad old days (or good old days depending on one's perspective), it was possible to secure patent protection far beyond the ordinary life of a patent. The trick was to prosecute an application to allowance, and then file a divisional application just before the patent issued. The first divisional could then be prosecuted to allowance, and then a second divisional filed before the first divisional issued. This could be done and over again, each time gaining a new 17 year term from the date of issuance. Just to show how ridiculous the system became, a patent was issued in 2000 on an application filed in 1936![67]

Congress tried to put a stop to these so-called submarine patents by requiring applicants to file a terminal disclaimer on these divisionals pending after an earlier member of the patent family had already issued as a patent, disclaiming any term beyond the term of the earlier patent. But there were still abuses to the system because the terminal disclaimer rule only applied to a pending application where the claims were obvious over the claims of the earlier issued patent. If the applicant chose to serially claim protection on different aspects

> **Applications can be kept secret with petition for non-publication**

of the invention, then the terminal disclaimer restriction would not apply. The result was grossly unfair to society, and a terrible abuse of the patent system. The Lemelson patents on the product bar codes are a case in point. The original application was filed in the 1950s, and yet many of the Lemelson patents were still in force in the 2000's.[68]

In 1995 a new law took place, limiting the term of a patent to 20 years from the earliest claimed U.S. priority date,[69] plus any applicable Patent Term Adjustment (PTA).[70] If that law had been in effect at the time of the Lemelson patent prosecution, the resulting patents would have expired in the 1970s at the latest. This is a very good change in the law, and advantageously also places the U.S. in accord with the patent laws of all the other countries on the planet.

One would have thought the U.S. had said goodbye to submarine patents in 1995. But that is not true. It is still possible to have a submarine patent of sorts, by filing a patent application with extremely narrow, irrelevant claims, waiting until the application publishes 18 months later, and then amending the claims to cover much more significant subject matter. By that strategy the competition falsely thinks it is free to practice embodiments outside the narrow scope of the published claims, and acts accordingly.

---

67 U.S. 6130946 (Oct. 2000) "Cryptographs."

68 *Symbol Techs., Inc. v. Lemelson Med., Educ. & Research Found.*, LP, 422 F.3d 1378, 2005 U.S. App. LEXIS 19439 (Fed. Cir. 2005); *affirmed, Symbol Techs., Inc. v. Lemelson Med., Educ. & Research Found.*, LP, 2005 U.S. App. LEXIS 24588 (Fed. Cir. 2005).

69 35 U.S.C. § 154(a)(2). Actually, patents on applications filed prior to June 6, 1995 have the longer of (a) 17 years from date of issuance or (b) 20 years from earliest claimed priority date.

70 35 U.S.C. § 154(b). Patent term adjustments begin accruing after 3 years of prosecution, subject to numerous exceptions. Under the American Inventors Protection Act of 1999, the automatic patent term extension under 35 U.S.C. §154 is only applicable for patent applications filed on or after May 29, 2000. (Pub. L. No. 106-113, § 4405, 113 Stat. at 1501A-560). The term of a patent may be extended under a separate section of the Patent Statute for up to 5 years for patents on products involving human drugs, medical devices, food additives, and color additives subject to regulation under the Federal Food, Drug, and Cosmetic Act (21 U.S.C. §§301-399f)35 U.S.C. § 156(f)(1)-(2).

The trick is to be sure to provide both enablement and best mode for whatever is going to be claimed in a child application.[71] The applicant can continue to secure additional subject matter by filing terminal disclaimers, but competitors cannot do so because they do not have overlap of inventors and ownership with the original application.

This is a classic one-two punch. The applicant forces the competitors to alter their products to circumvent an original set of claims, and then sues them under the subsequent sets of claims for producing and selling the altered products.

Since March 2001, U.S. patent applications are generally published 18 months after their earliest claimed priority date. It is possible to delay that publication, however, by filing a petition for non-publication at the time the application is filed. That tactic is often used to keep the application below the surface, where it is hidden until the patentee wants the world to see it.

B)   Public Disclosure Documents

Inventors often want to evidence their invention date in some manner, without going through the cost of filing a formal or even a provisional application. The USPTO's disclosure document program is intended to satisfy that need, and according to their literature "should provide a more credible form of evidence than that provided by the popular practice of mailing a disclosure to oneself or another person by registered mail."

All an applicant needs to do is describe the invention "in sufficient detail to enable a person having ordinary knowledge in the field of the invention to make and use the invention," and file the disclosure with a $10 fee.[72] The description can be of any length, and might commonly be only a page or two. A drawing is desirable, but not required.

Depositing a document under the public disclosure document program has no legal benefit with respect to securing any patent rights in the invention, does not provide any sort of priority filing date, and is not examined by the Patent Office. The document simply kept on file for two years, and then destroyed unless it is specifically referred to in an action in a then-pending patent application. In short, filing of a disclosure document is generally a waste of time and money. The better strategy is to pay a few dollars more and file a provisional patent application.

C)   Statutory Invention Registrations

In some cases an inventor doesn't want to pursue a patent application. Instead, he just wants to make sure that (a) he gets credit for having invented the technology, and/or (b) no one else gets the patent. That approach can make good sense where a strong claim is unlikely to issue in view of the prior art, or perhaps the market demand is so low that the inventor will never make back the money he paid his patent attorney.

In such cases an inventor or company should consider filing a statutory invention registration.[73] The patent office will publish the disclosure, and it will thereafter be considered prior art. There aren't very many Statutory Invention Registrations (SIRs). Only about 2100 have ever been published, all of which can be accessed

---

through the usual USPTO patent database. They are given "H numbers" such as H342. Note that it is possible to retract the SIR from publication, upon filing of a timely petition for express abandonment.[74]

35 U.S.C. § 157(a) provides for voluntary publication of specification and drawings of a regularly filed patent application for a patent, without examination. The rule can be used to advantage if the applicant wants to see his application published, but intends to abandon the application before it would normally be published at 18 months. The kicker is that the applicant must waive the right to receive a patent on the invention within such period as may be prescribed by the Director; and he still has to pay application, publication, and other processing fees.[75]

D) Patent Pending Status

A patent application is "pending" as of its filing date. This applies to non-provisional utility applications, as well as to provisionals and PCT applications.

References to "patent pending" status are often done to keep competitors at bay. Depending on their own patent pending status, research efforts and direction, cost of entry to market, expected lifespan of the product, perceived likelihood of being sued, expected profitability on the product, knowledge of prior art, and several other factors, competitors may decide to stay away from the market. But there is no legal enforceability until a patent is actually granted (issues). Thus, even though a patent application may have been pending for three or four years, the applicant has no right to try to enforce the patent.[76] Indeed, attempting to enforce claims of a pending application can strip the patentee of the liability exemptions that the patent law generally provides patentees, and can itself be actionable as an antitrust violation.[77] At the very least such an effort can be considered patent misuse, and may well render the patent unenforceable against the targeted party.[78]

It is possible to obtain a reasonable royalty for acts that would have been infringing during the window between publication of a patent application (at 18 months from earliest claimed priority date) and the issue date of the patent. As discussed elsewhere herein, enforcement under these circumstances requires that the competitor have actual knowledge of the patent application, and that the published claims are substantially the same as the claims that actually issue. Use of the "patent pending" notation could conceivably be used to bolster the actual knowledge requirement.

Pending patent applications can also be utilized in helping to determine royalties with respect unpatented aspects of patented products. In addition to the somewhat intangible benefit during negotiation of being able to describe a more comprehensive patenting strategy, a 1996 Federal Circuit case held that it is permissible to calculate royalties in part on the unpatented features.[79] In particular, the Court held that such licensing activity falls within 35 U.S.C. § 271(d)(1) and (2) and cannot, as such, constitute patent misuse. Aside from § 271(d), royalties may be based upon unpatented components of a patented system if done for the convenience of the parties in determining the value of the patented invention.[80]

---

74   37 C.F.R. § 1.138 https://www.ecfr.gov/current/title-37/chapter-I/subchapter-A/part-1/subpart-B/subject-group-ECFR-98ba3a7401adec0/section-1.138

75   https://www.govinfo.gov/content/pkg/USCODE-2015-title35/pdf/USCODE-2015-title35-partII-chap14-sec157.pdf

76   35 U.S.C. § 271 https://mpep.uspto.gov/RDMS/MPEP/e8r9#/e8r9/d0e305527.html , Infringement Of Patents.

77   *Unitherm Food Sys. v. Swift-Eckrich, Inc.*, 375 F.3d 1341 (Fed. Cir. 2004).

78   *C.R. Bard, Inc., v. M3 Sys., Inc.*, 157 F.3d 1340, 1372 (Fed. Cir. 1998); *Mallinckrodt, Inc. v. Medipart, Inc.*, 976 F.2d 700, 703-04 (Fed. Cir. 1992).

79   *Engel Indus. v. Lockformer Co.*, 96 F.3d 1398, 1408 (Fed. Cir. 1996).

80   *Id.*, 1407-1408.

Chapter VI - Controlling Patent Costs

It is an article of faith among many patent attorneys, inventors, investors, and a good number of corporate executives, that good patent protection is necessarily very expensive. Unfortunately, that attitude is both wasteful and dangerous. Acceptance of the inevitability of high patent costs leads to sloppy patent drafting, misallocation of prosecution funds, and reduced funding for research and development.

Part of the problem is that patent attorneys have enormous discretion in drafting claims, and often exercise that discretion in a self-serving manner that maximizes the eventual costs of securing the patent portfolio. The problem is exacerbated by the fact that most clients have little or no ability to evaluate the quality or cost-effectiveness of the work. This chapter addresses both problems, by providing a realistic view of the costs involved, and guidance with respect to distinguishing "good" patents from "bad" patents.

A) Why Patent Expenses Are So High

People are often told that the cost of securing a patent is about $15,000 - $20,000. That statement is probably correct for simple applications. As of 2023 it costs about $8,000 - $12,000 to search, brainstorm and draft the application, and pay the government filing fees. It costs another $2,500 to $7,500 to argue the application before the patent office, and another $1,500 to review the notice of allowance, pay the issue and printing fees, and examine the final patent for errors. This is all assuming small entity status. [81]

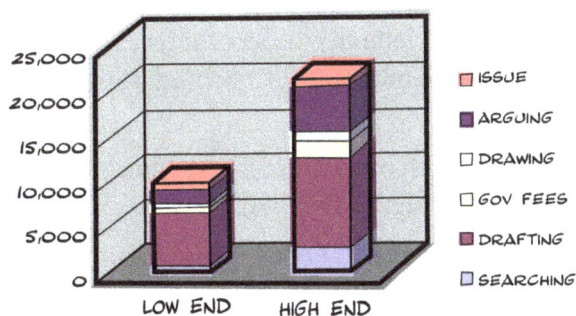

The problem is that such charges are often only the beginning. As described below, a single utility application can easily spawn numerous divisional or other continuation applications, and those other applications can increase the costs many fold. Add to that the costs of foreign prosecution, and what originated as a $20,000 budget can very quickly grow to $750,000 or more! To get a handle on that, let's review the costs of different types of U.S. utility applications, and then focus on the costs of foreign prosecution.

B) Costs Of Getting A Primary Application On File

As discussed above, the cost of getting a formal application U.S. utility patent application *on file* application filing is usually about $8,000 - $12,000, depending on the difficulty in searching and drafting the application. Where do these numbers come from?

---

81   All fees described in the Patent Shock Series are subject to change, and might well be outdated. Indeed, the patent office updates their fees several times a year as they try to balance competing interests.

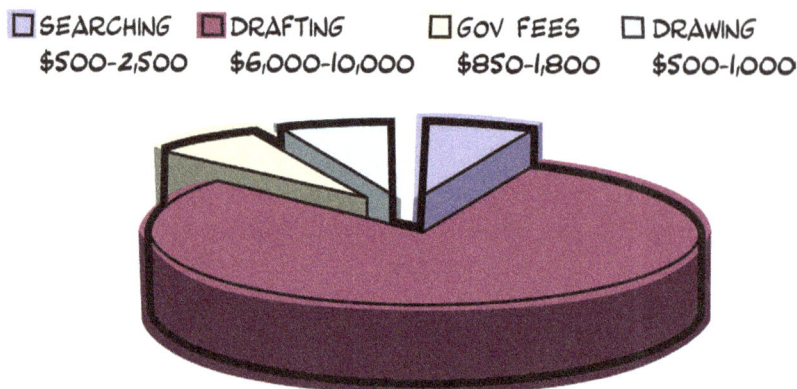

SEARCHING   DRAFTING   GOV FEES   DRAWING
$500-2,500 $6,000-10,000 $850-1,800 $500-1,000

- An experienced patent attorney or agent[82] usually takes two to four hours to run a patentability search[83], and another fifteen to twenty hours to draft a typical patent application. At about $500 an hour that comes to about $7,000 - $10,000. Less experienced attorneys (or patent agents) may charge less per hour, but are typically slower, so that the total charges remain about the same. Of course, searching and drafting charges on complicated inventions can run higher, as much as $5,000 or more. There are patent firms that charge $30,000 or more to draft a patent application, but such fees are unconscionable. It should not take eighty to a hundred hours to draft a patent application.

- In 2020, on top of the drafting charges, one needs to add the filing costs. The normal government filing fee is $728 for a U.S. utility application ($1,820 for so-called "large entities", entities that have at least 500 employees, and $364 for micro entities). But note that since many attorneys can't seem to draft concise applications, the patent office charges an extra $96/$192/$480 (micro/small/large) for each independent claim in excess of three, $20/$40/$100 for each dependent claim in excess of twenty, and $84/$168/$420 for each additional 50 sheets in excess of 100 sheets.[84]

- There are also drawing charges, which run about $80 per sheet. Most applications can be drafted to require only 5-10 sheets of drawing, so the total drawing charges should be less than $500.

Ironically, one very common cause for high charges is that the invention is very simple. A new pair of scissors, for example, is incredibly difficult to patent broadly. The concept of scissors has been around for so long that the prior art is a virtual minefield of ideas.

Another common cause for high charges is that the inventor keeps changing his mind about what the invention is. It is one thing to work with an inventor to search for prior art, derive claims, draft the application, and then get final sign-off with relatively few changes. It is quite another thing to spend the better part of a month discussing claims and writing the application, only to start the process all over again when the inventor decides that he wants to claim something different. On occasion, we have worked on applications where the inventors' vacillations more than doubled the cost. Indeed, inventor vacillation is probably a major reason that patent attorneys are loath to write patent applications at fixed cost.

A third common cause for high patent application costs is that the inventor has a large number of designs and/ or a huge amount of undigested data to consider. Running through all that information can be incredibly time

---

82   Patent Agents and patent attorneys are equal before the Patent Office. For simplicity in writing, references in this book are usually made to patent attorneys as opposed to "patent attorneys/agents."

83   Note that a patentability search is not the same thing as a right-to-practice search.

84   Fees shown are effective January 2023. See https://www.uspto.gov/learning-and-resources/fees-and-payment/uspto-fee-schedule

consuming, and patent attorneys sometimes take on the chore because they don't otherwise have a full plate. Nevertheless, the task of reviewing and consolidating such material is best done by the inventor, or at most by the inventor with help from the patent attorney or others. Forcing that work back on the inventor can significantly reduce patent drafting charges.

Some patent offices offer to draft, file, and prosecute an application through issuance or final rejection for a fixed price. This is usually a mistake because the incentive is for the patent attorney to draft extremely narrow claims that are easy to get allowed, but likely are worthless.

General information about patent fees is available on the Internet,[85] including the latest fee schedule, and related notices. Note that the USPTO's schedule can be misleading since many of the fees need to be combined. In general, a PCT filing through the U.S. receiving office runs about $3,500, and a PCT filing through the International Bureau (or through the USPTO designating the European Patent Office as the searching authority) runs about $4,500 (including attorney and paralegal fees).

C)   Costs Of Getting A Secondary Application On File

A first (primary) non-provisional utility or PCT application is often followed in the U.S. by additional (i.e., secondary) applications, such as divisionals, continuations, CIPs, and so forth. The primary and secondary applications can quickly form a complicated and expensive *family* of applications, even though these other applications are usually much less expensive to file than the primary application.

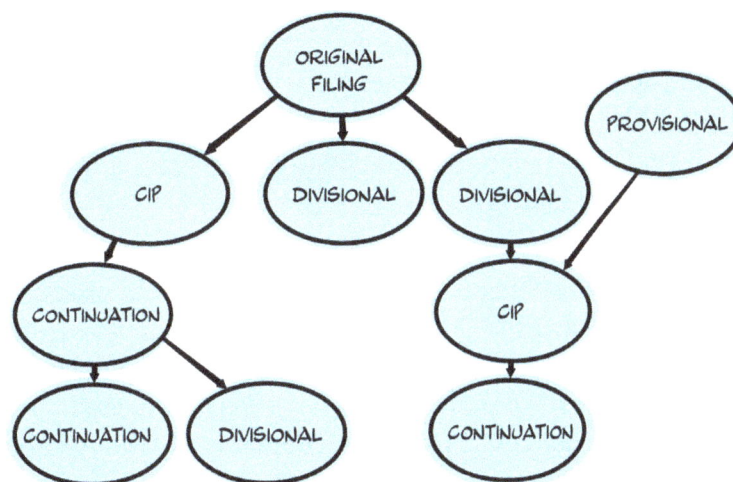

A "divisional" is one of the most common types of secondary applications. Divisionals are basically child applications that are filed off the parent. They receive a new serial number, but start with an exact copy of the Specification and claims as originally filed in the parent. A patent attorney cannot substantively change the Specification in a divisional application, so all the effort goes into changing the claims. That sometimes involves another one or even two thousand dollars, but often the patent attorney just files claims in the divisional that were withdrawn or rejected claims from the parent. Thus, the cost for filing a divisional application, including filing fees and paralegal charges, is often less than $2,000 (for a small entity).

A straight continuation is another type of child application, which again receives a new serial number. The difference is that the starting point of the continuation is the ending point, rather than the beginning point, of the parent, and changes made to the Specification and Drawing during prosecution of the parent are therefore reflected in the continuation. Here again most of the work is in altering the claims. The cost for filing a

---

continuation application, including filing fees and paralegal charges, is thus once again often less than about $2,000 (for a small entity).

A request for continuing examination application (RCE) is a continuation of the current application that was necessitated by repeated rejections of the pending claims. An RCE is very similar to the now obsolete File Wrapper Continuation, except that an RCE application keeps the same serial number as the parent. Here again only the claims are amended, and indeed failure to amend the claims when filing an RCE will result in an immediate final rejection. The Specification can usually only be modified to correct spelling and punctuation, and to make other relatively insubstantial changes. Unless there are significant changes to the claims, the cost for filing a RCE application, including filing fees and paralegal charges, should once again be less than about $2,000 (for a small entity).

There is still another type of child application called a "Continuation-In-Part" or CIP for short. CIP applications use an existing application as a springboard, and then add additional subject matter to the Specification. CIP applications also almost invariably add new claims. These applications are intermediate in difficulty (and cost) between a new utility application or PCT application, and a divisional application or straight continuation application. Thus, CIPs can run $3,500 and up.

A provisional patent application is an informal application that never issues as a patent. Its main purpose is to give the applicant a filing date to which the applicant can later claim priority in a formal non-provisional application. Indeed, unless the applicant files a formal application (utility or PCT) that claims priority to the provisional within a year of the provisional filing date, the provisional application dies at the one-year anniversary, and the effect is as if no application had ever been filed. Provisionals can be as simple as a single paragraph, or as complete as a formal application, with the patent attorney charges varying accordingly. In our office we have charged as little as $350 for essentially adding a cover sheet to pages copied from a lab notebook, and paying the $168 filing fee (for small entities). On the other hand, we have charged several thousands of dollars to draft what was effectively a non-provisional utility application, which we filed as a provisional application. It all depends on the filing strategy.

A design application focuses on the ornamental (non-functional) appearance of something. Designer sunglasses, for example, are often protected with design patents (and possibly a product configuration trade dress application as well). There is nothing at all to drafting design patent claims because every design patent has only one claim, and that claim is always worded in substantially the same manner. The claim always reads substantially as follows: "A <<something>> as shown and described in the accompanying drawing." The cost of a design application is mostly in preparing the Drawing. These should always be done by a professional patent drawing draftsman because of the many nuances peculiar to drawing design patent applications. Among other things an applicant must be very careful to avoid unnecessary detail, and to depict the non-claimed subject matter using dashed lines. Preparation and filing charges for a design patent, including drawing sheets, is often under $1000 (small entity).

D)   Variations In Charges From Firm To Firm

There are firms that charge a lot more than the fees and costs identified above. As unbelievable as it may seem, there are law firms that charge $2000 - $3000, *in addition to the government filing fees*, to basically refile a utility application as a PCT application. In another example, a well-known law firm charged $30,000 just to file a provisional!

Indeed, some law firms *routinely* charge $20,000 and even $30,000 to draft a patent application. Those charges are absurd. Just think about it. Let's say a patent attorney having a medium level of experience charges $500 per hour. If he drafts a $30,000 application, he effectively billed for 60 hours of work. That's 1.5 solid weeks of work. Absent very unusual circumstances, no competent patent attorney should have to spend that much time writing a single application.

The absurdity of some of the patent charges was captured in the Patent Beast™ comic strip[86], with respect to a radio show hosted by a hypothetical law firm named Berry, Olsen, Marvel and Bean.[87]

Of course, there are plenty of smoke and mirrors that attorney use to justify excessive charges. Sometimes the trick is to file a very long application. Along those lines some firms routinely submit patent applications that are 80, or even 100 pages long. Yes, there are possible circumstances that justify such a long application, but those circumstances rarely justify the high price. If the unusual length is due to an extensive listing of preferred embodiments or experiments (as is often the case in the pharmaceutical and other chemical fields), then the high cost is unjustified because those long listings are almost invariably compiled by the inventor(s). In most other instances, the excessive length is the result of the attorney's laziness or incompetence. Anyone can make something difficult. It takes hard work and intelligence to make something simple.[88]

Another common trick is to bill large amounts for work of a "supervising" attorney, who doesn't (or shouldn't) spend anywhere near the amount of time billed to the client. One patent attorney told me that he regularly drafted applications for about $5,000 of time, and that the firm billed about $25,000 for his work! These things are just unconscionable.

Still other trick is to use "standard" fees for simple administrative functions. Some firms, for example, charge a $500 administrative fee for opening a new matter, $150 per month docketing fee (even if there is nothing to docket), and up to $1500 per foreign application just for opening the file.

---

86   www.patentbeast.com

87   https://www.patentbeast.com/category/bomb/

88   Apologies here to Charles Mingus, Composer, 1922-1979, who said "Making the simple complicated is commonplace; making the complicated simple, awesomely simple, that's creativity."

(1)   Invention Companies And Patent Mills

One should be very careful to avoid filing patent applications through one of the patent mills. They are fairly easy to spot because they advertise the large quantity of applications they file each year. One such firm even brags that they file more applications than any other firm in the country. Whether these are styled as "invention companies" or law firms, the bottom line is that they pump out hundreds or even thousands of applications a year, usually with mechanistically drafted specifications and extremely narrow claims. The problem, of course, is that when the patent holder tries to enforce his patent years later, he quickly discovers that all of the claims can be readily circumvented, and that his patent is therefore essentially worthless.

From time to time one of the government agencies takes aim at one of the patent mills, and raises the level of awareness by bringing civil or even criminal charges.[89] Relevant information regarding patent mills can also be found on the website of the National Inventor Fraud Center.[90] But in general, inventors and patent holders need to watch out for themselves. Unfortunately, it can be very difficult for those outside the patent field to distinguish patent mills from legitimate patent firms and practitioners. One red flag is that patent mills often charge a *fixed fee*, usually about nine or ten thousand dollars, to draft and file a patent application. They can charge a fixed fee regardless of the difficulty of searching and drafting the application because they do a crummy job on all of the applications. Another red flag is that patent mills often promise to advertise the patent rights and/or the patented product. There are instances in which such efforts have been successful, but they are few and far between.

(2)   Costs Of Unproductively Arguing With The Patent Office

Another area where people waste a lot of money is in unproductively arguing back and forth with the patent examiner. In U.S. prosecution, an applicant is usually entitled to two bites at the apple before final rejection -- one response after a first substantive office action, and then a second response after a second substantive office action. Office actions for technicalities such as missing signatures in filing the application, or restriction requirements (see below) don't count towards the two bites.

After the final rejection, the applicant can file a request for continued examination, to get another two office actions. The process continues until allowance or the applicant gives up.

The arguing phase is usually completed within about two years from the first office action, and usually costs less than about $3,500. But the process can go much longer and cost much more. We once took over prosecution of a patent application that had been languishing in the patent office for ten years! We got the application allowed in just a few months, but the cost to the client before we took over, including a series of continuations, was $80,000!

The key is to know when to fight and when to give up. Attorneys are happy to carry the battle to the death, but of course it's the client's money that the attorneys are fighting with. There are diminishing returns here just as anywhere else.

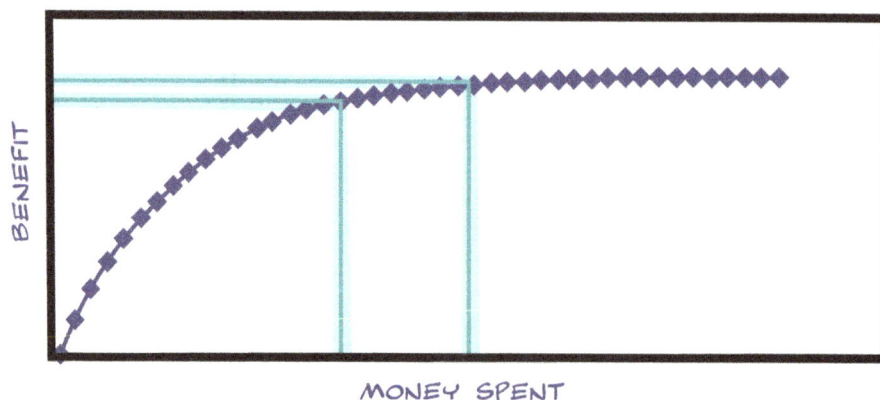

89   See, e.g., *FTC v. Davison Assocs.*, 431 F. Supp. 2d 548 (D. Pa. 2006).
90   http://www.inventorfraud.com/

One problem in excessively long prosecutions is where the patent attorney views the examiner as his enemy. That results in communications that sound like two children arguing in a playground. One says "x," and the other says "not x." Then the first one repeats "x," and the other repeats "not x." In the patent world, this can go on for years, with the patent attorney developing a hugely thick file to justify all his work. If a patent application is still pending after a third continuation, one has to seriously consider whether the attorney has the right strategy.

The solution is for the patent attorney to do the heavy mental lifting involved in figuring out where the invention lies relative to the prior art, and to write concise, commercially relevant claims that focus on the point of novelty. Merely focusing on technical distinctions is anathema to good patenting. The emphasis should be on claiming improvements that can be broadly patented, and that have significance in the marketplace. Once the patent attorney clearly understands *and claims* the novelty over the prior art, the patent examiners are usually quite supportive.

It is also true that high charges can sometimes be justified. From time to time an applicant pulls a bad examiner, and costs run up because the examiner doesn't know, or won't follow, the law. We once had an examiner who insisted upon rejecting a dependent claim on the grounds of obviousness, while admitting that the independent parent claim was allowable! Such a rejection is completely illogical, and charges to fight the examiner on that issue were completely justified. In other instances patent prosecution charges can run up because the inventor/applicant is keeping an application alive to allow for future claim amendments against a competitor that has circumvented previously issued claims. High prosecution costs can also be justified where the applicant chooses to keep his application pending rather than have narrow claims issue. In such instances the patent pending status of the application can be more valuable in the marketplace than an issued patent with narrow claims.

(3) Be Careful About Patent Applications With Many Independent Claims

As explained above, the cost of getting a U.S. patent application *on file* should be $8,000 - $12,000 (for small entities). In rare cases the cost can go up to $15,000. By the time the patent issues, the total cost may run from $20,000 to as high as $25,000 or more. So far so good.

But many companies want to file foreign application. It is quite common, for example, for patent applications on medical devices to be filed in Europe, Japan, China (PRC), Korea, Canada and Mexico. In those circumstances the added cost of at least $10,000 - $15,000 per country can be justified by the extremely high profits generated in each of the various foreign countries.

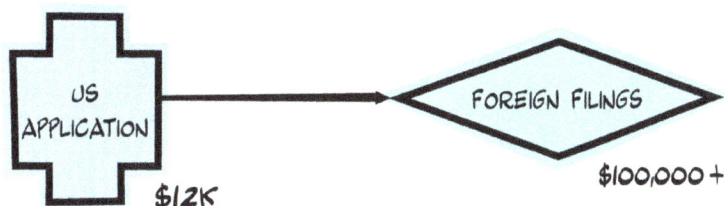

Now look at what happens when the single U.S. application spawns both divisionals divisional application and foreign filings foreign application. The patent budget will easily rise above $300,000.

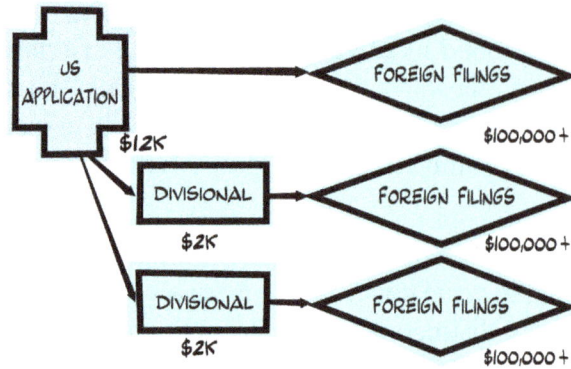

Finally, look at what happens when there are multiple U.S. applications. The original $20,000 - $25,000 U.S. patenting costs eventually run up a bill nearing half a million dollars. Of course, for most individuals, and many companies, those numbers are just unacceptable. This is why companies should be focusing on cost effectiveness. As discussed below, there *are* strategies for achieving the desired results, without triggering all that cost.

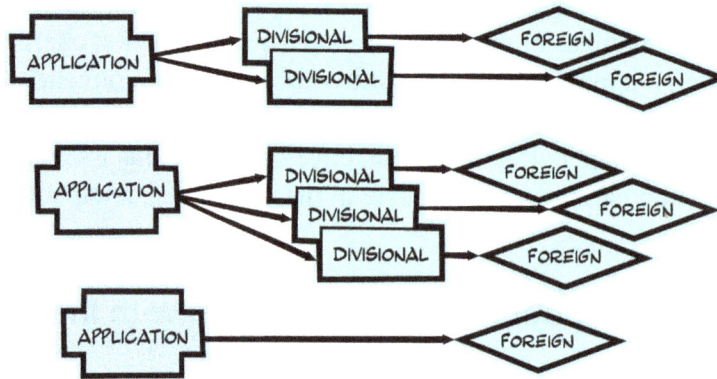

The bottom line here is that you shouldn't let your patent attorneys play games with your money. They shouldn't be filing applications with dozens of independent claims, and fifty or more dependent claims. All that does is result in high initial cost, and many-way restriction requirements. Your attorneys should be working for you, not the other way around.

E)   Software And Business Methods Applications

The Patent Office issued just over 374,000 patent applications in FY2021, a great many of which are software or business methods patents. Those statistics and many others are now readily available to the public on the patent office's Data Visualization Center.[91]

It is possible that such large numbers reflect great innovation in the software industry, but as the Bust Patents website[92] points out, it's a bit difficult to believe. Software and business methods patents can be quite difficult to get through the Patent Office with meaningful claims, and the process can easily take 3 - 5 years even if one is proceeding with Prioritized Examination. Before filing full-blown utility applications in these areas, it really behooves inventors and companies to take a long hard look at whether the cost justifies the benefits. Estimates are that 85% of patents are never commercialized at all, let alone make sufficient money to justify the attorney's fees.

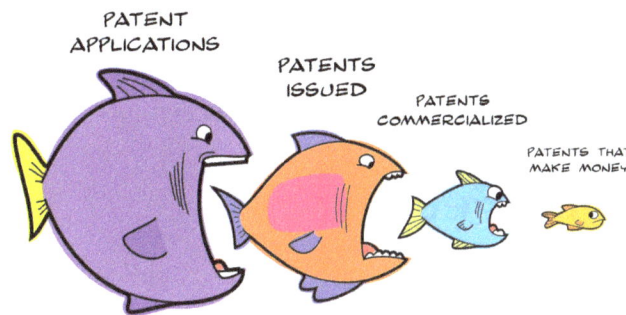

F)   Design Patents

Where the invention is mostly in the non-functional design of a product, the patent portfolio should be built around *design* patents rather than *utility* patents.

For several decades, design patents became less and less valuable due to the difficulty of establishing infringement. The Courts used a complex test that involved both "point of novelty" and an "ordinary observer" perspective. Beginning in 2008, however, the Federal Circuit established the "ordinary observer" test as the "sole test for determining whether a design patent has been infringed." *Egyptian Goddess, Inc. v Swisa, Inc.*, (Fed Cir 2008) 543 F3d 665, 678, cert denied (2009) 556 US 1167. Since then, there have been numerous high profile design patent infringement cases, including Apple's™ establishing infringement over Samsung™ and others regarding cell phone design.

Design patents are relatively inexpensive, with filing costs and fees usually less than $1000. Design patents are also prosecuted very quickly. A bar graph displayed in the January 20, 2013 Patently-O blog,[93] showed that about 45% of all design patent applications are resolved (issued or abandoned) by the end of the first year, and more than 90% are resolved by the end of two years. The same blog pointed out that Nike's Design Patent No. D659,988 issued in 2011 after less than three-months in prosecution. One drawback of design patents is that they expire only 15 years from the priority filing date.[94]

---

91   https://www.uspto.gov/dashboard/patents/

92   www.bustpatents.com

93   www.patentlyo.com/patent/2013/01/design-patents-are-still-relatively-quick.html?utm_source=feedburner&utm_medium=email&utm_campaign=Feed%3A+PatentlyO+%28Dennis+Crouch%27s+Patently-O%29

94   Patent Law Treaties Implementation Act of 2012.

G)   European Union Unitary Patent

U.S. companies tend to seek patent protection by filing EPO applications, and then registering the granted EPO application in countries of interest. There are many drawbacks to that approach, including the fact that the patent holder then has many different versions of the same patent (due to translation issues), and needs to enforce each of those patents separately in each of the registered countries.

The EPO is in the final preparatory stages of instituting the Unitary Patent and Unified Patent Court. This may be in effect as soon as spring 2023. This option will allow a single patent to have effect in throughout western and most of central Europe without registering in each member country. This will coexist for some time with an option to file in single European countries. A unified patent will likely only be a cost savings if patents would be sought in more than 4 member countries. For those seeking protection in one or two European member countries, filing in those countries separately would likely be a cheaper option.

Infringement proceedings are to be held in one of the Unified Patent Courts, and their decisions are to be binding upon all countries. Of course, patent holders need to carefully consider whether such "all or nothing" approach is advantageous. There will likely still be separate proceedings for validity and infringement.

H)   Maintenance Fees

Before 1980 the U.S. patent office had no maintenance fees. The applicant paid his patent issue fee, and that was that. Foreign countries did have maintenance fees even back then, but they were fairly inexpensive. More recently the U.S. and foreign governments realized that maintenance fees are an excellent source of income, one for which they don't even have to provide any services. The net effect is that patent owners now have quite considerable maintenance fees in the US, and throughout the world. It is not at all uncommon for a company with a 10 or 15 U.S. patents, and perhaps 100 foreign equivalents, to pay upwards of $75,000 a year in maintenance fees alone. As of January 2023, maintenance fees of U.S. utility patents are as follows:[95]

Deadline	Large Entity	Small Entity	Micro Entity
Due at 3.5 years	2,000	800	400
Due at 7.5 years	3,760	1,504	752
Due at 11.5 years	7,700	3,080	1,540
Surcharge - Late payment within 6 months	500	200	100

Maintenance fees are problematic not only because of the out-of-pocket costs involved, but also because they are a terrible nuisance and liability. Most countries have annual maintenance fees, and failure to pay those fees results in the patents being irrevocably lapsed.

Some large patent offices have their own inside maintenance department. Unfortunately, this means that the maintenance function is a profit center for them, and that cost is passed along to the patentees. It is very common for a law office with an internal maintenance department to tack on an extra several hundred dollars per patent per country per year for their maintenance service even if no maintenance fees is due that year!

The better solution is to utilize an outside service for maintenance. There are basically only a few independent maintenance systems that are widely used, including CPI (Computer Packages Inc.)[96], Clarivate[97], Dennemeyer[98],

95   https://www.uspto.gov/learning-and-resources/fees-and-payment/uspto-fee-schedule
96   https://www.computerpackages.com/products-and-services/annuity-service/
97   https://clarivate.com/products/ip-services/patent-and-trademark-maintenance-services/
98   www.dennemeyer.com/

and Maxval[99]. We currently use Dennemeyer, but each of those services has been in business for many years, and is extremely reliable. There are all sorts of packages available, with the average monitoring and processing cost running ranging from $50 to $250 per patent per country per year.

If a patent holder *wants* to pay its own U.S. maintenance fees, that task is quite easy in the U.S. The USPTO provides a convenient snapshot of the status of an application,[100] as well as detailed information on payment of fees.[101]

One should also be very careful about paying fees on patents that are no longer worthwhile. Many firms are paying so much for maintenance fees that it is negatively impacting their current innovation program.

I)   Be Realistic Regarding Expected Charges

Patent applicants often have an unrealistic view of the costs of patent protection. The bottom line is that an applicant usually needs to allocate at least $20,000 to $25,000 get a patent issued in the United States. In cases where the prosecution is likely to be especially difficult, he needs to allocate $30,000 or more. When confronted with those figures applicants often want to discuss how they can reduce the charges. There are indeed ways of addressing the high charges, including asking the attorney to take an equity position, or grant extended payment terms. One solution that seems to work for start-ups is for the company to give the attorney a few percent equity,in exchange for attorney fees. Some firms take 4-5% of equity in the applicant, cover all costs during prosecution, but then get back all of the prosecution costs upon a buyout or other equity event.

---

99   https://www.maxval.com/ip-renewal-services/

100 http://portal.uspto.gov.

101 https://www.uspto.gov/learning-and-resources/fees-and-payment/uspto-fee-schedule

Patent Beast

© FISH 2006

I HAVE DOZENS OF IDEAS....

....AND I WANT TO PATENT ALL OF THEM!

THAT WILL COST HUNDREDS OF THOUSANDS OF DOLLARS....

I WANT TO DO IT FOR $5,000... ...TOTAL!

Remember, the only thing an attorney has to sell is his time. Squeezing a reasonably priced attorney just means that he won't be able to do a decent job.

Sometimes, when considering how much money to devote to patent prosecution, it's helpful to view a patent as a product, with an expected return on investment (ROI). And whereas designing, producing and marketing a product may have a five- or ten-fold return on investment, a patent application may well have a fifty- or hundred-fold return on investment. It's not at all uncommon that a patent portfolio that costs a hundred thousand dollars can be sold for several million. Moreover, if a startup company finds itself on the auction block after a few years, it may discover that the only thing it has to sell is its patent portfolio.

Patent Beast

© FISH 2006

I HAVE THE WORLD'S GREATEST INVENTION!

IT WILL MAKE A MILLION DOLLARS PER YEAR!

FILING A UTILITY WILL COST ABOUT $8,000.

OH, NO... I CAN'T AFFORD THAT...

Applicants also inquire from time to time whether we can guarantee that a patent will issue. The answer to that question is "no". It is impossible for an attorney (or anyone else) to know in advance how broadly an invention can be patented. Among other things, the new AIA version of 35 U.S.C. § 102, provides that prior art includes anything "described in a printed publication, or in public use, on sale, *or otherwise available to the public* before the effective filing date of the claimed invention", with very few exceptions. And even if somehow one could magically know everything available to the public before the effective filing date, one still couldn't know all the prior art. Among other things, because patent applications are generally not published until 18 months, and they become prior art *as of their filing dates* once they are published.

J)   Cost-Effective Does Not Mean "Cheap"

My first book on patenting was called *Cost-Effective Patenting*. Since business people focus on cost-effectiveness when purchasing office equipment, hiring employees, and buying supplies, I just assumed they would be attracted to that title because they would want to use the same level of acumen when dealing with patents that they use in other areas of their business. I was wrong. Somehow, when it comes to securing legal protections, many business people blindly equate quality with price. Either that, or they opt for the least expensive filings, and compensate by filing lots and lots of applications. Both strategies are misguided.

One of the core concepts of this book is that business people are completely capable of learning about patenting, just as they learn about accounting, taxes, marketing, human resources, and a myriad of other fields. It's just not that difficult to understand what makes a good patent, what an intelligently crafted patenting strategy looks like, and how that strategy can be executed without wasting monies that could be put to better use. Cost-effective patenting is getting the most bang for the buck, not getting the least expensive application, or getting sucked into paying for what the attorney claims is "the best possible" application.

One quick point about selecting a patent attorney. Everyone tries to sell what they have. Big firms sell their size and resumes, and small firms and individual attorneys sell their particular educational and experiential backgrounds. What we have found is that neither firm size, nor years in practice, nor particular expertise in a given field are good predictors of patent quality.

Years ago I worked for one of the largest patent firms on the planet. Their low associate to partner conversion rates (1:15) made it unprofitable to spend much time training associates, and that translated into bloated charges, and poorly drafted applications. Obviously, that is not to say that all patent applications by large firms are poorly written. But it is true that even the largest and most respected firms can put out a lot of garbage.

The same, of course, can be said for small shops. It is not at all uncommon for an inventor to ask about enforcing a patent against a competitor, only for us to discover that the claims are so poorly drafted that litigation is untenable. What good did it do for the inventor to spend even a relatively small amount of money, to get a patent that is unenforceable?

The key is to know what to look for. When reviewing patent applications, the key is to figure out whether the applications (when viewed in the portfolio as a whole) are sufficiently broad to constitute a commercially significant barrier against the competition. When reviewing attorneys and agents, the key is to look for individuals who: (1) have a broad-based scientific background; (2) are creative thinkers; and (3) are sufficiently personable to effectively brainstorm the White Space and Green Fields surrounding the inventive subject matter. Unfortunately, that's a rare combination. A specific technology can be learned, but these other factors, especially the last two, are almost impossible to teach.

Bottom line here, don't be fooled by the number of pages or claims in a patent application, or the credentials of the firm or the attorney. Look carefully at the work product.

Patent Beast

© FISH 2009

BUT I DON'T HAVE A PhD IN THE FIELD, AND I'M THE INVENTOR!

YES, BUT IT TAKES A PhD TO UNDERSTAND THE INVENTION.

YOU'RE KIDDING?

ACTUALLY, WE DO IT BECAUSE PhD'S LOOK IMPRESSIVE ON THE LETTERHEAD....

Patent Beast

© FISH 2009

HOLD ON THERE. I'M A TRIPLE PhD, AND I OFTEN ...

... BRAINSTORM WITH PEOPLE OUTSIDE MY FIELDS ...

... TO GET A DIFFERENT PERSPECTIVE.

AND YOU DO THAT BECAUSE...?

K)   Put Patenting Costs Into Perspective

Although conceptualizing and patenting new inventions is much less expensive than actually creating new products and getting them on the market, patenting can still be a waste of money. It all depends on how the money is spent. The best strategy has the patent attorney involved in both the R&D and strategic planning efforts, helping to secure broad monopolies and creating roadblocks against competitors.

Some engineers, scientists and programmers have a difficult time with this concept. They tend to focus on actually building things, optimizing their performance, and reducing production costs. But that doesn't necessarily create a commercially relevant monopoly. As demonstrated by the myriad companies that went bust during the dot com frenzy of the late 1990s,[102] successful companies have to find some way of creating a monopoly or some other barrier to entry against competitors. In the patent world this means finding a creative patent attorney who understands how to manipulate the patent laws for commercial benefit, implementing a policy of creative and cost-effective patenting, and then helping to locate the funds needed to make it happen.

---

102 Go.com was in existence for only four years, but supposedly cost the Walt Disney Company almost $800,000,000. Webvan™ raised $375,000,000 in an IPO, and went bust less than a year later. kosomo.com™ raised $280,000,000 and even secured a $150,000,000 deal with Starbucks, but was out of business within two years. Pets.com™ raised more than $80,000,000 in an IPO and went bust nine months later. eToys.com™ and boo.com™ each managed to run through more than $150,000,000 in only a few years. Aside from the fact that these were all Internet ventures, the key similarity is that they were pure "action plays." They added nothing to science or technology.

L) Don't Pay For Phony Patent Services

Patent applicants sometimes receive official looking solicitations that provide no substantive benefit whatsoever to the prosecution, maintenance or enforcement of their patents or applications. For a typical fee of between $1400 and $2500, these services merely list the patents or applications in their "private company directories." Two that we commonly see are from the Commercial Center for Industries and Trade, and the F.I.P.T.R Service. While these solicitations may be legal, we always recommend that they be thrown out, or even better, reported to appropriate agencies. WIPO has an extensive collection of such solicitations, both for patents and trademarks.[103]

103 https://www.wipo.int/pct/en/warning/pct_warning.html

Chapter VII - Valuing Patents And Applications

The value of a patent can range from zero to many billions of dollars. Unfortunately, such things are often very difficult to measure, and in some cases patent valuation is little more than an educated guess. Here's why.

A)   Quantitative Valuation Of A Patent

Patents and other forms of intellectual property are intangible assets. The asset is merely a legal right conferred upon the patent holder. Yes, one can physically hold a registration certificate or other indicia of the asset, but one cannot physically feel, touch, smell, or hold, the underlying legal rights. Add to a patent's intangibility the fact that the legal right is by definition unique (because a patent must be something novel), and one has the very essence of a difficult-to-value asset.

On the other hand, patents are given valuations all the time. One possible valuation model focuses on the price that a willing buyer and a willing seller would agree upon for sale of the patent. Of course, if the willing buyer/seller model is to yield a result that is anything other than an estimate, there must be a ready market for the patent. In addition, for the result to be accurate the patent must have either been recently sold, or there must at least have been a recent arms-length negotiation. If there is no ready market, or the last transaction is a bit long in the tooth, the willing buyer/seller model is just an educated guess.

Many Ways To Value Patents

- Willing Buyer-Seller
- Marginal Profit Margin
- Costs of R&D
- Number of patents or claims

A second valuation model focuses on the market for the product (or products) covered by the patent. In the *marginal profit model* one makes assumptions about the market size, market penetration, cost of entry, cost of production, lifespan, and profitability of the patented product, and then runs a spreadsheet to estimate profit. The value of patent is then taken to be the discounted present value of the estimated marginal profit, i.e., the profit over and above profit that which one would expect to be generated without the patent.

Unfortunately, the validity of the marginal-profit model depends entirely upon the validity of the underlying assumptions, and those assumptions can vary wildly among different analysts. At the end of the day, it all boils down to experience and judgment. My advice is to use a company that specializes in valuing patents, and preferably that has experience in valuations in the particular field of interest. Two good choices are Joseph Hirsch[104] at Globalview Advisors and Stout[105].

A third valuation model focuses on the costs incurred in developing the technology and securing the patent, and in some instances the replacement cost of re-creating the technology. The *cost/replacement model* is perhaps useful for bookkeeping purposes, and may be important to shareholders to understand where their funds have disappeared. But costs incurred in developing technology and securing patent protection often have little or nothing whatever to do with the value of the resulting patent. One can easily spend millions of dollars securing a patent that is worthless, and one can also spend less than ten thousand dollars to secure a patent worth many millions.

---

[104] jhirsch@globalviewadvisors.com. Globalview advisors is an ESOP
[105] https://www.stout.com/en/services/intellectual-property-intangible-assets

For the willfully blind or the just plain lazy, there is a fourth valuation model that focuses on simple metrics, such as the number of patents in a portfolio, the number of claims in a patent, or the number of times that a given patent is cited by later patents. From perusal of the rest of this book, it should be completely obvious that those numbers have little to do with value of a patent. The one exception is where the owner holds a very large patent portfolio. In those instances the *simple metrics* model has at least some validity because every additional patent has intrinsic value regardless of the independent value of the patent. The whole is greater than the sum of the parts. IBM, for example, has so many patents on desktop and portable computers that it is essentially impossible to build a commercially viable computer without stepping on one of their patents. Years ago IBM threatened one of my clients with patent infringement for building and selling desktop computers. The IBM licensing agent sent me five patents to review, and we diligently found either work-arounds or invalidating prior art for all five patents. When we presented that information to the licensing agent, he merely offered to send me another twenty patents for consideration. The point is that IBM has so many patents, and is so reasonable with their licensing rates, that it makes no sense whatsoever to fight them. Independently of any other analysis, the sheer size of IBM's patent portfolio means that the portfolio has inherent value.

A fifth valuation model focuses on the management team charged with exploiting the patent. That *management team* model is the darling of investment capital firms because startup companies rarely have an "A" management team, let alone an "AAAA" team. Indeed, the venture capital firms regularly use that deficiency as a cudgel to beat the patentee over the head, declaring that the patent is worth very little without an adequate team to build and market the product. They have a point, of course, but the argument is illogical. The value of the patent is often entirely dependent on the people who are exploiting it.

The valuation analysis is analogous for both licenses and assignments, with the proviso that there is somewhat greater perceived value for the assignee to hold a patent than for a licensee to hold a license. That perception is not necessarily justified, however, because in many ways it may be better to hold a license than a patent. One factor is venue of litigation. It is not uncommon for an infringer to bring a declaratory judgment action against the patent holder to declare the patent invalid. But the owner of a patent is a necessary and indispensable party to the litigation, and an individual owner can only be sued where he/she resides. Thus, maintaining the patent ownership in the name of the inventor can often prevent the licensee from being dragged into court in the middle district of some locality where the judge is the brother of the infringer. Another factor is cost of litigation and maintenance. Where a patent is assigned, the assignee becomes responsible for defending the patent (by suing infringers) and for paying maintenance fees. With licenses it is common for the licensee to cover those costs.

B)   Royalty Rates

> Reasonable royalty often calculated to be 20 – 25% of the marginal value to the licensee

If a patent is licensed, the valuation often turns heavily on the expected royalty rate. Estimating royalty rate is a matter of experienced judgment, and depends upon all the factors mentioned above, as well as the relative bargaining strengths of the parties, and the competitive landscape. Inventors often want to know what a reasonable range of royalties for their invention is. Thankfully, the process is not entirely guesswork. For most mechanical patents the starting point for royalties is about 3%, with extremely valuable patents fetching values of 7 - 10%. On the other end, it is not uncommon for a patent royalty to be down in the 1 - 2% range. Pharmaceuticals can fetch royalty rates of 20% and more, but only because the margins can run 80 - 90%, and the barrier to entry of competing products is extremely high.

The Licensing Executives Society[106] (LES) spent many years trying to rationalize licensing rates. What they found after reviewing thousands of licenses is that a licensor generally receives 20 - 25% of the *marginal value* of the license to the licensor. As a simple example, let's say a product costs $25 to manufacture. If the patent allows the licensee to sell his product for $100 instead of $75, then the marginal benefit of having the patent is $25/unit. The licensee should get 20 - 25% of that amount, or $5 - $6.25 per unit sold, which is about 5 to 6 % of the sales price. A similar analysis can be made with respect to increased sales volume. If holding a license to a patent allows the licensee to double his sales, then 20 - 25% of the marginal profit from those marginal sales should go to the licensor. Most likely, a license results in increased profit on a per unit basis, as well as increased the total sales. Thus, the royalty should be calculated as a function of both increased profit per sale and increased sales.

When making these calculations it is extremely important to account for all of the marginal costs. This means evaluating both direct costs (e.g., raw materials and manufacturing), and indirect costs (e.g., product distribution, administrative overhead, borrowing costs, and the risk of opening a new market). In addition, marginal profit must amortize the start-up and shutdown costs of producing, advertising, and distributing the product over its estimated life span. If the licensee fails to properly account for those indirect costs, a licensee could end up losing money by licensing a patent.

When licensing an inventive part of larger product, it is also important to appreciate that the proper royalty rate depends on how important the part is to the entire product. A patent on a new way of stitching the leather on an automobile seat has a value relative to the seat. The manufacturer might save some money in producing or buying the seat, but likely cannot charge any more for the automobile. In that case, an appropriate royalty may be rather low relative to the price of the car. On the other hand, an improvement to the fuel injection system that increases mileage by 15% may be worth hundreds or even thousands of dollars per vehicle to the manufacturer.

Another major factor is the relative bargaining powers of the licensor and licensee. If the licensee has a great need for immediate cash, the equation tilts in favor of the licensor. Similarly, if a product requires multiple licenses, then a single licensor cannot control the licensing process, so the value of its portfolio goes down. In such instances it is very common to include an anti-stacking provision in the license agreement. Under such a provision, the royalty rate and/or other licensing fees are automatically reduced as the licensor is forced to take on licenses from third parties.

Of course, there are other factors involved, including allocation of risk. If the intellectual property is still in the application stage (no patent issued yet), if development, production and marketing of a patented product requires millions of dollars in investment, and/or if it is not clear that the market for the product will be robust or long-lasting, then the licensor is taking a tremendous risk in licensing the patent rights. That would tend to reduce the value of the license to the licensor. One way to address the risk issue is to back-load the payments with little or no upfront licensing fee, and a larger royalty. One can also address the risk issue by staging the licensing fees and royalty rates according to milestones, e.g., upon issuance of a patent, regulatory approval, first sale, and so forth.

The bottom line here is that determination of a correct license fees and royalty rates can be quite complicated. A rule of thumb is that most licenses have royalty rates in the 2 - 6% range. There are rare instances where the royalty rate is in the 10 - 15% range, but very rarely does it go above that.

106 www.lesi.org.

C)   Royalties From Pending Applications

In the U.S. one cannot enforce a patent against a competitor until the patent actually issues. That makes abundant sense because no one can be certain about the scope of the claims of a patent until the patent issues. And since infringement is determined by reading a claim on an accused product or method, one cannot determine infringement until the patent issues.

Patents can be licensed in the application stage

That result is a bit harsh on an applicant who was unable to license out the patent rights or secure risk capital because he didn't have an issued patent. With that difficulty in mind, Congress changed the law in about 2000 so that it became possible for a patent holder to obtain a "reasonable royalty" for activity of a competitor in the window between publication of the patent application and the date of the patent issuance. Unfortunately, there are so many loopholes in the law that it has little or no value. The royalty is only available if: (a) the issued claims are substantially the same as the published claims; *and* (b) the competitor had "actual" knowledge of the published application. These are significant stumbling blocks. There are precious few published cases in which a court enforced a "reasonable royalty" for activity during the window period.

Even though enforcement is not possible until a patent issues, it is possible to license or sell a pending application. In fact, this happens frequently. In effect the licensee assumes the risk that the patent will never issue, or that the issued claims will have little commercial use, in exchange for a confidence that it can push forward with researching or commercializing the invention without having to later try to negotiate a royalty. To the extent that the license is exclusive, there is also a benefit in possibly precluding a competitor from acquiring a competing license down the road, after the patent issues.

D)   Payment Schedules

Yet another aspect of patent valuation involves the timing of payments to the assignor or licensor. A royalty of one million dollars could be paid out as a lump sum payment, over time with nothing up front, or with some payment up front with some royalty. Although the net present value of all the options should theoretically all add up to the same million dollars regardless of the timing, in practice the valuation is heavily discounted (up to 75%) where there is a large up-front payment. There are many reasons for this, mostly having to do with allocation of risk. Greater up-front payment means the assignee/licensee is taking more risk, whereas lower upfront payment means that the risk is being shared. In theory, that risk should already have been incorporated into the net present value calculations, but the psychology is that large up-front payments tend to double-count that risk.

E)   Things To Watch Out For

Valuation also depends upon who is doing the manufacturing. If the patent holder is merely licensing the patent to a manufacturer, the estimated profit will be considerably lower (by three quarters or more) than if the patent holder were to manufacture and sell the product. However, that difference is misleading because it fails to account for the risks and costs involved in production, distribution, and patent enforcement. Most electronic products, for example, cost much more for a newcomer to manufacture than for an established business. From the distribution standpoint, an established player will likely sell many times that of a smaller player, just because of name recognition and store placement. For example, one can easily imagine a great new breakfast cereal that will never see the light of day unless it is being marketed by one of the giant food product companies. From an infringement standpoint, one needs to consider that a competitor will think very hard about trying to outrun the patent of a multi-billion dollar company, but may well be willing to chance an infringement action brought by an individual or small player.

Another issue concerns the purpose for which a patent is being valued. There is currently somewhat of a scam going on with companies donating their unused patents to charities. There, the tendency is to value the patent as high as possible because the company can write off the donated value. Since patents are notoriously difficult to value, it is quite difficult for the tax authorities to challenge the valuation. Other errors in valuation can also arise from biases of the persons valuing the patent. A seller or licensor will almost always make assumptions that increase the value, while a buyer or licensor will almost always make assumptions that decrease the value. It is absolutely fascinating to see the patent valuation given by an investor when he is seeking to buy into a company, and the valuation he gives the very same patent when seeking a later round of financing from some other investor.

Another factor of considerable importance is stacking. Royalties can only go so high. If a licensee is already paying a first licensor a 5% royalty on his product, he is unlikely to pay a second licensor another 5%, regardless of the value of the second licensor's patent. That situation is usually handled in the license agreement by an anti-stacking clause, which limits total royalties to be paid. Thus, in the example above the licensor may end up paying each of the licensors 3.5 - 4%. At the end of the day, given the usually stark difference in bargaining power of licensor and licensee, the possibility of multiple royalties, and all the other factors, most licenses still come down to 2 -6% royalty.

> **Consider anti-stacking provisions**

F)   Qualitative Valuation

There are many instances in which one needs a *quantitative* (i.e. monetary) valuation of a patent. For example, quantitative valuation is critical in evaluating assets for a merger or acquisition, for allocating R&D development costs, for establishing collateral, and for determining damages during litigation. In many other instances, however, the greater need is for a *qualitative* valuation. Is this patent worth pursuing? Should one continue to pay the maintenance fees? Should one file corresponding foreign applications?

The qualitative value of a patent is based to some extent upon the factors discussed above (expected market size, profitability, and so forth), but also upon scope and enforceability of the claims. The real issue with respect to claim scope is how difficult it is to circumvent the claims. In making that determination one must evaluate every element of a claim, and determine whether there is a commercially feasible way of avoiding that element. If there is at least one element in every claim of a patent that can be avoided, then the claims of that patent have little value. For example, in the following claim of U.S. 5695532, there are at least three elements that can readily be avoided.

> **If the claims can be circumvented, a patent may have little or no value**

1. A process for gasifying a particulate solid carbonaceous fuel with a ***moisture content greater than 50%***, said process comprising:

> introducing said fuel into a predryer at ***atmospheric pressure***;...
>
> partially drying said fuel in said predryer...
>
> introducing said partially dried fuel into said at least one
>> pressurized drying vessel ***without adding water*** to the partially dried fuel;...
>
> introducing at least a portion of said hot product gas into said at
>> least one drying vessel at a temperature such that pyrolysis of the fuel particles in the drying vessel is essentially avoided.

One can circumvent the "moisture content" requirement in the preamble by feeding the device with fuel having moisture content less than 50%. One can circumvent the "atmospheric pressure" requirement by introducing the fuel into the predryer under a slight vacuum. Not only would one circumvent the claim, but it would help dry the material. One can circumvent the "without adding water" requirement simply by adding a little water to the partially dried fuel. In short, the claim is worthless.

In evaluating the scope of a patent, it is critical to consider all of the claims. If a product circumvents claims 1-8 but infringes claim 9, then the product infringes the patent.

That being said, when evaluating the scope of protection afforded by a patent, one usually just focuses on the independent claims because the dependent claims are always proper subsets of their parent independent claims. Dependent claims contain all the limitations of the parent (and grandparent, great-grandparent, etc.) claim(s), plus at least additional limitations from the dependent claim. It is thus logically impossible to fall outside the scope of an independent claim, and still fall within the scope of one of its dependencies. A good analogy is shooting an arrow at a target. If you miss the target (independent claim) then you necessarily missed the bullseye (dependent claim).

The law regarding claim scope is set forth in considerable detail in the sample opinion letter of Appendix B - Sample Patent Infringement Opinion. From a qualitative valuation standpoint, it suffices to say that claim scope should be determined by reading the claims as broadly as possible, within the constraints imposed by the so-called intrinsic evidence, i.e., the claims, the written description (specification), and the prosecution history. Yes, it is true that the stilted language of most patent claims presents a considerable barrier to their analysis. But the only way to determine the intrinsic value of a patent is to read the claims, claim-by-claim, and element-by-element, and then to read the entire specification and prosecution history to boot. If the reader can't understand the technology, he needs to get someone (preferably a patent attorney) who does understand it.

A potentially important problem in determining scope of a patent claim involves application of the doctrine of equivalents (also sometimes referred to as the doctrine of equivalence). Under that doctrine a product can be deemed to infringe a patent claim even though the product falls outside the literal scope of the claim. For many years the dominant test was the function-way-result test, which focuses on whether the accused process [performs] substantially the same steps as the patented process, in substantially the same way, to obtain the same result. But that test is problematic in that the result depends entirely on the level of abstraction used for the analysis. For example, in considering whether a door latch is equivalent to a doorknob one could focus on the fact that both devices operate the hand of a user, and both operate a mechanism that frees a door from a doorjamb. They may even be interchangeable in a given door. On the other hand, a door latch can be opened with an elbow, but the doorknob cannot, and a door latch will not receive a globe type baby protector, but a doorknob will receive the protector. Thus, on a usage abstraction a door latch and doorknob may or may not be equivalent. But on a higher level of abstraction, focusing on the fact that both latch and knob are both types of door hardware, there is no question that they are equivalent. The bottom line is that equivalence depends upon the level of abstraction used in the analysis. A patent holder usually wants to interpret the claims using a very high level of abstraction that ignores details, while an alleged infringer wants to interpret the claims using a low level of abstraction that focuses on the details.

A more recent test is whether there is an "insubstantial difference" between the accused product and the claimed subject matter. That test avoids the abstraction problem to some extent, but substitutes a substantiality test where the difference is still a matter of perspective. Is a method claim reciting an alkaline pH of 10-13 infringed by process that uses a pH of 9? If the pH 9 process only produces 75% of the yield of the pH 10-13 process, is the difference in yield substantial or not? Is analysis of yield even relevant to determining substantiality of differences? Sometimes the "insubstantial differences" test is clarified by an interchangeability test, but that still doesn't help. The question then becomes interchangeability for what purpose. These are very difficult questions.

Despite the difficulties, however, one can usually make a reasonable assessment of equivalence by focusing on what is emphasized in the specification. For example, U.S. patent 6431092 (Aug. 2002) claims a portable folding utility table with a center support assembly. Claim 1 recites a blow molded plastic table having first and second pivotally extendable pedestal supports, and a center support assembly connected to a cross-brace member using support braces. The specification goes on at length explaining how the claimed configuration allocates counter-forces in a desirable manner, making it clear that a competitor's table that omits both a center support and a cross bar member falls outside the scope of that claim. The competitor's table is not only missing the claimed elements, but it also fails to provide the counter-forces.

One significant development is that a few years ago the Federal Circuit made the doctrine of equivalents analysis much simpler in its *Festo* decision. In spite of being partially overturned by the U.S. Supreme court, the current law is that an amendment of claims that narrows the scope of the claims is presumed to constitute a disclaimer of the relinquished subject matter, and the reality is that amendment of the claim in any manner very likely eliminates doctrine of equivalents for that claim, and its dependencies.[107] Thus, one can often eliminate the doctrine of equivalents assessment for a given claim by establishing that the claim was amended during prosecution of the underling application.

Another aspect of patent valuation is the practical enforceability of the patent. One would think that a really broad patent will do the trick, but the reality does not always bear out that assessment. It may well be, for example, that the patent holder doesn't appear to have the funds to bring a lawsuit. It may also be the case that there are potential gorilla defendants that will spend the patent holder into oblivion. On the other hand, a patent holder can buy offensive insurance that pays for the offensive litigation against an infringer.

Other factors that often affect evaluation and enforceability are prior art related. It may be, for example, that a competitor had a product on the market more than a year before the priority date of the patent application. In that case the competitor's product is prior art, and the claims cannot correctly be interpreted to read on the competitor's product. It may also be the case that the patent holder or alleged infringer knows of some prior art, or perhaps some irregularity during patent prosecution that would be brought out during discovery. Another entirely preventable reason for un-enforceability is that the patent holder jumped the gun in trying to enforce its patent. Patents can only be enforced upon issuance. Prior to that time there is no patent, and nothing to enforce. If a patent applicant sends a cease and desist letter to a competitor prior to issuance of the patent,

107 Festo Corp. v. Shoketsu Kinzoku Kogyo Kabushiki Co., Ltd. et al., supra, 122 S. Ct. at 1831.

that act can be deemed to be patent misuse and an antitrust violation. Until "corrected" (whatever that means) the patent is unenforceable against that particular competitor.[108]

All of those circumstances could either invalidate the critical claims, or render them unenforceable.

G) Resolving Disparate Valuations

Minimum royalties and buyout clauses can sidestep many valuation issues

It will come as no surprise that patent owners tend to value their patents more highly than potential assignees or licensees. The question is how such disparities can be resolved. A good idea in that circumstance is to use the marginal profit model of patent valuation. At the very least, that model provides a mathematical foundation upon which to start negotiations. Yes, the assumptions will lead the model, but at least one can argue the assumptions more intelligently that one can argue the final number.

At Fish IP Law, LLP, we strongly suggest that the parties allocate risks and benefits using: (a) minimum royalties; and (b) buy-outs. A patent assignee or licensee is usually willing to forgo a large upfront payment if he is guaranteed a minimum royalty. Such minimums should usually start within a year of signing the contract, and should usually escalate to a maximum over the next four or five years. The punishment for failure to meet the minimum can range from loss of exclusivity (favors the assignee/licensee) to reversion of the patent rights (favors the assignor/licensor). Similarly, a patent assignee or licensee is usually willing to pay a higher royalty rate if he can buy out of the contract at some future date. For example, a contract can be drafted such that the assignee/licensee can purchase the entirety of the patent at the end of five or ten years. The buy-out can be set in advance at a particular dollar amount (e.g. ten million dollars), or can be set at a multiple of the prior year's royalties, or some other mathematically calculable benchmark.

H) Securing Value Through Donation

If a patent holder cannot seem to secure the value he wants for his patent, he may do well to donate the patent to a non-profit organization. He can secure a tax break, and he may even be able to continue practicing the claimed invention. That can be accomplished by the donor carving out a license for himself, at little or no royalty, and then donating the remainder.

For several years patent donation was somewhat of a scam. The IRS finally took notice, and issued a new rule in which a donor's initial charitable deduction is limited to the lesser of: (a) the donated property's tax basis; and (b) its fair market value.[109] Additional deductions may be allowed in later years based on specified percentages of income received by the charity from owning the donated property. These additional amounts are calculated using sliding-scale percentages that decline over the years. No deductions are permitted with respect to income received by the charity after the legal life of the patent or intellectual property has expired.

Also under the new rules, additional deductions after the year of contribution aren't allowed for donations of patents and other intellectual property to a private foundation - unless it's a private operating foundation or a private foundation described in 26 U.S.C. § 170(b)(1)(E).

To take advantage of the rule allowing additional deductions after the contribution year, the donor must inform the charity that the gift will be treated as a donation eligible for that treatment. The donor must then obtain annual written substantiation from the charity of the amount of income earned from the donated property.

---

108 Unitherm, supra, 375 F.3d 1341.
109 IRS Publication 561, Determining The Value Of Donated Property (2005).

Finally, the charity must file an annual information return with the IRS to report the income amount and other information.

I)   Valuation Due Diligence

In valuing patent portfolios it is often helpful to have a due diligence checklist. A simple such checklist is included in Appendix C – Due Diligence Checklist.

J)   Choosing A Valuation Firm

It has been extremely disappointing to work with the large general practice valuation consulting firms. In general, they provide a nicely prepared, impressively thick report that tell their clients exactly what their clients hired them to say. But usually, the client won't know how they accomplished their analysis, and won't be able to assess the validity of the analysis.

Perhaps the most frustrating aspect is that such firms tend to prepare their analysis at a level of abstraction that more or less ignores the specific language of the patent claims. Instead of delving into the nitty gritty of: (a) how large a piece of the technology is being captured by the patent claims; and (b) the difficulties entailed in circumventing those claims, they focus on the marketplace and the technology as a whole. Yet knowing the size of the market for pencils only helps determine the value of a pencil patent if one understands how effective that specific patent will be in cornering the market on pencils. And to do that one has to focus on the verbatim language of the claims.

A second problem is that valuation consulting firms tend to be very secretive about their methodology. Sure, the marketing person will provide a laundry list of the myriad steps they will take in performing their analysis. But at the end of the day, instead of explaining why the royalty rate should be this or that, the firm will simply divine the rate from their "proprietary database." That doesn't help very much because it forecloses any realistic scrutiny of the results or methodology. Clients deserve to know what goes on behind the curtain.

> **Valuation firms often just tell their clients what they want to hear**

To secure a valid analysis, one needs to understand and be comfortable with the methodology. One should force that the valuation firm to take a position on the scope and validity of the claims, and the likelihood and costs of circumventing the claims. Don't let them get away with the pabulum that they "can't analyze the scope of a patent because that would be practicing law." Valuing a patent while ignoring the scope and validity of the specific patent claims makes about as much sense as appraising a diamond while ignoring the size, cut, color, clarity, and defects of that specific diamond. It can be done, but it can't be done well.

All that aside, there is one valuation firm that seems to stand out among the rest, Stout[110]. To cite just one example, their valuation of an international company will take into account currencies, working capital and capital expenditures, taxation, non-operating and other assets/liabilities, indicated negative equity value, investment in subsidiaries, and valuation date vs reorganization transaction dates.

---

110   https://www.stout.com/en/services/intellectual-property

Chapter VIII - Patent-Related Agreements

A) Assignments

Assignments are extremely important in the patent world. Failure to properly assign rights can lead to unnecessary litigation, and possible liability on the part of both the inventor and the patent attorney. This can happen for all sorts of reasons, including death or disability of an inventor, reluctance of an inventor to file an assignment due to a separation from a company, divorce, and so forth. It thus behooves a patent attorney to at least consider getting an assignment on file quite early in the patenting process.

(1) Format Of An Assignment

The basic format of an assignment is straightforward. One essentially grants rights in and to one or more patents and/or applications in exchange for consideration. (See example in Appendix D - Sample Assignment Form). The same applies to licenses, which in reality are merely assignments of licensed rights as opposed to assignments of all right, title, and interest. Assignments of both types must be recorded using the official Recordation form[111].

Of course, one must be very careful when using assignments drafted by someone else. Template contracts in particular cannot be written in a "fair" manner for all purposes, primarily because terms that might be correct for one situation might be entirely wrong for another situation. Moreover, it depends what side a person is on as to what he thinks is "fair." A company that hires a software house to develop software probably thinks it is fair for the software to be a "work for hire" that is owned *ab initio* by the hiring company. On the other hand the software house probably thinks it is only fair that it owns the software that it developed, and that the hiring company only receives a copy. Architects, for example, almost always own the plans they develop, and merely let the customer use the plans on his particular building.

There are numerous websites that provide sample contracts for less than $50 each, and many of those sites even provide an interface that captures important information and preferences, and uses the information to select among various options[112]. It is also possible to find verbatim text of contracts actually used by Fortune 500™ and other public corporations[113]. The texts are made public record through SEC filings. One should note, however, that template forms are just that, templates. They need to be modified for particular purposes.

It is not technically necessary to re-file assignments for divisional or continuation applications. A properly worded prior assignment recorded in the patent office with respect to a parent application is automatically effective for a child application because the assignment recorded against the parent gives the assignee rights to the subject matter common to both applications[114]. On the other hand, the Office's assignment records will only reflect an assignment of a division or continuation application if a request for recordation is filed with respect to the child.[115]

---

111 www.uspto.gov.
112 See e.g.,www.legalcontracts.com
113 http://contracts.onecle.com.
114 MPEP § 306; https://mpep.uspto.gov/RDMS/MPEP/E8r8#/E8r8/d0e18955.html
115 MPEP § 306; https://www.govinfo.gov/app/details/CFR-2002-title37-vol1/CFR-2002-title37-vol1-sec3-28

One does need to consider state law in determining ownership, and therefore in drafting assignments. In California, for example, an employee may well have a duty to assign an invention to his / her employer, if the invention was relevant to the job[116]. Other states have different rules on this.

(2)   Multiple Inventors

Without agreement, co-inventors have independent right to commercialize an invention

Still another issue arises where there are multiple inventors. The rule is that a named co-inventor has a separate right to make, use, sell, import, export, license, and assign his/her undivided interest in the patent rights, unless that inventor assigned or licensed away his rights. Thus, if only one inventor assigns the patent rights to a company, a co-inventor could compete against the company, either directly or indirectly by assigning or licensing his portion of the patent rights. This could possibly destroy the value for everyone.

(3)   Recordation

Patent assignments should be recorded immediately

Under U.S. law, assignments must be recorded to be effective as against third parties who do not have actual knowledge of the assignment. The statute is similar to recording statutes used for recording real property.

Recordation is straightforward. The attorney simply completes the recordation form, and sends it off to the patent office with the appropriate fee (currently $40[117]) and the document to be recorded. About six months later the patent office returns the documents submitted, stamped to show the date and microfilm reel/frame number of the recordation. The process can be expedited by filing the recordation through EPAS, the Electronic Patent Assignment System. One simply scans the assignment, completes the recordation form[118], include an electronic signature, and hit the send button. Recordations submitted over the Internet are recorded at least by the following business day.

Prior to 2014, the office charged $40 for each patent or patent application listed on the recordation form. Thus, if an assignment references a family of 5 patent applications, the recordation fee was $200. Of course paralegal charges would also apply, and possibly attorney time. But in 2014 the fee dropped to zero for electronically recorded assignments!

Patent Beast   ©FISH 2022

GUYS, WE SHOULD FILE ASSIGNMENTS ALONG WITH THE APPLICATION.

DON'T WORRY, WE'RE ALL REALLY GOOD FRIENDS.

I GET IT. BUT WHAT IF...

UGH, LET'S JUST CELEBRATE FINISHING THE APPLICATION.

---

116 California Labor Code § 2870. https://leginfo.legislature.ca.gov/faces/codes_displaySection.xhtml?lawCode=LAB&sectionNum=2870

117 37 C.F.R § 1.21(h). https://www.law.cornell.edu/cfr/text/37/1.21

118 http://epas.uspto.gov.

Note also that it is important to clearly identify whether the document being recorded is an assignment, license, or other document. The recording branch does not generally read the documents to verify the content. Following recordation, we usually return any original assignment form to the client. We do not want the liability of keeping the document secure, and paying for its storage.

Absent some unusual circumstance, patent assignments do not have to be notarized for use within the United States. It is, however, a good idea to notarize assignments, and many patent assignment forms include a space for notarization. But the notarization is not strictly required. The opposite is true of assignments for use in foreign patent practice. Many countries require notarization, and many even require an apostille, which is generally done at the foreign country's U.S. consulate. Some people seem to have success sending documents directly to the various foreign consulates in Washington, D.C., San Francisco, or wherever. In other cases obtaining an apostille can be almost impossible. We typically use a company named Parasec[119] in Sacramento, CA, which we have found to be quick, reliable, and relatively inexpensive.

Confusion sometimes arises in terminology between an assignment and a license. The confusion is exacerbated by the practice of the patent office to refer to a license as a type of assignment. In a strict legal sense, that designation is correct. A license is a grant (assignment) to the licensee of licensed rights. The situation can be further obscured by the fact that one can assign the licensed rights from one entity to another. Thus, the first recordation of a license may be recorded as a "license," while the assignment of those same licensed rights to another entity may be recorded as an "assignment." The only way to really understand the situation is to review the actual documents, which are all readily available, for a fee, from the recordation branch of the patent office.

With respect to foreign applications and patents, one needs to carefully consider whether and when to record assignments in the various countries. The main advantage of early recordation is that many countries (including most or all of Europe) consider an assignment to be a taxable transfer, and charge VAT (Value Added Tax) on the estimated value of the application or patent. Since the value is often low in the early days, and can rise considerably during the life of the patent, the tax cost of registering is usually much lower early in the game. Another advantage of early recordation is that patent infringement damages accrue in some countries only from the date the assignment was actually recorded at the relevant Patent Office. Thus, delay in registering can cost a patent holder dearly in reduced patent infringement damages. The main disadvantage to recording assignments is that such recordation does cost something, and that such recordation is not absolutely necessary, at least until the patent holder wants to enforce his patent.

(4)   Tax Considerations

U.S. tax code is more favorable to those involved in the development and securing of a patent than in those who later acquire an issued patent. Reasonable costs of research and development of patentable subject matter are fully deductible[120], and the costs of patent attorneys and agents are also deductible to the extent that they were involved in filing and perfecting (i.e. prosecuting) a patent application[121]. Of course one can only expense those costs if they were incurred in connection with the taxpayer's trade or business. In contrast, the costs of purchasing patent rights are amortizable over a 15 year period[122]. The amount of the deduction is determined by amortizing the adjusted basis over a 15-year period beginning with the month in which a patent was acquired. Patents do not count as qualified export assets under section 993.[123]

---

120 26 U.S.C. § 174, Research and Experimental Expenditures. https://www.govinfo.gov/content/pkg/USCODE-2011-title26/html/USCODE-2011-title26-subtitleA-chap1-subchapB-partVI-sec174.htm

121 IRS Reg. 1.174-2(a)(2). https://www.govinfo.gov/content/pkg/CFR-2011-title26-vol3/xml/CFR-2011-title26-vol3-sec1-174-2.xml

122 26 U.S.C. § 197, Amortization Of Goodwill And Certain Other Intangibles https://www.govinfo.gov/content/pkg/USCODE-2011-title26/html/USCODE-2011-title26-subtitleA-chap1-subchapB-partVI-sec197.htm

123 https://www.govinfo.gov/content/pkg/USCODE-1994-title26/html/USCODE-1994-title26-chap1-subchapN-partIV-subpartA-sec993.htm

Licensing income from rentals or royalties relating to patents is treated as ordinary income[124]. This applies to both income from within the United States and income from without[125]. There are strategies for avoiding that outcome, but they must be set up in advance. Transfers of patents are taxable as capital gains, so long as the holder is transferring all substantial rights to a patent, or an undivided interest therein which includes a part of all such rights. The favorable rate applies regardless of whether or not payments in consideration of such transfer are: (1) payable periodically over a period generally coterminous with the transferee's use of the patent; or (2) contingent on the productivity, use or disposition of the property transferred. The term "holder" means: (1) any individual whose efforts created such property, or (2) any other individual who has acquired his interest in such property in exchange for consideration in money or money's worth paid to such creator prior to actual reduction to practice of the invention covered by the patent, if such individual is neither (A) the employer of such creator, nor (B) related to such creator (within the meaning of subsection (d))[126].

> **Transfer of all right, title and interest can be taxed as capital gains**

For those considering more sophisticated tax issues, it should be noted that section 483, dealing with present value of deferred payments, does not apply to sales of patents;[127] gain from sale of a patent between certain related taxpayers is subject to the allowance for depreciation provided in section 167;[128] and exchanges of patents may be considered same-kind transfers.[129] The era in which patent holders could receive excessively high tax deductions by donating their patents to charities has now been closed.[130] Currently, the patents must be donated at "fair value."

While assignments of U.S. patent applications from an employee to the company typically have no tax consequences, assignment of foreign patent applications and patents can be a very different story, because such transfers can be subject to a value added tax. Foreign taxes are also a consideration where a company assigns

124 26 U.S.C. § 861, Income From Sources With The United States. https://www.govinfo.gov/content/pkg/USCODE-2011-title26/html/USCODE-2011-title26-subtitleA-chap1-subchapN-partI-sec861.htm

125 26 U.S.C. § 862, Income From Sources Without The United States. https://www.govinfo.gov/content/pkg/USCODE-2011-title26/html/USCODE-2011-title26-subtitleA-chap1-subchapN-partI-sec862.htm

126 26 U.S.C. § 1235, Sale Or Exchange Of Patents. https://www.govinfo.gov/content/pkg/USCODE-2011-title26/html/USCODE-2011-title26-subtitleA-chap1-subchapP-partIV-sec1235.htm

127 26 U.S.C. § 483, Interest On Certain Deferred Payments. https://www.govinfo.gov/content/pkg/USCODE-2011-title26/html/USCODE-2011-title26-subtitleA-chap1-subchapE-partIII-sec483.htm

128 26 U.S.C. § 1239(e), Gain From Sale Of Depreciable Property Between Certain Related Taxpayers. https://www.govinfo.gov/content/pkg/USCODE-2006-title26/html/USCODE-2006-title26-subtitleA-chap1-subchapP-partIV-sec1239.htm

129 IRS Publication 544, Sales and Other Dispositions of Assets (2021). https://www.irs.gov/publications/p544

130 26 U.S.C. § 186, Recoveries Of Damages For Antitrust Violations, Etc.

In many countries, assignment of patents is subject to value added tax, which can be very expensive

intellectual property to an off-shore company, division, or subsidiary as a means of shunting profits out of the country. In such circumstances it may be wise to make the assignment or license early on, before the intellectual property has significant value. Otherwise the consideration may be viewed as inadequate, and the transaction viewed as a sham. One should also be cognizant that many countries having value-added taxes place a tax on transfer of intellectual property. In the case of extremely valuable patents, such a transfer (even to a related company) can unwittingly incur very significant taxes.

Patent infringement payments or obligations incurred are deductible, but only to the lesser of: (1) the amount of such compensatory amount, or (2) the amount of the un-recovered losses sustained as a result of such compensable injury.[131] The term "compensatory amount" means the amount received or accrued during the taxable year as damages as a result of an award in, or in settlement of, a civil action for recovery for a compensable injury, reduced by any amounts paid or incurred in the taxable year in securing such award or settlement.

(5) Designation of Assignee On The Face of A Patent

One cannot necessarily rely upon the designation of "assignee" as set forth on the face of a patent. For one thing, the patent office obtains the "assignment" information directly from the issue fee transmittal form, and there is no verification whatsoever that such information is, or even ever was, correct. The entry could well have been an error on the part of an attorney, paralegal, or secretary, and the issue fee transmittal form even warns that designation of an assignee of that form does not, in and of itself, effect an assignment. Second, information that was correct at one point in time may well be superseded down the road. Third, even if the "assignee" information is correct, one cannot know from the face of the patent what rights were assigned. It might well be that only licensed rights were assigned, or that such rights are subject to a reversion. The only thing one can rely upon is to obtain copies of the underlying documents from the patent office.

(6) Patents And Applications Must Be Identified By Number.

This little-known rule expressly states that patents and applications must be identified by their respective numbers in the assignment.[132]

> *An assignment relating to a patent must identify the patent by the patent number.* An assignment relating to a national patent application must identify the national patent application by the application number (consisting of the series code and the serial number, e.g., 07/123,456). An assignment relating to an international patent application which designates the United States of America must identify the international application by the international application number (e.g., PCT/US90/01234).

(7) Escrow Agents

It is sometimes helpful to use an intellectual property escrow agent in handling assignments. One suggestion is InnovaSafe Technology Escrow Services.[133]

131 26 U.S.C. § 186, Recoveries Of Damages For Antitrust Violations, Etc. https://www.govinfo.gov/content/pkg/US-CODE-2011-title26/html/USCODE-2011-title26-subtitleA-chap1-subchapB-partVI-sec186.htm
132 37 C.F.R § 3.21, Identification of patents and patent applications. https://www.uspto.gov/web/offices/pac/mpep/s302.html
133 InnovaSafe Technology Escrow Services, www.innovasafe.com/

B)   Licenses

(1)   Considerations In Drafting License Agreement

Patent licenses come in myriad different formats, with widely varying content. An exemplary license is set forth in Appendix E - Sample License Agreement, but there are many others available on the Internet, including a good collection of actual licenses utilized by well-known companies.[134] By comparing the provisions of all the contacts in a given area, one can at least get a good idea of the complexities involved, and the potential issues that may arise. Following are several factors that tend to arise in assignments and licenses.

A patent owner often has the upper hand in deciding whether to assign or license. Unless a court orders otherwise, there is no requirement in the U.S. to ever license a patent.[135]

(2)   Designation Of Parties And Property

Designation of the parties is critical. If one of the parties is a Delaware corporation and the assignment refers to that party as a California corporation, then the assignment may be declared invalid down the road. It also happens from time to time that the assigning party doesn't actually have the right to assign. To help avoid errors in drafting, attorneys traditionally employ a "Whereas" clause to identify the source of patent rights being assigned from any entity other than an inventor (where they originate), usually even including the reel/frame number of any earlier transfers of rights.

The property being assigned must be described accurately. Does the property include only issued patents, or both issued patents and pending applications? Does the property include continuations, divisionals, and/or Continuations-In-Part? This is often a critical issue because a very broad grant can tie up an inventor's future efforts for 20 years or more. Are foreign rights included? Does the property include technical know-how, which may or may not be addressed in the Specification, or just the specific subject matter *claimed* in the patents?

The grant of rights can be restricted in any number of ways, by any combination of time, geography, product line, and so forth. Licenses are often worded such that the grant of rights is for Licensed Products within The Field within the Territory for the duration of the Term, with each of the initial cap terms being defined in a separate paragraph.

Patent Beast   © FISH 2022

AND WHAT ABOUT IMPROVEMENTS?

UNDER THE LICENSE AGREEMENT...

Bob

...DO YOU GET OWNERSHIP OF ALL IMPROVEMENTS?

NOT MY FINEST HOUR.

---

134 See e.g., http://contracts.onecle.com.

135 35 U.S.C. 271(d)(4) "No patent owner otherwise entitled to relief for infringement or contributory infringement of a patent shall be denied relief or deemed guilty of misuse or illegal extension of the patent right by reason of his having done one or more of the following:… (4) refused to license or use any rights to the patent…."

(3)   Improvements

Be very careful about who owns improvements. Typically, the assignee wants to own all future improvements created by the assignor. But unless the assignor is leaving the field, a broad assignment of future improvements can so hamstring the assignor that he is in virtual economic slavery to the assignee. Anything he develops is considered an "improvement," and the improvements are handed to the assignee with little or no additional compensation.

The assignor, of course, wants to keep all of the improvements to himself. But that solution is usually unacceptable to the assignee because of the risk that the "old" invention will be eclipsed in the marketplace by the improvement. The problem is usually resolved with a clause specifying that the assignment encompasses all new patents and applications that claim priority to the expressly assigned patent matters. However, even that resolution is problematic, because the priority claim is entirely in the hand of whomever controls prosecution. An alternative solution is to assign improvements, but define the term "improvements" in some restrictive manner. Following is a typical definition:

> **Be very careful about who owns new inventions and improvements**

"Improvement" shall mean a) any modification or variation of a Covered Product (the subject of Patents) or component thereof, b) any method of manufacturing or using a Covered Product, or c) any modification or variation of a Covered Method or step thereof, which affects a Covered Product or a Covered Method by 1) reducing its production or use costs, 2) improving its performance, 3) increasing its service life, 4) broadening its applicability, 5) increasing its marketability, or 6) otherwise enhancing its competitive value.

Consideration for transfer of patent rights can be almost anything. There is often some combination of a royalty and a lump sum payment, but assignments are also common where one of these types of consideration is absent. It is not at all unusual for royalties to change over time, or for different royalties to apply to types of products, or in different countries. Where the consideration includes a royalty stream, that royalty stream should terminate upon expiration, lapsing or other termination of the patent rights, usually on a country-by-country basis. If the royalty continues after the patents expire, there can be an allegation of patent misuse. There can be an exception, however, where the parties contract that the transfer includes something other than patent rights (such as trade secrets). In that case it can be perfectly valid for a royalty to continue after the patent(s) are no longer in force.

(4)   Control Of Prosecution

> **A nonexclusive license usually confers no standing to the licensee to bring suit**

Unless all right, title, and interest is being assigned, it is important to establish what entity will control the prosecution, and who will pay for it. For example, who decides whether to file continuation after final rejection? It is unfair to the assignor/licensor (who expects a royalty) for the assignee/licensee to allow an application to die on the vine. On the other hand, it may be unfair to the assignee/licensee for the prosecution to be controlled at the sole discretion of assignor/licensor. Even if the patents are already issued, it is important to decide who is to pay for maintenance fees, and what happens if the paying party decides to terminate such payments.

These issues are especially important with respect to foreign filing, where the costs can easily spiral to hundreds of thousands of dollars. Whichever party is responsible for paying could wind up bankrupt. Assignments typically grant all foreign rights, whether or not any exist. Usually the assignee controls all the foreign prosecution and bears all the costs.

(5)   Litigation

Unless all right, title, and interest is being assigned, it is also very important to designate who has what rights and responsibilities with respect to litigation. Patent litigation can easily run $500,000 to $1,000,000 before trial even begins, and twice that if the case goes through trial and appeal. Typically, both parties are given the right, but not the duty, to sue for infringement, and damages are usually allocated first to the out-of-pocket costs of the parties, and then to the parties pro-rata based upon their monetary involvement in the litigation.

One "gotcha" is that a nonexclusive license confers no constitutional standing on the part of the licensee to bring suit.[136] Thus, unless the licensor is willing to be dragged into court for every patent infringement or invalidity action, the license must be exclusive. A contrary provision in the contract is ineffective to create standing.

The licensee will want the license to specifically address what happens if the underlying patent is invalidated or otherwise rendered unenforceable. In *Medimmune, Inc. v. Centocor, Inc.*,[137] a licensee sued the licensor to invalidate the license after the underlying patent was invalidated. The trial court dismissed the case on the grounds that there was no actual controversy, and the Federal Circuit affirmed. Unless materially breached, the existence of a license obliterates any reasonable apprehension of a lawsuit.

A patent licensee can usually keep the license if the licensor goes bankrupt

(6)   Reversion

Reversion is often an important consideration, and is applicable to both assignments and licenses. It is very common to provide for a reversion clause where the consideration is not fully paid at the time of the transfer of rights, and also where the assignee/licensee fails to prosecute or maintain the intellectual property rights. There are all sorts of issues with respect to reversion, some of which are addressed below.

A licensee can generally keep its license even though the licensor files for bankruptcy protection. Under 11 U.S.C. § 365(n), a licensee can elect to retain its license rights despite a debtor's rejection. The statute states:

136 *Sicom Sys. v. Agilent Techs., Inc.*, 427 F.3d 971 (Fed. Cir. 2005).
137 *Medimmune, Inc. v. Centocor, Inc.*, 2005 U.S. App. LEXIS 9965 (Fed. Cir. 2005).

"If the trustee rejects an executory contract under which the debtor is a licensor of a right to intellectual property, the licensee under such contract may elect . . . (B) to retain its rights . . . under such contract . . . to such intellectual property . . . as such rights existed immediately before the case commenced." The same is likely true where the license is worded as a "promise not to sue".[138]

(7)   Non-Patent Rights

Be careful when designating patents what other rights are being transferred. Attorneys that specialize in areas other than intellectual property will often include transfers of trademark and copyright in a patent assignment. There is nothing wrong with assigning all of them in the same document, and indeed in assigning patent rights to software one should be careful to also assign the underlying copyrights to the software. But beware that those other areas of law have their own special considerations. For example, a trademark (service mark, trade name, web site name, etc) should be assigned "along with the goodwill appurtenant thereto".[139] Licensing of such rights should include a right to control quality of goods and services bearing the mark or name, restriction upon challenging the rights, and so forth. A copyright assignment should be careful to assign only rights that do not already belong to the purported assignee by virtue of an employment relationship or a "work for hire" clause. Copyright assignment should also be sure to waive moral rights ("*droit moral*") on the part of the author.

Beware! Licensing practices might be discoverable	Be careful about what you say (especially in writings) during licensing negotiations. At least one district court has held that licensing practices are not protected from discovery by attorney-client privilege.[140] The attorney-client privilege doctrine only protects confidential communications between lawyer and client made to facilitate legal services for the client. It is questionable whether licensing practices are developed to facilitate legal services. Defendant shall produce documents that reflect its licensing practices or procedures relative to location technology.

(8)   Avoid Illegal Tying Arrangements.

Although patent holders are generally allowed to extract monopolistic value from the marketplace for their patents, there are limits on the extent to which a patent holder can extend patent monopoly outside the scope of the patent claims.

This issue typically arises in a so-called tying arrangement, where a patentee tries to use the market power derived from his patent to extract monopolistic profits from non-patented goods or services, or from other presumably less valuable patents. Illegal tying arrangements can be attacked under several legal theories, including an equitable defense against patent infringement called patent misuse.[141] The patent misuse defense used to be quite strong, but has diminished in recent years, as Congress[142] and the courts have required the

---

138 *In re Spansion, Inc.*, 2012 U.S. App. LEXIS 26131 (3d Cir. Del. Dec. 21, 2012), *cert denied, Spansion, Inc. v. ITC*, 132 S. Ct. 758 (U.S. 2011).

139 "Appurtenant thereto" is a term of art, basically meaning "relating thereto".

140 *Skyhook Wireless, Inc. v. Google, Inc.*, 2012 U.S. Dist. LEXIS 131403 (D. Mass. Sept. 14, 2012).

141 Tying arrangements have been condemned as improper extensions of the patent monopoly: (a) under the patent misuse doctrine; (b) as unfair methods of competition under § 5 of the Federal Trade Commission Act, 15 U.S.C. § 45; (c) as contracts tending to create a monopoly under § 3 of the Clayton Act, 15 U.S.C. § 13a; and (d) as contracts in restraint of trade under § 1 of the Sherman Act, 15 U.S.C. § 1. Ill. Tool Works Inc. v. Indep. Ink, Inc., 126 S. Ct. 1281 (U.S. 2006).

142 35 U.S.C. 271(d)(5). "No patent owner otherwise entitled to relief for infringement or contributory infringement of a patent shall be denied relief or deemed guilty of misuse or illegal extension of the patent right by reason of his having done one or more of the following: ...(condition) the license of any rights to the patent or the sale of the patented product on the

party propounding the defense to prove "market power" in the relevant market, separate from market power arising merely as a function of existence of the patent. From a practical standpoint this shift in presumption means that the misuse defense is only likely to prevail in cases of *per se* patent misuse, where a patentee conditions a license under the patent on the purchase of a separable, staple good, and arrangements in which a patentee effectively extends the term of its patent by requiring post-expiration royalties."[143] The patent misuse defense is likely to fail in most other cases because they are analyzed under the rule of reason.[144] For example, we do know that it is not a *per se* patent misuse to license a bundle of patents for recording compacts disks (CDs), as opposed to offering licenses for individual ones of the patents.[145] We also know that it is not *per se* patent misuse to require OEM licensees of inkjet printhead technologies to purchase their (non-patented) ink exclusively from the patent holders.[146]

(9) Sub-Licenses

Consider sub-licensing penalties. It sometimes occurs that a licensee sublicenses the patent rights to a third party, which might well be owned by the same principals as the licensee. That little trick allows the licensor to pay its license fee as a percentage of monies received from the sub-licensee, rather than on gross revenue or even net profit of selling the patented product or service. The sub-licensee then goes on to make a lion's share of the profits. One approach to avoid that scenario is to contractually preclude the licensee from sub-licensing. Another approach, which is commonly used by Universities, is to include in the licensing agreement some sort of sub-licensing penalty. Both approaches are good for licensors, and bad for licensees.

Consider sublicensing penalties

Here is some boilerplate language for handling sublicensees.

> LICENSEE may grant sublicenses under LICENSED SUBJECT MATTER consistent with the terms of this AGREEMENT provided that LICENSEE is responsible for its sublicensees relevant to this AGREEMENT, and for diligently collecting all amounts due LICENSEE from sublicensees. If a sublicensee pursuant hereto becomes bankrupt, insolvent or is placed in the hands of a receiver or trustee, LICENSEE, to the extent allowed under applicable law and in a timely manner, agrees to use its best reasonable efforts to collect all consideration owed to LICENSEE and to have the sublicense agreement confirmed or rejected by a court of proper jurisdiction.

---

acquisition of a license to rights in another patent or purchase of a separate product, unless, in view of the circumstances, the patent owner has market power in the relevant market for the patent or patented product on which the license or sale is conditioned...."

143 *Virginia Panel Corp. v. MAC Panel Co.*, 133 F.3d 860, 868-69 (Fed. Cir. 1997).

144 *Monsanto Co. v. McFarling*, 363 F.3d 1336, 1341 (Fed. Cir. 2004) (under the rule of reason, a practice is impermissible only if its effect is to restrain competition in a relevant market).

145 *U.S. Philips v. ITC et al.*, 424 F.3d 1179 (Fed. Cir. 2005).

146 *Ill. Tool Works Inc. v. Indep. Ink, Inc., Supra.*

> In addition to other royalties and payments, [Licensee should pay] 50% of all consideration, other than research and development money, received by LICENSEE from either (i) any sublicensee pursuant to Section --- herein above, or (ii) any assignee pursuant to Section --- herein below, including but not limited to, royalties, upfront payments, marketing, distribution, franchise, option, license, or documentation fees, bonus and milestone payments and equity securities.

(10)   Taxation Of Licenses

Be careful about tax consequences. Although income from the sale or exchange of all substantial rights to a patent can be taxes as capital gains,[147] sale or exchange of less that substantially all rights, and royalty from an assignment or license will likely be viewed as ordinary income, and subject to the corresponding taxes. Where the assignor wants ongoing royalty, one option is to have two agreements, a transfer agreement for the sale of the patent rights, and a consulting agreement for either stock in a going concern, or perhaps a percentage of revenue or other income in a new company. Since income from the consulting agreement will likely be taxed as ordinary income, a further improvement to the arrangement would provide the seller with stock options in the new company, where exercise of the option would terminate the royalty. This gives the seller the best of both worlds. While the company is still new, his income is based upon sales rather than profits (albeit taxed as ordinary income), but when the company is generating sufficient profits he can convert to having his compensation paid as dividends, which would be taxed at a lower rate.

Check whether foreign licensing incurs value-added taxes

Foreign taxes are also a consideration. Many companies assign their intellectual property to an off-shore company, division, or subsidiary as a means of shunting profits out of the country. In such circumstances it may be wise to make the assignment or license early on, before the intellectual property has significant value. Otherwise the consideration may be viewed as inadequate, and the transaction viewed as a sham. One should also be cognizant that many countries having value-added taxes place a tax on transfer of intellectual property. In the case of extremely valuable patents, such a transfer (even to a related company) can unwittingly incur very significant taxes.

(11)   Drafting To The Interest of An Owner/Inventor

Filing a pure assignment of all right, title, and interest may or may not be a proper course of action. Many inventors in small, inventor-controlled companies want to keep the patents in their own names. That way the inventors may try to gain leverage over their partners or other business associates in the event of a breakup. The problem for the patent attorney is that he or she usually represents the company, and not the inventor - even if the inventor controls the company. The patent attorney therefore has a duty to protect the company by requiring either: (a) an assignment; or (b) explicit instructions from the company that an assignment is not desired. If an assignment to the company is not desired, then there should be a license agreement from the

---

147 26 U.S.C. § 1235. A good article on this topic can be found on the web at https://www.finnegan.com/en/insights/articles/favorable-capital-gains-taxation-rates-apply-to-payments-for.html

inventor (as licensor) to the company (as licensee). Delineation of the terms of the license may well raise the assignment issue to the fore.

There is also a litigation consideration. The owner of a patent is a "necessary and indispensable party" in federal court litigation regarding patent infringement or patent invalidity. This is true even if the owner has granted an exclusive, worldwide license to another. Leaving title in the name of an inventor ensures that all litigation brought by an infringer must take place in the district of the inventor's residence. This is a very useful trick to avoid getting "home-towned" where the infringer resides, and also may go a long way towards reducing the cost of litigation.

If an assignment is desired, there are several considerations. First, one must decide who is granting the rights. In the United States, all patent applications are filed in the name of the inventor(s), and the patent rights remain in the inventor(s) unless contracted away. Thus, even if the invention is made by a company employee, on company time, using company facilities, within the course and scope of the employee's duties, the invention still belongs to the employee unless he assigns those rights to the company. Now it is true that many companies have their employees sign employment agreements stating that the patent rights must be assigned to the company. It is also true that under state law such an employee may have a legal obligation to assign his invention to the company. But an obligation to assign is not the same as an assignment. It is important for the patent attorney to address the assignment issue head on.

Another consideration is whether the grant includes only the current application, or all continuations, divisionals, and so forth. This is a particularly tricky issue because many assignments routinely grant rights to all improvements made or acquired by the assignor. That approach benefits the assignee, but can be extremely burdensome to the assignor (inventor). Where the inventor basically owns or control the company, the inventor will likely insist that the assignment cover only the currently pending application(s), as well as continuations and divisionals. If the agreement between inventor and company is a bit ore tilted towards the company, then the assignment should also include all applications that claim priority to the assigned application(s). Note that language purporting to assign all improvements can be attacked as being unclear. After all, who knows where to draw the line between an improvement to the previous invention, and a new invention?

> **Consider whether the license includes all family members, and IP acquired after signing**

Along the same lines it a licensee will want to limit the license to a specific set of patents and applications, and not those that might later be acquired by the licensor.

One possible solution to assignment of patent rights where the inventor owns/controls the company is to include a term in the assignment that triggers a change in royalty, ownership, or control of the patent rights upon a change in ownership or control of the company. That strategy has the benefit of acting as a "poison pill" against a hostile takeover. Another possibility is for the assignor/ inventor to retain an undivided 50% interest in the patent rights, and only assign 50% to the company. That way the assignor (inventor) could negotiate assignment of the remaining interest upon leaving the company. Still another possibility is for the assignor/inventor to grant responsibility for enforcement of the patent to the company, with a reversion of some or all of the assigned rights if the company fails to adequately enforce the patent against an infringer. That strategy can be especially advantageous where the assignor/inventor has no responsibility to enforce the patent upon return of the previously assigned rights.

> **Consider a license rate that varies according to scope of portfolio, market conditions, etc.**

Be reasonable. Licensing a first patent is a bit like an actor getting into the movies. The first role, even a leading role, often produces very little revenue for the actor because he/she has little market power. The real money comes with subsequent roles, where the actor can negotiate from a position of strength. In the patent world, a first patent is usually followed by several others, in the same or even a different field. Once a patentee has pursued a few infringers into federal court, its market power could well increase markedly.

(12)   Where To Find A Licensee

Inventors often ask their patent attorney or agent for assistance in finding a licensee. Certainly a patent attorney can help in that regard, but the better choice is usually to seek assistance from others. Patent attorneys are usually a poor choice for many reasons, including: (1) they are often singularly bad salesmen; and (b) their hourly rates are much too high to justify their traipsing around the country looking for deals. Marketing an invention requires an inordinate amount of legwork, and it can usually be done much better and more cost-effectively by someone who does not bill by the hour.

The better choices for marketing assistance are brokers, angel groups, venture capital groups, and corporate departments of the larger law firms. One can also seek advice and assistance from the local contractor for the Small Business Administration. Within the last few years it has even become possible to auction patents on the Internet,[148]

Entities willing to sell their patents should consider

a)   AST-Allied Security Trust[149]

b)   RPX-Rational Patent Exchange[150]

c)   OIN-Open Innovation Networks[151]

d)   Intellectual Ventures (for IT-related technologies)[152]

e)   Acacia (patent troll)[153].

There are companies that specialize in assisting inventors locate suitable licenses. That effort carries a cost, of course, and unfortunately the cost often far outweighs the benefits. We recently reviewed a draft agreement under which the inventor would have received nothing up front, would have been on the hook for essentially unlimited "marketing" costs on the part of the company, and would have ultimately lost substantially all of his rights to the company. There are undoubtedly some decent marketing assistance services out there, but we do not know of any. If a patent holder has decided to utilize the services of a commercialization assistance company, he should at least require the service to sign an agreement along the lines of that found in Appendix F - Commercialization Assistance Agreement.

C)   Employment Agreements

California and several other states provide that the work of an employee, performed during the course and scope of his employment, is automatically owned by the employer.[154] On that basis, many employers think

---

148 See e.g., https://patentauction.com/
149 https://www.ast.com/
150 https://www.rpxcorp.com/platform/patent-sales/
151 https://openinventionnetwork.com/
152 https://www.intellectualventures.com/
153 https://acaciaresearch.com/
154 California Labor Code § 2870. https://leginfo.legislature.ca.gov/faces/codes_displaySection.xhtml?lawCode=LAB&sec-

that employment agreements are unnecessary. Don't believe it. Failure to secure a clear assignment of rights, or at least a clear right to require assignment of rights, can cause an enormous headache for both employer and employee.

Moreover, the process is simple. Just print up a good employment agreement, such as that found in Appendix H - IP PORTION OF EMPLOYMENT AGREEMENT, and have each of the employees sign it. That strategy is most easily implemented when an employee starts working, but can be done at any time, even with employees that have been working for the company for a decade or more.

By the way, everyone should sign, including (and maybe especially) management, owners, board members and so forth. Several years ago we were embroiled in a difficult situation in which a board member at a first company assigned rights in one of his inventions to a second company where he was a full-time employee. That would have been fine, except that much of the information that triggered the invention likely came from board meetings of the first company. These issues are oh-so-easy to work through early on, and oh-so-expensive to deal with down the road.

Along the same lines a company should be very careful in its agreements with independent contractors and other vendors. Among other things it is important for a company to ensure that *all* research and development performed by its vendors under contract belongs to the company. It happens over and over, year after year. A company hires some computer programmer, architect, chemist, or other vendor to develop some technology, and then subsequently has a falling out with the vendor. The vendor walks away from the contract, and then turns right around and sues the company for using the technology that the company paid for in the first place. This all happens because the company failed to implement appropriate IP provisions with the vendor.

Of course, it is perfectly acceptable for an independent contractor, or even an employee, to contract with a company for whatever distribution of rights or benefits they can agree to. For example, an independent contractor might agree to forgo a high salary in exchange for a low salary plus an ownership right in intellectual property that he/she develops. This gets tricky, though, and the details should be discussed with an attorney. Among other things there will be issues as to handling of co-inventor situations, determining what subject matters gets patented, who controls patent prosecution, and who controls licensing or other commercialization.

D)   Non-Disclosure Agreements

Non-Disclosure Agreements (NDAs), are the same thing as Confidential Disclosure Agreements (CDAs). A sample is included as Appendix I - SAMPLE BILATERAL NDA. They are legal contracts between two or more parties, intended to stop information disclosed between the parties from being transferred to others. NDAs are commonly signed between companies at the beginning of a potential business relationship, but could be entered into between any parties, including for example between an employer and an employee, and between an inventor and a manufacturer to which the inventor is disclosing his invention.

> **NDA agreements vary widely as to whether confidential info needs to be marked "confidential" and whether failure to mark can be cured**

NDAs can be unilateral or bilateral, depending on whether only one or both of the parties is disclosing confidential information to the other.

One key consideration is what material is considered to be confidential. At one extreme, *only* information marked "confidential" at the time of disclosure is considered confidential. That restriction is extremely dangerous for the disclosing party because it doesn't cover additional information provided orally during a meeting.

A more liberal agreement considers confidential information to be that which is marked confidential, as well as other information that is identified as being confidential within some time period (usually 10 days) of disclosure. Under that term, a disclosing party can reveal confidential material orally during a meeting, or perhaps make drawings on a white board, and still retain confidentiality status of that material.

The most favorable provision for a disclosing party is where the NDA considers confidential information to be (a) that which is marked confidential, (b) other information that is identified as being confidential within some time period (usually 10 days) of disclosure, and also (c) information that would normally be considered confidential. With that clause, there is at least an argument that all of the confidential information disclosed is covered by the agreement, even though the disclosing party may have forgotten to mark each relevant piece of paper with a confidentiality notation, or may have failed to identify all of orally disclosed confidential information as confidential within the prescribed time period.

From the standpoint of the party receiving the confidential information, it is best to have a very restrictive provision with respect to what constitutes confidential materials. NDAs are especially problematic for a company receiving information about a possible invention, because broad confidentiality language leaves the company open to a lawsuit by the supposed inventor, who years later could claim to have disclosed something that was never disclosed.

It is quite common for consumer products companies to require disclosers to use an NDA form provided by the company. That is *extremely dangerous* for the discloser. Often those NDA forms provide that any information disclosed that is not already claimed in a pending patent application is considered public information to which no confidentiality is accorded. We have even seen company-provided NDAs that recite ownership of any and all disclosed material not otherwise claimed in a patent application is owned by the company!

Other clauses of NDAs are also important to consider, as for example where the recipient requires any dispute to be resolved in court, and where the prevailing party can be awarded attorneys fees. With those onerous conditions, an individual inventor might not have the resources to realistically enforce the NDA even if there is a clear breach by the receiving party.

Bottom line, NDAs can be quite problematic for inventors and other disclosing parties. If the designation of confidential material is too narrow, or there are other undesirable terms in the agreement, the discloser would be better off not signing the NDA. And, if the discloser tries to get the other party to sign and NDA, and the other party refuses, the situation is even worse than if there had been no effort to sign an NDA. A discloser's best bet is often to file a strong patent application prior to disclosure.

Chapter IX - Infringement

Patent Beast © FISH 2010

I WOULD LIKE TO GET A PATENT ON MY RECIPE FOR APPLE PIE.

AND HOW DO YOU PROPOSE TO ENFORCE THAT PATENT?

WOULD YOU GO HOUSE TO HOUSE?

DO I HAVE TO ENFORCE MY PATENT?

A) Infringement Under 35 U.S.C. § 271 et seq.

Patent infringement in the United States is governed by 35 U.S.C. § 271 *et seq.*

> (a) Except as otherwise provided in this title, whoever without authority makes, uses, offers to sell, or sells any patented invention, within the United States, or imports into the United States any patented invention during the term of the patent therefore, infringes the patent.

(1) Direct And Indirect Infringement

Section 271(a) quoted above refers to direct infringement, but patent infringement can also be found for either of two types of indirect infringement, (a) contributory infringement, and (b) inducement to infringe.

Liability for contributory infringement arises when one "sells within the United States... a component of a patented machine... knowing the same to be especially made or especially adapted for use in an infringement of such patent, and not a staple article or commodity of commerce suitable for substantial non-infringing use."[155] Liability for inducing infringement arises when one acts in a manner that actually induces infringement,[156] and the actor knew or should have known that his actions would induce direct infringement.[157] Both contributory infringement and inducement to infringe are dependent upon the proof of direct infringement by some other party. There can be no indirect infringement without direct infringement.[158] During litigation, the patent claims are presumed to be valid, and invalidity must be proven on a claim by claim basis by clear and convincing evidence.[159]

---

155 35 U.S.C. § 271(c) (2000); Golden Blount, Inc. v. Robert H. Peterson Co., 365 F.3d 1054, 1061 (Fed. Cir. 2004).
156 35 U.S.C. § 271(b); Golden Blount, Inc. v. Robert H. Peterson Co., 365 F.3d 1054, 1061 (Fed. Cir. 2004).
157 *Micro Chem. Inc. of the corresponding patent v. Great Plains Chem. Co.*, 194 F.3d 1250 (Fed. Cir. 1999).
158 *Met-Coil Sys. Corp. v. Korners Unlimited, Inc.*, 803 F.2d 684, 687 (Fed. Cir. 1986).
159 35 U.S.C. § 282; the application of the clear and convincing evidence standard is being challenged by Microsoft, and is currently under review by the U.S. Supreme Court. See *i4i Ltd. P'ship v. Microsoft Corp.*, 598 F.3d 831 (Fed. Cir. 2010), *cert. granted* 2010 U.S. LEXIS 9311 (U.S., Nov. 29, 2010).

(2)   Joint Infringement

There is also case law support for joint infringement, even for parties that are not technically contributory infringers of inducement infringers. In *Akamai v. Limelight*,[160] the Federal Circuit held that a defendant can be held liable for induced infringement if the defendant performs at least some of the claimed steps, and induces another to commit the remaining steps. This overrules the previous emphasis on vicarious liability.

In addition, joint infringement no longer requires an underlying direct infringement by a single entity or joint enterprise practicing all steps, either alone or vicariously. All steps of a claimed method must be performed in order to find induced infringement, but it is not necessary to prove that all the steps were committed by a single entity. *Akamai* establishes an "inducement only" rule, where the induced party does not have to be an agent of the inducing party.

(3)   No Infringement Of Pending Applications

Under current law it is not possible to infringe a pending application. This actually makes a lot of sense because one cannot know what the scope of the claims are until the patent actually issues. The situation is a bit like real property law. Until one is certain that one actually owns some property, and it has been decided where that property starts and ends, it is impossible to say whether a person is trespassing.

> **Recovery of royalties for activities between publication of an application and issuance almost never happens**

It is possible, however, to reach back into the past and obtain royalties from competitors who were making, selling, using, importing or exporting goods, or performing methods, for the period between the date the application was published and the date the application was issued. That is the so-called "provisional patent protection", and only applies: (1) from the time that the competitor had actual notice of the patent application; (2) where the competitor would have been infringing had the published patent claims issued; and (3) where at least one of the relevant claims upon issuance is substantially identical to the claim as published.

In practice that almost never happens. Actual notice is not satisfied merely by publication of the patent application. It needs to be established that the competitor actually knew of the application and its contents. Even sending a cease and desist letter might be inadequate if the letter fails to expressly allege possible future "infringement", and includes a copy of the actual publication of the patent application. In addition, the claims are almost never issued as published. There is almost always some change that affects the scope, even if only minor. One way that an applicant can try to minimize the effects of that provision is to file many independent claims with narrow scope. That way, a competitor might be found to have fallen within the narrow independent claim that was not modified following publication within the application. But of course that strategy can be quite expensive, and there is no guarantee that even the narrow claims will be allowed, or that they will read on the competitor's product or activities.

B)   Compulsory Licensing / Injunction

The Paris Convention for the Protection of Industrial Property[161] gives countries broad discretion to implement compulsory licensing. More recently, the WTO Agreement on Trade-Related Aspects of Intellectual Property Rights (TRIPS) imposed certain restrictions, namely that governments must: (a) consider cases on their

160 *Akamai Techs., Inc. v. Limelight Networks, Inc.*, 692 F.3d 1301 (Fed. Cir. 2012).
161 Full text at https://www.wipo.int/treaties/en/ip/paris/

individual merits; (b) make an effort to negotiate a voluntary license on reasonable commercial terms prior to authorizing third party use; and (c) require "adequate remuneration . . . taking into account the economic value of the authorization."[162] Currently, many countries require compulsory licensing of patents, including Australia,[163] Brazil,[164] France,[165] Germany,[166] Canada,[167] and Japan.[168] In some cases compulsory licensing applies across the board, and in other cases mostly to pharmaceutical and medically related patents.[169] A good general article can be found at Wikipedia.com,[170] and summaries of the laws for individual countries can be found at the website of the Consumer Project on Technology.[171]

Until 2006 the U.S. had no compulsory licensing, with only two exceptions. The Clean Air Act provides for compulsory licensing to a preferred manufacturer where development of the technology was funded by U.S. government grants. And the Atomic Energy Act authorizes forced sale of an atomic-energy invention or discovery to the government.

Nevertheless, in *eBay, Inc. v. MercExchange*[172] the Supreme Court effectively forced the country into the world of compulsory licensing by refusing to uphold mandatory injunctive relief. In particular, the Court held that District Courts must exercise "discretion consistent with traditional principles of equity, in patent disputes no less than in other cases governed by such standards." Thus, a patent holder of must satisfy the traditional "four-factor test" for issuance of an injunction: "(1) that it has suffered an irreparable injury; (2) that remedies available at law, such as monetary damages, are inadequate to compensate for that injury; (3) that, considering the balance of hardships between the plaintiff and defendant, a remedy in equity is warranted; and (4) that the public interest would not be disserved by a permanent injunction. . . . "

From a practical standpoint the *eBay* ruling means that patent holders who want injunctive relieve may want to refrain from ever even suggesting their willingness to license, and should certainly refrain from negotiating with the infringer. In the *eBay* case, the trial court found infringement of several of the claims, but went on to deny permanent injunction on the grounds that MercExchange had made public statements regarding its willingness to license its patents.[173] It also means that the value of a patent depends to

Injunctive relief is no longer automatic in patents

162 www.wto.org/english/docs_e/legal_e/legal_e.htm, see especially TRIPS Article 31, and also Articles 1, 7, 8, 27.1, 30 and 44.

163 The Patents Act of 1990, sections 133 and 135 permit applications to be made for compulsory licenses when "the reasonable requirements of the public" have not been met, and section 173 provides protection from infringement for "Crown use" for the services of the Commonwealth or State where "necessary for the proper provision of those services."

164 Law No. 9.279 of May 14, 1996, to Regulate Rights and Obligations Relating to Industrial Property, section III, article 68.

165 Code de la Propriété Intellectuelle, www.wipo.int

166 German patent law, www.wipo.int/, sections 13, 24 and 81.

167 Since 1993 the Commissioner of Patents has had discretion under Canadian Patent Act, § 66(1), to grant a compulsory license under specific limited circumstances: (a) demand is not being met; (b) trade or industry is being prejudiced and the patentee refuses to grant a license; (c) the patentee is only willing to grant a license under unreasonable terms; or (d) the patent unfairly prejudices the manufacture, use or sale of a product in Canada.

168 Patent Law, (Law No. 121 of April 13, 1959, as last amended by Law No. 30 of 1990), Chapter IV, section 83.-(1), see www.cptech.org/ip/health/cl/japan1.html.

169 For example, in Canada prior to 1993, the Commissioner was authorized to grant compulsory licenses to anyone who applied for a license for a patented invention intended or capable of being used for medicine or for the preparation or production of medicine ("pharmaceutical compulsory licenses"). Pharmaceutical compulsory licenses granted in Canada before December 20, 1991 may still be in effect.

170 http://en.wikipedia.org/wiki/Compulsory_licensing.

171 www.cptech.org/ip/health/.

172 *eBay Inc. v. MercExchange, L.L.C.*, 2006 U.S. LEXIS 3872 (U.S. 2006).

173 *MercExchange, L.L.C. v. eBay, Inc.*, 275 F. Supp. 2d 695, 2003 U.S. Dist. LEXIS 13842 (E.D. Va., 2003); *MercExchange, LLC v. eBay, Inc.*, 401 F.3d 1323, 1339 (Fed. Cir. 2005), *rehearing denied; eBay Inc. v. MercExchange, L.L.C.*, 2006 U.S. LEXIS 3872 (U.S. 2006).

some extent upon who owns it. A patent holder that is competing in the marketplace, for example, should have an easier time securing an injunction (or a higher royalty) than a patent holder that is not commercializing its patented technology.

Since the *eBay* decision, the District Courts have granted or denied injunctive relief based upon these very principles. For example, in T*ivo Inc. v. EchoStar Comm. Corp.*[174] a Texas District Court granted injunctive relief to the patent holder, largely on the grounds that EchoStar competes directly with Tivo, marketing their infringing products to potential DVR customers as an alternative to purchasing Tivo's DVRs. Just one day earlier the very same court denied injunctive relief in *Paice LLC v. Toyota*[175] on the grounds that the patent holder failed to prove irreparable harm. Among the significant findings were that the patent holder was not practicing the claimed invention, and that the patent holder offered to license the technology to Toyota. The court found that offer evidence that a monetary award would be sufficient compensation.

Although the Federal Circuit definitively proclaimed dead the *presumption* of irreparable harm in the context of patent infringement in the 2011 *Robert Bosch* case[176], there was some reluctance on the part of the Court to do so. In particular, the Federal Circuit distinguished traditional cases, where the patentee and adjudged infringer both practice the patented technology, and non-traditional cases, in which (1) firms use patents not as a basis for producing and selling goods but, instead, primarily for obtaining licensing fees; (2) the patented invention is but a small component of the product; and (3) those involving business methods. The implication of *Robert Bosch* is that the patentee's right to exclude weighs more heavily in a "traditional case," and less so in a "non-traditional case."

Relying on that distinction, some courts still seem to have a bias towards issuing injunction relief. In the widely publicized 2012 litigation of Apple against Samsung, a San Jose District Court issued a preliminary injunction even though Apple failed to come forward with direct evidence that specific Samsung customers would have purchased an iPhone but for the allegedly infringing Quick Search Box feature, and even though Apple failed to demonstrate other than meager sales for the accused product. That ruling was promptly stayed in part by the Federal Circuit, so the long term effect on the law is not yet known.[177]

Whether this shift to compulsory licensing is good for the country remains to be seen. Certainly there has been quite an outcry by established businesses against what they see as reduced value being allocated to innovation. On the other hand, pharmaceutical drugs are much less expensive in Canada, precisely because such drugs are subject to compulsory licensing. There are clearly situations where the benefits of innovation are excessively allocated to innovators.

C) Standing To Sue

(1)   Patent Holders

Patent owners clearly have standing to sue for patent infringement under the patent statutes.[178] Questions arise, however, when the entity bringing suit owns less than all substantial rights. For example, a licensee having less than all substantial rights in a patent likely cannot sue on its own, and must join the patent holder.[179] All substantial rights generally requires an exclusive license (even as to the licensor/patent holder), although the

---

174 *Tivo Inc. v. EchoStar Comm. Corp.*, 2005 U.S. Dist. LEXIS **** (D. Tex. Aug 17, 2006).

175 *Paice LLC v. Toyota Motor Company, Inc.*, 2005 U.S. Dist. LEXIS **** (D. Tex. Aug 16, 2006).

176 *Robert Bosch LLC v. Pylon Mfg. Corp.*, 659 F.3d 1142, 1149 (Fed. Cir. 2011).

177 *Apple Inc. v. Samsung Elecs. Co.*, 2012 U.S. App. LEXIS 13835 (Fed. Cir.2012).

178 35 U.S.C. § 281.

179 *Intellectual Property Dev., Inc. v. TCI Cablevision of Calif., Inc.*, 248 F.3d 1333 (Fed. Cir. 2001).

exclusivity can be for a limited period of time or for a limited geographical area.[180] In the *Aspex Eyewear* case, the Court appears to have been persuaded by the fact that the transfer was: (a) for exclusive right to make, use, and sell; (b) included the right to sue for infringement; and (c) included an unfettered right to sublicense.

Questions can also arise where there are multiple owners of a patent. In general, the rule is that all patent owners must be joined. However, there does appear to be one anomalous ruling, in which a district court allowed a case to proceed even though one of the patent holders was not joined in the lawsuit.

Issues of standing and joinder can be raised at any time during litigation, even during appeal. *Enzo APA & Son, Inc. v. Geapag A.G.*, 134 F.3d 1090, 1092 (Fed. Cir. 1998).

(2)   Declaratory Judgment

The Declaratory Judgment Act provides that "[i]n a case of actual controversy within its jurisdiction, . . . any court of the United States, upon the filing of an appropriate pleading, may declare the rights and other legal relations of any interested party seeking such declaration, whether or not further relief is or could be sought."[181] The Supreme Court reiterated the test in 2007 as "whether the facts alleged, under all the circumstances, show that there is a substantial controversy, between parties having adverse legal interests, of sufficient immediacy and reality to warrant the issuance of a declaratory judgment."[182].

The Federal Circuit has since interpreted the rule broadly, stating that "Article III jurisdiction may be met where the patentee takes a position that puts the declaratory judgment plaintiff in the position of either pursuing arguably illegal behavior or abandoning that which he claims a right to do."[183] In 2013 the Federal Circuit's willingness to allow declaratory judgment actions to proceed reached the stage where such actions can even be brought by a potential indirect infringer, (i.e., one who might be accused of contributory infringement or inducement to infringe), and even where direct infringement might not occur for more than a year.[184]

Filing a declaratory judgment action challenging the validity of a patent forfeits the right to subsequently file post-grant reviews and *inter partes* reviews on that patent.[185] One could, however, file a declaratory judgment and a post grant or *inter partes* review on the same day, in which case the court is likely to stay the declaratory judgment action. That preserves the venue (via the declaratory judgment action) without forfeiting the post grant or *inter partes* review processes. Alternatively, one could file a declaratory judgment action that only claims non-infringement (no invalidity claims), and file for post grant or *inter partes* review shortly thereafter.

(3)   Other Provisions

There are a few other ways of asserting patent invalidity or non-infringement besides raising the issues as counterclaims or defenses to an infringement action, or for a competitor to bring a declaratory judgment action (DJ action). One way is to file a so-called Walker Process claim, wherein a competitor has standing to bring suit under the antitrust laws, alleging that a patent was procured by fraudulent conduct.[186] There, standing in

---

180 *Aspex Eyewear, Inc. et al. v. Miracle Optics, Inc.*, 2006 U.S. App. LEXIS 501 (Jan. 2006); *Viam Manufacturing, Inc. v. Tesor Technology Corp.*, 243 F.3d 558 (Fed. Cir. 2000).

181 28 U.S.C. § 2201(a)..

182 *MedImmune, Inc. v. Genentech, Inc.*, 549 U.S. 118 (2007).

183 *SanDisk Corp. v. STMicroelectronics, Inc.*, 480 F.3d 1372, 1381 (Fed. Cir. 2007).

184 *Arkema Inc. v. Honeywell Int'l* (Fed. Cir. 2013) 2013 U.S. App. LEXIS 2520.

185 35 U.S.C. §§ 315(a)(1), § 325(a)(1).

186 *Walker Process Equip., Inc. v. Food Mach. & Chem. Corp.*, 382 U.S. 172, 177, 86 S. Ct. 347, 15 L. Ed. 2d 247 (1965) ("A patent ... is an exception to the general rule against monopolies and to the right to access to a free and open market.") (quoting *Precision Instrument Mfg. Co. v. Auto. Maintenance Mach. Co.*, 324 U.S. 806, 816, 65 S. Ct. 993, 89 L. Ed. 1381, 1945 Dec. Comm'r Pat. 582 (1945)).

the consumer is justified because the harm is not an invalid patent, but the use of the allegedly invalid patent to establish a monopoly.

In 2006 the District Court of D.C.[187] held that a consumer (who is not a competitor) also has standing to bring an antitrust claim for asserting patent invalidity. The court distinguished prior case law by insisting that the consumer be a direct purchaser of a product covered by the patent.

D) Jurisdiction

There are two types of jurisdiction, subject matter jurisdiction and personal jurisdiction. The federal courts have exclusive subject matter jurisdiction over issues of patent law.[188] Whether a case involves substantive issues of patent law is determined by the well-pleaded complaint rule, and both federal and state courts can make that determination.[189] If the plaintiff founds his or her suit directly on a breach of some right created by the patent laws, he or she makes a case arising under those laws and only a federal court has jurisdiction. But if the plaintiff founds his or her suit on some right vested in him or her by the common law, or by general equity jurisprudence, the plaintiff makes a case arising under state law and only a state court has jurisdiction. A case founded on a principle of tort, contract, or equity law is a case arising under state law.

A claim supported by alternative theories in the complaint may not form the basis for jurisdiction under 28 U.S.C. § 1338(a) unless patent law is essential to each of those theories. When an issue of federal law is merely possible, or doubtful and conjectural, or lurking in the background, this attenuated possibility will not extinguish the jurisdiction of the state.[190]

Personal jurisdiction requires that the court resolving the dispute have the power to haul the defendant into court. Personal jurisdiction is easy over an in-state defendant because any federal court in the state has jurisdiction over all of its residents. Jurisdiction over an out-of-state defendant is more complicated, and is appropriate only if the relevant state's long-arm statute permits the assertion of jurisdiction without violating federal due process."[191] Because the long-arm statutes of California and many other states are co-extensive with federal due process requirements, the cornerstone of personal jurisdiction is whether "the defendant purposefully established 'minimum contacts' in the forum State."[192]

There are two types of personal jurisdiction, general jurisdiction and special jurisdiction. General jurisdiction arises where a defendant's contacts with the forum are "continuous and systematic, "even if those contacts are unrelated to the plaintiff's claims.[193] This "fairly high" standard requires the contacts to be the sort that approximate physical presence within the state, and in that regard, "[f]actors to be taken into consideration are whether the defendant makes sales, solicits or engages in business in the state, serves the state's markets, designates an agent for service of process … or is incorporated there."[194]

The jurisdictional battle is not usually fought over general jurisdiction, but instead over special jurisdiction, where the plaintiff must show: (1) the defendant purposefully directed its activities at residents of the forum,

---

187 *Molecular Diagnostics Labs. v. Hoffmann-La Roche, Inc.*, 2005 U.S. Dist. LEXIS 30142 (D.D.C. 2005).

188 28 U.S.C. § 1338(a).

189 *Caldera Pharmaceuticals, Inc. v Regents of Univ. of Cal.*, 205 CA4th 338, 140 CR3d 543 (1st Dist, 2012).

190 *Gully v. First Nat. Bank 299 U.S. 109, 118, 117* [81 L. Ed. 70, 57 S. Ct. 96 (1936).

191 *3D Sys., Inc. v. Aarotech Labs., Inc.*, 160 F.3d 1373, 1376-77 (Fed. Cir. 1998),

192 *Burger King Corp. v. Rudzewicz*, 471 U.S. 462, 474, 105 S. Ct. 2174, 85 L. Ed. 2d 528 (1985) (quoting *Int'l Shoe Co. v. Washington*, 326 U.S. 310, 316, 66 S. Ct. 154, 90 L. Ed. 95 (1945)).

193 *Red Wing Shoe Co., Inc. v. Hockerson-Halberstadt, Inc.*, 148 F.3d 1335, 1359 (Fed. Cir. 1998) (quoting *Helicopteros Nacionales de Colombia, S.A. v. Hall*, 466 U.S. 408, 414 (1984)).

194 *Bancroft & Masters, Inc. v. Augusta Nat'l, Inc.*, 223 F.3d 1082, 1086 (9th Cir. 2000)

(2) the claim "arises out of" or "relates to" those activities, and (3) assertion of personal jurisdiction is fair and reasonable.[195] In establishing special jurisdiction, the plaintiff often has to rely on "other activities," which can be the source of considerable argument. We do know the following:

- Licensing efforts per se are insufficient to establish special jurisdiction where the licensor has no control and no dealings with licensees beyond the receipt of royalty income."[196]

- An agreement with a domestic company to pursue the field of the invention is not "analogous to a grant of a patent license,"[197] and is insufficient to establish special jurisdiction.

- Using conferences as a *de facto* office to meet potential customers is insufficient to establish special jurisdiction.[198]

- A single direct sale into the forum can be sufficient for to establish special jurisdiction.[199]

- Mailing offers to sell an allegedly infringing product into a forum state can be sufficient for personal jurisdiction.[200]

- Providing an "interactive website from which customers can purchase the allegedly infringing goods is sufficient for personal jurisdiction.[201]

One cannot establish personal jurisdiction merely by reciting blanket personal jurisdiction language in a complaint.[202]

In the context of a declaratory judgment action, where the patent holder is the defendant, the standards are different. The law has shifted back and forth on those standards, but at present:

- The patentee's own commercialization activities are not relevant to establishing special jurisdiction.[203] "What the patentee makes, uses, offers to sell, sells, or imports is of no real relevance to the enforcement or defense of a patent, because 'the federal patent laws do not create any affirmative right to make, use, or sell anything.'"

- The act of sending out cease and desist letters does not necessary invoke special jurisdiction over the patentee. "Principles of fair play and substantial justice afford a patentee sufficient latitude to inform others of its patent rights without subjecting itself to jurisdiction in a foreign forum. A patentee should not subject itself to personal jurisdiction in a forum solely by informing a party who happens to be located there of suspected infringement. Grounding personal jurisdiction on such contacts alone would not comport with principles of fairness."[204]

---

195 *Breckenridge Pharm., Inc. v. Metabolite Labs., Inc.*, 444 F.3d 1356, 1363 (Fed. Cir. 2006).

196 *Id.* at 1366 (Fed. Cir. 2006).

197 *Autogenomics, Inc. v. Oxford Gene Tech. Ltd.*, 566 F.3d 1012, 1021 (Fed. Cir. 2009).

198 *Id.*

199 *R.E. Davis Chem. Corp. v. Int'l Crystal Labs., Inc.*, No. 03 C 7288, 2004 U.S. Dist. LEXIS 19396 (D. Ill. Sept. 24, 2004); *Nuance Communs., Inc. v. Abbyy Software House*, 2010 U.S. App. LEXIS 23419 (Fed. Cir. 2010).

200 *3D Sys. v. Aarotech Lab.*, 160 F.3d 1373 (Fed. Cir. 1998) and *B & J Mfg. Co. v. Solar Industries, Inc.*, 483 F.2d 594 (8th Cir. 1973).

201 *O'Donnell v. Animals Matter, Inc.*, No. 3:07-CV-00241-FDW, 2007 U.S. Dist. LEXIS 70266 (D.N.C. Sept. 21, 2007).

202 *AFTG-TG, LLC v Nuvoton Technol. Corp.* (Fed Cir 2012) 689 F3d 1358, 1365.

203 *Avocent Huntsville Corp. v. Aten Int'l Co.*, 552 F.3d 1324, 1328 (Fed. Cir. 2008).

204 *Id* at 1360-61.

- Sending out cease and desist letters and "a number of related contacts," such as national advertisements, sales to distributors in the forum, trouble-shooting experts in the forum, and providing repair services in the forum, used to be sufficient for personal jurisdiction,[205] but that was overruled by *Avocent*.

- The fact that a patentee received large amounts of indirect revenue from a forum may be relevant to establishing personal jurisdiction[206] but it insufficient by itself.[207]

E) Venue

A still further consideration is venue. Patent holders often want any litigation to take place near their place of business, to have the "home court advantage" and to reduce cost. A potential infringer, of course, usually wants the litigation to take place near their place of business for the same reasons.

There are also two "rocket docket" venues, one in the Eastern District of Texas and one in the District of Delaware. Plaintiffs usually favor those venues because the cases move forward very quickly under the local rules, and both judges and juries frequently rule in favor of the patent holders. That situation is, of course, unfair to defendants, and the Federal Circuit has finally started to remedy the situation. In the *Acer*[208] case, the Court issued mandamus under the Federal Rules[209] to transfer the case from the Eastern District of Texas to the Northern District of California "[f]or the convenience of parties and witnesses, in the interest of justice." The ruling relied on the facts that (1) a substantial number of party witnesses reside in or near the Northern District of California, relative to the number of witnesses in Texas, (2) a significant portion of the evidence was in the Northern District of California, and (3) the Northern District had significant interest in the case resulting from the residence of many of the parties in that district.

In a November 2010 case, *in re Microsoft*,[210] the Federal Circuit went even further, making precedential an earlier decision transferring a case from the Eastern District of Texas to Washington State. In that case the Texas district court denied a request to transfer even though all individuals identified by the defendant, Microsoft, resided within 100 miles of the Washington court, and all but two of the witnesses identified by Allvoice resided outside Texas, and even those persons were peripheral to the case. Of particular interest was that the Federal Circuit refused to consider the plaintiff's presence in the Eastern district of Texas because it appeared that such presence was made solely for the purpose of manipulating venue.

Note that a patent holder does not always get first crack at determining venue. In most cases the patent holder cannot bring an infringement action against a potential infringer until an allegedly infringing product is on the market. In addition, it is possible for a potential infringer to the turn the tables on venue by bringing a declaratory judgment action against the patent holder for invalidity and non-infringement. That DJ action would usually be brought where the potential infringer resides, but there must be a "case or controversy" for the courts to proceed with the case. Thus, if the alleged infringer doesn't even have a product on the market, there may well not yet be a case or controversy.

---

205 *B & J Mfg. Co. v. Solar Industries, Inc.*, 483 F.2d 594, 597 (8th Cir. Minn. 1973).
206 *Mass. Inst. of Tech. v. Micron Tech., Inc.*, 508 F. Supp. 2d 112 (D. Mass 2007).
207 *Autogenomics, Inc. v. Oxford Gene Tech., Ltd.*, 2008 U.S. Dist. LEXIS 111756 (C.D. Cal. Jan. 17, 2008).
208 *In re Acer Am. Corp.*, 2010 U.S. App. LEXIS 24678 (Fed. Cir. Dec. 3, 2010).
209 28 U.S.C. 1404(a).
210 *In re Microsoft Corp.*, 2010 U.S. App. LEXIS 23121 (Fed. Cir. Nov. 8, 2010).

F)   Suing Multiple Infringers

Until September 2011, it was very common for patent holders to bring a single patent infringement action against multiple alleged infringers. In many cases this allowed a troll (a "non-practicing" entity that doesn't sell products) or other patent holder to sue in one of the rocket dockets (e.g., E. District of Texas), where at least one of the accused parties was doing business. Fortunately for defendants, and unfortunately for patent holders, the America Invents Act substantially put the kibosh on the strategy. At this point in time, plaintiffs in new court proceedings are prohibited from accusing multiple infringers in a single action *solely because* each defendant allegedly infringed the same patent.[211]

Notwithstanding the new law, the United States Judicial Panel on Multidistrict Litigation can still order consolidation of pre-trial procedures where common issues arose in cases pending in different district courts.[212]

(1)   Liability Of Corporate Officers

Although individuals can be sued for their individual acts of patent infringement, one cannot usually pierce the corporate veil to sue a CEO or other office for patent infringement by their company. In January 2013, Patently-O discussed a Federal Circuit case[213] that upheld that general rule by refusing to pierce the corporate veil, but also listed authority for holding a corporate officer could be held liable for inducing or contributory patent infringement, including the following quote:[214]

> [I]t is well settled that corporate officers who actively aid and abet their corporation's infringement may be personally liable for inducing infringement under § 271(b) regardless of whether the corporation is the alter ego of the corporate officer.

G)   Immunities

(1)   Foreign Government Immunity

The Foreign Sovereign Immunity Act (FSIA)[215] confers broad original jurisdiction on federal District Courts over claims arising from political, tortious acts of foreign governments. The primary purpose of the act was to assure litigants that their rights would be vindicated more on legal than sovereign immunity grounds, and the act permits plaintiffs to sue unless some discretionary function of government is involved.[216] Foreign governments can have immunity under the act, but that immunity is lost with respect to patents where the foreign government engages in commercial activity in the U.S. related to the patent.[217]

That particular situation applied in Intel Corp. v. Commonwealth Sci. & Indus. Research Org.,[218] where the CSIRO, Australia's national science agency, waived its immunity by entering into negotiations to license a patent it owned. The case is especially interesting because the waiver occurred even though the negotiations

211 35 U.S.C. § 299.

212 *In re Bear Creek Techs., Inc.*, (722) Patent Litig., 858 F. Supp. 2d 1375 (J.P.M.L. 2012).

213 *Hall v. Bed, Bath & Beyond, Inc. and Nachemin*, __ F.3d __ (Fed. Cir. 2013); *Wordtech Systems, Inc v. Integrated Networks Solutions, Inc.*, 609 F.3d 1308 (Fed. Cir. 2010); *Power Lift, Inc. v. Lang Tools, Inc.*, 774 F.2d 478 (Fed. Cir. 1985) and *Manville Sales Corp. v. Paramount Systems, Inc.*, 917 F.2d 544 (Fed. Cir. 1990).

214 *Orthokinetics, Inc. v. Safety Travel Chairs, Inc.*, 806 F.2d 1565 (Fed. Cir. 1986).

215 28 U.S.C. §§ 1602-1611.

216 *Letelier v Republic of Chile*, 488 F Supp 665 (DC Dist Col 1980).

217 28 U.S.C. § 1605(a)(2).

218 *Intel Corp. v. Commonwealth Sci. & Indus. Research Org.*, 455 F.3d 1364 (Fed. Cir. 2006).

did not result in a fully-executed, binding contract, and even though the proffering of licenses was exercised by private citizens.

(2)   State Immunity

Although one can sue the federal government for patent infringement,[219] states are generally immune from prosecution unless the state chooses to waive immunity.[220] Congress does not even have the authority to abrogate state sovereign immunity absent particularized findings of state violations of constitutionally protected rights.[221] The immunity usually attaches to state universities, hospitals and other facilities owned by the state, is applied on a state by state basis, and is not impliedly waived by the state's entry into commerce.[222]

On the other hand, prospective injunctive relief that does not reach the state treasury is not necessarily barred by the Eleventh Amendment.[223] In addition, professors and others that work for a university are not automatically immune from prosecution in their personal capacities. "[T]he mere fact that [a party's] conduct was undertaken in the course of . . . State employment does not of course relieve [the party] of individual liability, even if [the] employer could not be sued for it."[224] And even where damages are not available against the individuals, it is possible to secure injunctive relief against the actions of individual infringers acting in their official capacities under the *Ex parte Young* doctrine.[225]

The State of Utah improperly claimed immunity for a highly profitable commercial medical laboratory that was run out of the University of Utah.[226]

(3)   Immunity For Medical Practitioners And Researchers

Doctors, nurses and other medical practitioners, and related health care entities are also immune as to direct infringement and inducement to infringe, (but not contributory infringement) for treating patients ("performing a medical or surgical procedure on a body).[227] In any event, that exception does not extend to infringement with respect to: (a) use of a patented machine, manufacture, or composition of matter; (b) the practice of a patented use of a composition of matter; or (c) the practice of a process in violation of a biotechnology patent.

There is yet another immunity against patent infringement that is available to pharmaceutical companies, physicians, hospitals, and others that are preparing a submission for FDA approval.[228] That provisional is intended to prevent patentees from effectively gaining an effective extension of their patent beyond its expiration date, which would otherwise result from FDA filing requirements imposed upon generic manufacturers.

> (1) It shall not be an act of infringement to make, use, offer to sell, or sell within the United States or import into the United States a patented invention (other than a new animal drug or veterinary biological product (as those terms are used in the Federal Food, Drug, and Cosmetic Act and the Act of March 4, 1913) which is primarily manufactured using recombinant DNA, recombinant RNA, hybridoma technology, or other processes involving site specific genetic

---

219 28 U.S.C. § 1498(a)

220 *College Sav. Bank v. Fla. Prepaidpostsecondary Ed. Expense Bd.*, 527 U.S. 666, 675 (U.S. 1999).

221 *Pennington Seed, Inc. v. Produce Exch. No. 299*, 2006 U.S. App. LEXIS 20363 (Fed. Cir. 2006).

222 *Tegic Communs. Corp. v. Bd. of Regents*, 2006 U.S. App. LEXIS 20475 (Fed. Cir. 2006); *Xechem Int'l., Inc. v. Univ. of Tex. M.D. Anderson Cancer Ctr.*, 382 F.3d 1324, 1330 (Fed. Cir. 2004).

223 *Kersavage v. University of Tennesse*e, 731 F. Supp. 1327, 1330 (D. Tenn. 1989), citing

224 *Id.*

225 *Pennington Seed, supra.*

226 *United States ex rel. Sikkenga v. Regence Bluecross Blueshield*, 472 F. 3d 702, 722 (10th Cir. 2006).

227 35 U.S.C. § 287(c).

228 Food and Drug Administration, 35 U.S.C. § 271(e)(1).

manipulation techniques) solely for uses reasonably related to the development and submission of information under a Federal law which regulates the manufacture, use, or sale of drugs or veterinary biological products.

The so-called "safe-harbor" immunity "extends to all uses of patented inventions that are reasonably related to the development and submission of any information under the FDCA."[229] "This necessarily includes preclinical studies of patented compounds that are appropriate for submission to the FDA in the regulatory process …. [and is not] limited to research conducted in clinical trials.[230]

(4) Experimental Use Immunity

There is a very limited "experimental use" exception in the medical field, but that exception has historically only been applied when the use is "solely for amusement, to satisfy idle curiosity, or for strictly philosophical inquiry."[231] The exception is generally inapplicable whenever the alleged infringer is acting in furtherance of a business or commercial purpose, even where that business or purpose is non-profit, such as educating and enlightening students and faculty.[232]

H) Defense To Infringement Based On Prior Commercial Use

Determining validity and scope of business method patents has been a real thorn in the side of the patent office at least since the State Street case of 1989.[233] Ten years later, congress passed 35 U.S.C. § 273, which provided a limited form of prior user rights with respect to methods of doing business. In 2011 the AIA amended the statute to cover any patent (not just method patents), provided the person asserting the defense reduced the subject matter of the patent to practice, and commercially used the subject matter, at least 1 year before the effective filing date of the patent. The defense was also expanded to include situations where the subject matter was derived from the patent holder or persons in privity with the patent holder.

The new law specifically covers premarketing regulatory review period during which the safety or efficacy of the subject matter is established, 35 U.S.C. §273(c)(1), and laboratory use by a nonprofit research laboratory or other nonprofit entity, such as a university or hospital, for which the public is the intended beneficiary, 35 U.S.C. § 273(c)(2).

Section 273 is not, however, a blanket license, and there are several exceptions. In general, a defense under section § 273 may be asserted only by the person who performed, directed or controlled the prior commercial use, at sites of the prior commercial use, and only if the prior commercial use was not derived from the patent holder. In addition, the defense cannot generally be licensed, assigned or otherwise transferred.

I) Exhaustion

Authorized sale of an article that substantially embodies a patent exhausts the patent holder's rights and prevents the patent holder from invoking patent law to control postsale use of the article. This same principle

---

229 Food, Drug, and Cosmetic Act, *Merck KGaA v. Integra Lifesciences I, Ltd.*, 125 S. Ct. 2372, 2380 (U.S. 2005).
230 *Id.*
231 *Madey v. Duke Univ.*, 307 F.3d 1351, 1362 (Fed. Cir. 2002).
232 *Id.*
233 *State Street Bank & Trust Co. v. Signature Financial Group*, 149 F.3d 1368 (Fed. Cir. 1998).

applies to methods, such that authorized sale of a product produced with a patented method relinquishes the patent monopoly with respect to the article sold".[234]

But what happens when the product is self-replicating, such as a seed? Under 2012 Federal Circuit precedent, the patent rights are not exhausted. Thus, a farmer can be sued for patent infringement by harvesting seeds grown from patented seeds.[235]

J)   Failure to Mark

Marking is now easier than ever, by listing patent numbers on the Internet

Failure of the patentee to properly mark his product, (or literature regarding a service), does not provide immunity or any other defense against infringement. Failure to mark only provides a limitation with respect to damages.[236] Note that marking is easier than ever under the America Invents Act, which allows for virtual marking.[237] Under that statute, marking can be satisfied by placing information on the patented article that uses the word "patent" or "pat", and directs the public to a free access internet site that associates the patented article with the number of the patent.

K)   Remedies In General

Remedies for patent infringement can be severe. Injunctive relief is no longer mandatory, (see discussion below regarding compulsory licensing), but damages are still supposed to adequately compensate the patent holder for all injury arising from infringement.[238] Damages should at least equal a reasonable royalty, and in the hands of creative counsel the damages can be several times a reasonable royalty, including for example an infringer's profits, the patent holder's lost profits, damage to the marketplace, and so forth. There is no specific statute of limitations for bringing an infringement claim (except against the U.S. government), but damages are limited to six years prior to filing the infringement complaint or counterclaim.[239]

The patent law provides for enhanced damages (up to three times the amount found or assessed) and attorneys fees for "willful infringement."[240] One should not automatically assume, however, that each infringement will be found to be willful.

Patent damages can be severe, including triple damages, in addition to attorneys' fees

Since the *Seagate* case of 2007 the Courts have used what is essentially a recklessness standard. To establish willfulness a patentee must show by clear and convincing evidence (1) that the infringer acted despite an objectively high likelihood that its actions constituted infringement of a valid patent, and (2) that this objectively-defined risk was either known or so obvious that it should have been known to the accused infringer.[241] Following Seagate, the Federal Circuit established the rule that generally

234 *Quanta Computer, Inc. v. LG Electronics, Inc.*, 553 U.S. 617 (U.S. 2008).
235 *Monsanto Co. v. Bowman*, 657 F.3d 1341 (Fed. Cir. 2011).
236 35 U.S.C. § 287(b)(1).
237 35 U.S.C. § 287.
238 35 U.S.C. § 284.
239 35 U.S.C. § 286.
240 35 U.S.C. § 284.
241 *In re Seagate Technology, LLC*, 497 F.3d 1360 (Fed. Cir. 2007) (en banc).

the "'objective' prong of Seagate tends not to be met where an accused infringer relies on a reasonable defense to a charge of infringement."[242]

Proof that a risk was "known or obvious" can be established by demonstrating "deliberate indifference", such as where a party failed to inform its attorney that it had copied a competitor's product.[243]

L) Proactive Strategies – From The Potential Infringer's Standpoint

(1)   Keeping Track Of A Competitor's Patent Portfolios

Every company involved with newer technologies should keep current on the intellectual property of their competitors. It may be far better to change a product than to fight a lawsuit, and even if product change is not a realistic option, it is usually less expensive to secure a license before the applicant has a product on the market than afterwards wnen fighting a lawsuit. Monitoring a competitor's patents and patent application is fairly straightforward with modern databases. Many firms rely on NERAC,[244] a searching and monitoring service that has electronic access to essentially all of the public patent databases, as well tens of thousands of journals. They charge a fixed annual fee regardless of number of searches and concurrent TechTracks, so that the marginal out-of-pocket cost for additional services is substantially zero. Other good choices are STNeasy,[245] Lexis Total Patent,[246] and Google Patent Searches.[247]

Companies generally do not need a full search and opinion on every worrisome patent and patent applications. Published patent applications with ridiculously broad claims are usually not a problem. The patent office can generally be relied upon to find any prior art that the patent attorney could find, and to force narrowing of the claims. If there is a particular reference of interest, the patent office is usually very receptive to considering the reference, as long as it is timely presented. Most patent applications are published 18 months after the earliest claimed priority date.

Issued patents require considerably more deference. If one or more of the claims appear problematic, one should obtain the file wrapper, which is a copy of all of the official correspondence between the patent office and the attorney, (or the applicant if he has no attorney). File wrappers for patents published after December 2000 can usually be downloaded from the Patent Office.[248] File wrappers for older patents can be ordered very inexpensively directly from the USPTO, but the lag time can be several months. We prefer to use Lexis, which has stored hundreds of thousands of file wrappers electronically, and can deliver them almost immediately. It is usually a good idea to obtain histories of related applications (parent and grand-parent applications, CIPs, divisionals, PCTs, and so forth).

Another word of caution involves the necessity to review both independent and dependent claims when considering whether a patent claim is invalid. Where infringement is avoided because an independent (or other parent) claim is invalid over the prior art, the dependent (child) claims can still be valid and still need to be

242 *Spine Solutions, Inc. v. Medtronic Sofamor Danek USA, Inc.*, 620 F.3d 1305, 1319 (Fed. Cir. 2010).
243 *SEB S.A. v. Montgomery Ward & Co.*, 594 F.3d 1360, 1377 (Fed. Cir. 2010), *affirmed Global-Tech Appliances v. SEB S. A., 131 S. Ct. 2060, 179 L. Ed. 2d 1167, 2011 U.S. LEXIS 4022 (U.S., May 31, 2011)*.
244 https://www.nerac.com/
245 https://stneasy.cas.org/
246 https://www.lexisnexisip.com/products/totalpatent-one/
247 https://patents.google.com/
248 Patent Application Information Retrieval, http://portal.uspto.gov/external/portal/pair.

considered for patent infringement. But where infringement is avoided because the accused device or method falls outside the scope of an independent (or other parent) claim, then there is no need to review possible infringement of the corresponding dependent (child) claims. The reason is that it is logically impossible to fall outside the scope of a parent claim, but still fall inside the scope of a corresponding dependent (child) claim.

Of course, one of the best defenses is a strong offense. It may be that a competitor's patent claims could be invalidated over prior art that was not cited to the Patent Office. Good invalidation searches can, however, be quite expensive. It is not unusual for a defendant to spend $50,000, $100,000 or even more searching for prior art to invalidate patent claims.

(2)   Keeping Track Of One's Own Prior Usage

> Pending applications can be attacked by filing a §301 statement, making a §122(e) sub-mission, by protest, and by public use proceedings

Under the America Invents Act of 2011, there is a prior use defense for entities that commercially used a claimed invention in the U.S., either internally or in an actual sale occurring at least one year before the claim's effective filing date, or as a qualified pre-filing disclosure. There are some restrictions and exceptions, and of course, the prior use defense does not apply if the prior use was derived from the patentee.

(3)   Citing Prior Art Against Patent Applications

There are several actions that one can take upon discovering that a competitor has filed an application with claims that should never be allowed.

- One of the best ways to attack a patent application having overly broad claims is to identify "killer" prior art, and submit it to the patent office by filing a 35 U.S.C. § 301.[249] Submissions can be anonymous. Preparing a 301 statement is easy, but finding relevant prior art could wind up costing thousands of dollars.

- Since September 16, 2012, any person can also file a pre-issuance submission of prior art under 35 U.S.C. § 122(e). There is no fee for submitting three or fewer documents in a pre-issuance submission, but the submitter must provide a concise description of the asserted relevance, a fee if needed, and a statement of compliance. The kicker here is the deadline. A pre-issuance submissions must be filed prior to the latter of the first office action rejecting any claims or within 6 months of notice of publication, but no later than the notice of allowance. They may be filed in any utility, design, or plant application, as well as in any continuing or reissue application.

- File a protest. Any member of the public may file a protest against a pending application, but it must be filed before publication or before mailing of the Notice of Allowance, whichever is earlier.[250] The fact that protests may not be filed against a published application is a good reason for an applicant to keep quiet about a pending application that is due to be granted before the usual 18 month application. ("Loose lips sink ships"). The protest must include: (a) a listing of the patents, publications, or other information relied upon; (b) a

---

249 35 U.S.C. § 301 "(a) IN GENERAL.--Any person at any time may cite to the Office in writing ... (1) prior art consisting of patents or printed publications which that person believes to have a bearing on the patentability of any claim of a particular patent...."

250 37 C.F.R § 1.291. https://www.uspto.gov/web/offices/pac/mpep/s1901.html

concise explanation of the relevance of each item listed; (c) a copy of each listed item or at least the pertinent portions thereof; (d) an English language translation of all the necessary and pertinent parts of any non-English language item. If the submission is not the first such submission by the real party in interest, there must be an explanation as to why the latter protest is significantly different from the former. Unfortunately, the patent office will not respond to the initiator of the protest, other than to return a self-addressed postcard.

• Initiate a public use proceeding. Any member of the public may file a request for a public use proceeding against a pending application, but as in the case of a protest, the request must be filed before publication or before mailing of the Notice of Allowance, whichever is earlier.[251] The request must be supported by affidavits or declarations that provide a prima facie showing that the invention claimed in an application had been in public use, or on sale, more than one year before the filing of the application. Upon receipt of the request, the Director will decide whether to institute public use proceedings. The petitioner will be heard in the proceedings but after decision therein will not be heard further in the prosecution of the application for patent.

(4)   Derivation Proceedings During Prosecution

It often happens that two or more people independently invent similar things at about the same time. If each of those individuals files a patent application on their inventions, there has to be some means of determining who gets to own the patent rights.

In the past that was accomplished by the U.S. patent office conducting an interference proceeding under 35 U.S.C. § 135(a). Basically, interferences involved a mini litigation conducted within the patent office. Such proceedings were generally less costly than litigation in federal court, but could still be quite expensive and time consuming.

As of March 16, 2013, the AIA eliminates interference practice in favor of derivation proceedings.[252] New section 35 U.S.C. § 135 (a) is fairly limited, however, and as currently interpreted by the patent office,[253] _only_ _applies_ in situations where an alleged wrongdoer files an earlier patent application "claiming" the original inventor's (but late filer's) "claimed invention." The final proposed rules only authorize derivation proceedings when the petitioner's claims are "substantially the same" as the alleged deriver's claim, with "substantially the same" defined as "patentably indistinct."[254]

> **Derivation proceedings only cost $420 out-of-pocket, but have very limited applicability**

The derivation proceeding must be filed before the earlier of (i) one year from the petitioner application's publication date, or (ii) one year from the issuance of the patent being challenged.[255] In this context, "earlier" means that the petitioner application's _effective_ filing date is earlier than the _effective_ filing date of the patent or application being challenged.[256]

---

251 37 C.F.R § 1.292. https://www.govinfo.gov/content/pkg/CFR-1998-title37-vol1/xml/CFR-1998-title37-vol1-sec1-292.xml

252 Interference proceedings are theoretically still available under § 135 to the extent that they are limited to the issue of derivation

253 37 C.F.R.. 42.405(a)(2), Final Rule on Changes to Implement Derivation Proceedings. https://www.law.cornell.edu/cfr/text/37/42.405

254 37 C.F.R. 42.401. https://www.law.cornell.edu/cfr/text/37/42.401

255 37 C.F.R. 43.403. https://www.law.cornell.edu/cfr/text/37/42.403

256 This definition of "earlier comes from H.R. 6621 signed into law January 2, 2012.

A petition seeking to institute derivation proceedings must show that the claimed invention is the same or substantially the same as at least one claim of the petitioner's application, and was derived from another without authorization. The petition must also be supported by substantial evidence, including corroboration of the showing of derivation.[257] Rules, trial practice guides, etc, for derivation proceedings are all available online.[258]

It remains to be seen how this will play out. One worry is that the law will encourage applicants to file for patents on minimal improvements on technologies that were actually invented by others. While this may be troubling for some, it just goes to reinforce the strategies taught in the book. Inventors should be brainstorming their inventions with their patent counsel, and filing applications that cover the white space of the applicant's own ideas, as well as green fields that could be occupied by competitors in the future. And inventors should be filing patent applications as soon as possible.

(5)   Derivation Proceedings After Issuance

It sometimes happens that an inventor files and prosecutes his own patent application without knowing that someone else stole his invention, and secured a competing patent. Under pre-AIA 35 U.S.C. § 291, the inventor could file suit to invalidate the thief's patent at any time. Under revised § 291, there is a one year statute of limitations for bringing such an action, calculated from the issued date of the challenged patent.

(6)   Post Grant Review

Post Grant Review

• Within 9 months

• $20K+ petition fee, plus $27.5K+ if the case moves forward

Patents issued to others can be attacked in the patent office rather than in the courts. In the past this was done by either *ex parte* reexamination (in which the petitioning entity had no part in the proceedings other than to file a petition to get the process started), or an *inter partes* reexamination (in which the petitioning entity could take an active part in the proceedings).

Under the America Invents Act, only patents that are <u>less than nine months old</u> can be attacked using post grant review.[259] Patents can be attacked on any ground of invalidity that can be raised as a defense in an infringement action. However, the process will not commence until the Director makes a determination that "the information presented ... if not rebutted would demonstrate that it is more likely than not that at least one of the claims challenged in the petition is unpatentable." Review may also proceed if the initial determination shows that the petition raises a novel or unsettled legal question that is important to other patents or patent applications.

Discovery is permitted, but limited to "evidence directly related to factual assertions advanced by either party."

The process should move forward quickly, with the patent office making a final decision within one year, subject to a possible six month extension "for good cause." Each party has the right to an oral hearing. Appeals lie only to the Federal Circuit Court of Appeals. Rules, trial practice guides, etc, for post grant review are all available online.[260] The Patent Office also has great FAQs.[261]

257 37 C.F.R. 42.405(c). https://www.law.cornell.edu/cfr/text/37/42.405
258 https://www.uspto.gov/patents/laws/america-invents-act-aia/inter-partes-disputes
259 35 U.S.C. §§ 321-329. https://www.govinfo.gov/content/pkg/USCODE-2011-title35/html/USCODE-2011-title35-partIII-chap32.htm
260 https://www.uspto.gov/patents/laws/america-invents-act-aia/inter-partes-disputes
261 https://www.uspto.gov/patent/laws-and-regulations/america-invents-act-aia/america-invents-act-aia-frequently-asked#type-post-grant-review

Filing a declaratory judgment action challenging the validity of a patent forfeits the right to subsequently file post-grant reviews and *inter partes* reviews on that patent.[262] One could file a declaratory judgment and a post grant or *inter partes* review on the same day, in which case the court is likely to stay the declaratory judgment action. That preserves the venue (via the declaratory judgment action) without forfeiting the post grant or *inter partes* review processes. Alternatively, one can file a declaratory judgment action that only claims non-infringement (no invalidity claims), and file for post grant or *inter partes* review shortly thereafter.

Post grant review is expensive. The fee for challenging up to 20 claims is $47,500, and increases by $475 for each additional claim challenged.[263]

Until 2019, there was a special post grant review process[264] for business method patents that claim "a method or corresponding apparatus for performing data processing or other operations used in the practice, administration or management of a financial product or service," except for patents for technological inventions. Determination was made on a case-by-case basis "whether the claimed subject matter as a whole recites a technological feature that is novel and nonobvious over the prior art; and solves a technical problem using a technical solution."[265]

(7)   Transitional Program for Covered Business Method Patents

Until September 16, 2020, one could have attacked business methods through a TPCBM proceeding. Such proceedings employ the standards and procedures of a post grant review, with certain exceptions. Rules, trial practice guides, etc, for TPCBM proceedings are all available online.[266] The Patent Office provided great FAQs.[267]

> **Special proceedings to attack business methods patents**

(8)   Inter Partes Review (IPR)

Patents that are *more than nine months old* can be attacked using inter partes review.[268] This was also a new procedure started in 2011 by the America Invents Act, and has now replaced the old *inter partes* reexamination for all patents, regardless of when they were issued. Under the new procedure the patent owner can respond to the petition, and the review will only take place if the Director makes a determination that a reasonable likelihood exists for the petitioner to succeed on at least one of the challenged claims.

Inter Partes Review is a hybrid between interference and re-examination. The review should take place rather quickly, and is supposed to be resolved within 1.5 years. The PTAB can, however, continue the review even if the matter settles between the parties. As with other post grant proceedings, the Patent Office has great FAQs.[269]

---

262 35 U.S.C. §§ 315(a)(1). https://mpep.uspto.gov/RDMS/MPEP/e8r9#/e8r9/d0e306745912.html ; 325(a)(1). https://www.law.cornell.edu/uscode/text/35/325
263 37 C.F.R. 42.207. https://www.law.cornell.edu/cfr/text/37/42.207
264 37 C.F.R. 42.300 – 304. https://www.govinfo.gov/content/pkg/CFR-2013-title37-vol1/xml/CFR-2013-title37-vol1-part42-subpartD.xml
265 37 C.F.R. 42.301.
266 at https://www.uspto.gov/patents/laws/america-invents-act-aia/inter-partes-disputes
267 https://www.uspto.gov/patent/laws-and-regulations/america-invents-act-aia/america-invents-act-aia-frequently-asked#-type-derivation-proceedings
268 35 U.S.C. § 311-319, and 37 C.F.R. 42.100 – 123, and under H.R. 6621 signed into law January 2, 2013, at any time for patents that have a filing date prior to March 16, 2013.
269 https://www.uspto.gov/patent/laws-and-regulations/america-invents-act-aia/america-invents-act-aia-frequently-asked#-type-inter-partes-review

Unless otherwise necessary in the interest of justice, discovery is limited to depositions of witnesses who have submitted affidavits or declarations. The patent owner is given only one opportunity to file an amendment to

> ### *Inter Partes* Review
>
> • <u>After</u> nine months
> • $19K+ petition fee, plus $22.5K+ if the case moves forward

cancel challenged claims, and to replace them with a reasonable number of substitute claims. See 2019 Pilot Program for handling claim amendments.[270] Each party has the right to an oral hearing. Appeals lie only to the Federal Circuit Court of Appeals. Rules, trial practice guides, etc, for inter partes review are all available online.[271]

Under the AIA, parties can now submit to the PTO written statements of a patent owner filed in a federal court case, or in a proceeding before the PTO. That change is hugely significant because patent holders may well make an argument or admission against interest in a court case that the PTO could use to invalidate the patent.[272]

Inter partes review can only be filed by a patent infringement defendant within one year of being sued. One trick for a defendant is to wait for the end of the 12 month period. If the patent holder files a preliminary statement, then the petitioner can re-file if within 12 months.

Filing a declaratory judgment action challenging the validity of a patent forfeits the right to subsequently file post-grant reviews and *inter partes* reviews on that patent.[273] One strategy is to file a declaratory judgment and a post grant or *inter partes* review on the same day, in which case the court is likely to stay the declaratory judgment action. That preserves the venue (via the declaratory judgment action) without forfeiting the post grant or *inter partes* review processes. Alternatively, one can file a declaratory judgment action that only claims non-infringement (no invalidity claims), and file for post grant or *inter partes* review shortly thereafter.

Inter partes review is expensive, but somewhat cheaper than post grant review. For all entity sizes, the fee for challenging up to 20 claims is $41,500, and increases by $375 for each additional claim challenged.[274] Total cost could easily be $75,000 to pursue an inter-partes review to completion. Interestingly, the high fees have apparently had little effect on the number of filings.

(9)   Ex Parte Reexamination

> ### *Ex Parte* Reexamination
>
> • Anytime
> • $5,040 small entity, or $2,520 micro entity

Anyone can request ex parte reexamination at any time during the period of enforceability of the patent. The prior art considered during reexamination is, however, primarily limited to prior art patents or printed publications applied under the appropriate parts of 35 U.S.C. 102 and 103, and therefore excludes prior art that might otherwise be available in a district court proceeding. On the other hand, as with inter partes review, the AIA allows parties to submit to the PTO written statements of a patent owner that had been filed in a federal court

270 https://www.uspto.gov/sites/default/files/documents/12720201212020BoardsideChatMultiplePetitionMTAS-tudyandSOP2relatedforms.pdf
271 https://www.uspto.gov/patents/laws/america-invents-act-aia/inter-partes-disputes
272 https://www.uspto.gov/patents/laws/america-invents-act-aia/inter-partes-disputes
273 35 U.S.C. §§ 315(a)(1), https://www.govinfo.gov/content/pkg/USCODE-2020-title35/pdf/USCODE-2020-title35-partIII-chap31-sec315.pdf ; 325(a)(1). https://www.govinfo.gov/content/pkg/USCODE-2015-title35/pdf/USCODE-2015-title35-partIII-chap32-sec325.pdf
274 https://www.uspto.gov/learning-and-resources/fees-and-payment/uspto-fee-schedule

case, or in a proceeding before the PTO.[275] As with other post grant proceedings, the Patent Office has great FAQs.[276]

In addition, after making the request for reexamination, the requester is out of the picture. There is no opportunity for the requester to make comments to the examiner, for example to argue against false or misleading comments made by the patentee, or to point out to the examiner positions that could be taken by the patent office.

Upon receiving a request for *ex parte* reexamination, the patent office has three months to review the cited art, and determine whether that art presents a "substantial new question of patentability". If the answer is yes, a reexamination proceeding is begun, and is supposed to proceed with "special dispatch" within the Office. Reexamination proceedings are normally conducted to conclusion and the issuance of a reexamination certificate. Reexamination and patent files are available to the public in electronic format through public PAIR. Reexamination is governed by 35 U.S.C. §§ 301 – 307.

> **Invalidation of patent may invalidate all family members!**

Patent holders must be especially careful about conducting reexaminations or post-grant reviews on patents having other family members. If patent is invalidated pursuant to either of those procedures, then all children of the invalidated patent are presumed to be invalid.[277] The patent holder has the burden of proving patentably distinct claims, which may be impossible if the applicant filed a terminal disclaimer instead of insisting on distinctiveness over the parent during prosecution.

Ex parte re-examination is expensive, although less expensive than *inter partes* review. Here, however, the high fees have apparently been a significant factor in the number of filings. Since the fee increase for *ex parte* reexamination on September 16, 2012, the annual number of cases has dropped from almost 800 (FY2012) to 186 in FY2021.

(10)   Litigation Versus Patent Office Review

There is quite a bit of disagreement within the patent community as to whether one should file some form of redress within the patent office (e.g., post-grant review, inter partes review, ex parte reexamination, etc), or litigate in district court to attack another's patent.

Many attorneys have told me that they would prefer to litigate invalidity in federal court, rather than fight the battle within the patent office. It could be that they don't trust the patent office, or perhaps they are litigators, and stand to gain a much larger fee by pursuing invalidity in court than in the patent office.

Another possible reason for being leery about proceedings within the patent office is that they can create an estoppel. Under 35 U.S.C. § 315(e)(2) provides that a third party requestor is estopped (precluded) from later asserting that a claim is invalid based upon grounds that were "raised or could have been raised" during inter partes review. Thus, prior art used during a failed inter partes review likely cannot be used again during a subsequent district court infringement litigation. This sounds draconian, but in fact the same thing occurs in federal district court. Once the court rules that claims are allowable over a given set of prior art, that ruling becomes the law and likely cannot be re-litigated in a subsequent case.

---

275 https://www.uspto.gov/patents/laws/america-invents-act-aia/inter-partes-disputes
276 https://www.uspto.gov/patents/ptab/trials/ex-parte-appeals-faq
277 37 CFR 42.73(d)(3). https://www.govinfo.gov/content/pkg/CFR-2016-title37-vol1/xml/CFR-2016-title37-vol1-sec42-73.xml

Despite these considerations, our office usually recommends patent office proceedings over litigation, for the reasons listed below:

- First, there is a huge difference in cost. While the whole process of *inter partes* review might run less than $100,000, including arguments, invalidating a patent in the court system can cost upwards of one and a half million dollars at the District Court level, and then easily that much again going through appeals, remands, and so forth.

- Second, there is a huge difference in timing. Whereas the patent office will quickly grant or deny the petition for *inter partes* review, and the entire proceeding can be over within a year or two, a court battle over invalidity might have no quick indication of outcome, and can realistically go on for five years or more.

- Third, there is a huge difference in expertise. The fact is that most federal court judges are only minimally schooled in both the intricacies of patent law and whatever technology is being discussed. Moreover, the Federal Circuit reverses the District Courts in a staggering 50% of all cases.[278] At least decisions by the examiners are reviewed by the Patent Trademark and Appeals Board,[279] which provides some oversight before having to incur the major expense of an appeal to the Federal Circuit.

- Fourth, there is a difference in motivation. The patent office has strong pressure from the public and the media to fix its own errors. In a famous recent reexamination case, the patent office rejected broad claims[280] to a crustless peanut butter and jelly sandwich, and the Federal Circuit took only two days to affirm![281] Moreover, the reexamination almost always goes to an examiner other than the one who granted the patent.[282] According to patent office statistics, just over 90 percent of reexamination petitions are granted, and at least 80% percent of granted petitions result in either revocation or narrowing of patent claims. In contrast to the strong motivation of the patent office to fix mistakes, the federal courts really don't seem to care one way or another whether a patent stands or falls. If anything, the courts tend to side with patent validity, granting considerable administrative deference to the patent office.

- Fifth, there is no loss of appellate rights. An adverse decision in an inter partes review can still be appealed to the Federal Circuit.[283]

- Sixth, many district courts are willing to grant stay of patent infringement litigation during the reexamination process, especially if the petitioner chose the inter partes route. In one of the EchoStar proceedings,[284] a District Court judge gave a very well-reasoned

---

278 Petherbridge and Wagner, "The Federal Circuit and Patentability: An Empirical Assessment of the Law of Obviousness", U. of Penn. Law School, (2006), *citing Cybor Corp. v. FAS Techs.*, 138 F.3d 1448, 1476 (Fed. Cir. 1998).

279 Effective March 16, 2013, the Board of Patent Appeals and Interferences is replaced by the Patent Trial and Appeal Board.

280 U.S. 6004596 (Dec. 1999) "Sealed crustless sandwich"; Exemplary claim: "A ... crustless sandwich, comprising: a first bread layer ...; a ... (peanut butter and jelly) filling ...; a second bread layer ...; a crimped edge ...for sealing ... said first bread layer and said second bread layer; wherein a crust portion ... has been removed."

281 *In re Kretchman, supra,* 124 Fed. Appx. 1012.

282 37 C.F.R. 1.931(b) Order For *Inter partes* Reexamination. https://www.govinfo.gov/content/pkg/CFR-2009-title37-vol1/xml/CFR-2009-title37-vol1-sec1-931.xml

283 35 U.S.C. § 315(b) Appeal. https://www.law.cornell.edu/uscode/text/35/315

284 *Echostar Techs. Corp. v. TiVo, Inc.*, 2006 U.S. Dist. LEXIS 48431, 4-5 (D. Tex. 2006).

analysis in support of granting stay of a long-pending patent infringement action in view of a late-filed reexamination petition.

There are a few downsides of filing for review by the patent office, but they are not particularly weighty. One problem is that bringing an *inter partes* review forecloses the same party from raising invalidity as a defense based upon the same prior art in a litigation with the patent holder.[285]

This is a valid consideration, but the whole idea of *inter partes* review is to avoid litigation. Being foreclosed against raising the same prior art as a defense to infringement is somewhat beside the point. If the patent cannot be invalidated, the accused infringer should either take a license or stop infringing. In any event, a reexamination can potentially be brought in federal court by a party other than the accused infringer.

> **Review at the patent office is much less expensive than litigation**

Still another downside of filing for reexamination is that the patent holder has an opportunity during *inter partes* review to amend the scope of the claims so that they are valid. One has to assume that the patent holder has clever attorneys, and can potentially re-write the claims in such a manner as to circumvent the prior art, while still covering embodiments of the alleged infringer.

Note that the America Invents Act modified the threshold for getting a patent reexamined. Instead of the old "substantial new question of patentability", the standard is now "a reasonable likelihood that the requester would prevail with respect to at least 1 of the claims challenged."

Before actually filing for *inter partes* review of another's patent, one should at least consider licensing. If the patent holder is an individual, or otherwise not a serious competitor, he is often willing to license the patent for a royalty of somewhere between 2 and 6 percent. And even if the patent holder is a competitor that has no intention of giving you a license, he might well be swayed by seeing that you are serious about filing a *inter partes* review proceeding. A useful strategy is to draft a petition, and send a copy to the patent holder with a note advising that it will be filed within two weeks unless a fully paid up license is agreed to. The fact that the petition is fully drafted seems to light a fire under the patent holder, and push along the licensing process very quickly. Indeed, if the prior art is strong, it makes very good sense for the patent holder to grant a license, even if the royalty is zero. The reason is that it is better to have the patent appear to be valid, and thereby keep other competitors away. The patent holder can likely still maintain oligopolistic profits with only a few players in the field.

(11)   Contacting The Patent Holder

Post-grant review and litigation are not the only choices to deal with a competitor's patent. One can also contact the competitor early on (to proactively forestall litigation), or just wait to see whether the patent holder issues a cease and desist letter. To a large extent that depends upon the stage of development of the potential infringer's product or service. If the potentially infringing product or service is at a fairly early stage of development, then it may be a very good idea to engage the patent holder in some sort of discussion regarding validity and infringement. If changes need to be made to the product/service it is almost always less expensive to make them earlier rather than later. Another timing factor is cash flow. It may well be that the patent holder

---

285 35 U.S.C. 315(c) Appeal "A third-party requester whose request for an inter partes reexamination results in an order under section 313 is estopped from asserting at a later time, in any civil action arising in whole or in part under section 1338 of title 28, the invalidity of any claim finally determined to be valid and patentable on any ground which the third-party requester raised or could have raised during the inter partes reexamination proceedings. This subsection does not prevent the assertion of invalidity based on newly discovered prior art unavailable to the third-party requester and the Patent and Trademark Office at the time of the inter partes reexamination proceedings."

has a lot more monetary and other resources than the potential infringer, so that the latter may well want to gain strength in the marketplace, complete another round of funding, or achieve some other milestone before doing something that might trigger the expense of litigation.

Beyond timing, one should evaluate broad strategic considerations. It may be, for example, that the potential infringer is looking to sell its own patent portfolio (or market position) to the patent holder, and offering a friendly challenge to the patent holder may assist in the bargaining position. This is especially true if the potential infringer has critical information (such as on-sale bar information) that is not generally accessible to other competitors.

(12)   Opinion Letters

(a)   Is An Opinion Letter Cost Effective?

It is a commonplace event for an individual or company to seek some sort of right-to-use opinion regarding a new product. Such opinions, also called right-to-practice, non-infringement, or freedom to operate opinions, can save a lot of money that would otherwise be wasted by putting a product on the market and then having to withdrawn it in the face of potential patent infringement litigation. The question is, when should a right-to-use opinion be commissioned, and when is it not cost-effective to do so.

- Probably the best reason for securing a right-to-use opinion is that a decision is being made on whether to place a given product into the marketplace, and the scientists, engineers, programmers or other designers are trying to figure out how to roll out a product that doesn't infringe. A good opinion is extremely helpful in that regard because it identifies what features must be avoided to steer clear of litigation, and can usually point to non-infringing alternatives. If a right-to-practice opinion wasn't prepared prior to introduction of the product in the marketplace, then it certainly should be commissioned as soon as a cease and desist letter is issued.

- Another viable justification is risk assessment. Any good product manager wants to know in advance what the likelihood is of the company being sued, and of having the new product enjoined from the marketplace. Indeed, if the manager is seeking defensive product infringement insurance, the insurance company will often require the company to secure a right-to-practice opinion as a condition of issuing the insurance.

- A third justification is damage control. A losing defendant in a patent infringement lawsuit can be liable for a penalty of up to three time damages, plus attorneys' fees.[286] Although failure of an accused infringer to obtain a non-infringement opinion may not be used to prove that the accused infringer willfully infringed the patent,[287] obtaining such an opinion before the product hits the market can be helpful in avoiding enhanced damages.

- On the flip side of the coin, the biggest downside of commissioning a formal right-to-practice opinion is that such an opinion typically costs $5,000 to $25,000 or more. It is certainly possible to secure an informal analysis, for $5,000 or even less, but of course the value of such an analysis is less than that of a formal opinion.

---

286 35 U.S.C. § 284. https://www.govinfo.gov/content/pkg/USCODE-2009-title35/html/USCODE-2009-title35-partIII-chap29-sec284.htm

287 35 U.S.C. § 298 (only as to civil actions filed on or after September 16, 2011, per H.R. 6621 signed into law January 2, 2013).

- Another consideration in deciding against commissioning a right-to-practice opinion is minimal sales. If the sales are low enough, especially in a crowded marketplace, the seller may well be under the radar screen of the patentee, and it may well be cost-effective to just throw the dice and see what happens. After all, the damages are likely to be so small that litigation is not cost effective for either side.

- Another consideration in deciding against commissioning a right-to-practice opinion is easy substitution or modification of the allegedly infringing product. If the product at issue (or method) can be readily modified to clearly circumvent the claims, then the money spent on the formal opinion would probably be better spent just making those substitutions or modifications.

Formal opinion letters take anywhere from a few weeks to several months to complete, depending on how many documents are needed and how difficult they are to acquire. For example, an opinion addressing validity or infringement with respect to only a single patent is fairly straightforward. But a more global opinion stating that the client's product or method appears to be clear of all infringement of issued patents is much more difficult and time consuming. As noted above, costs vary widely from a low of about $5,000 to $25,000 or more. It all depends upon how crowded the field is, and how much confidence the client wants to buy. Below is a graph that sometimes helps clients grasp the idea of buying a level of confidence.

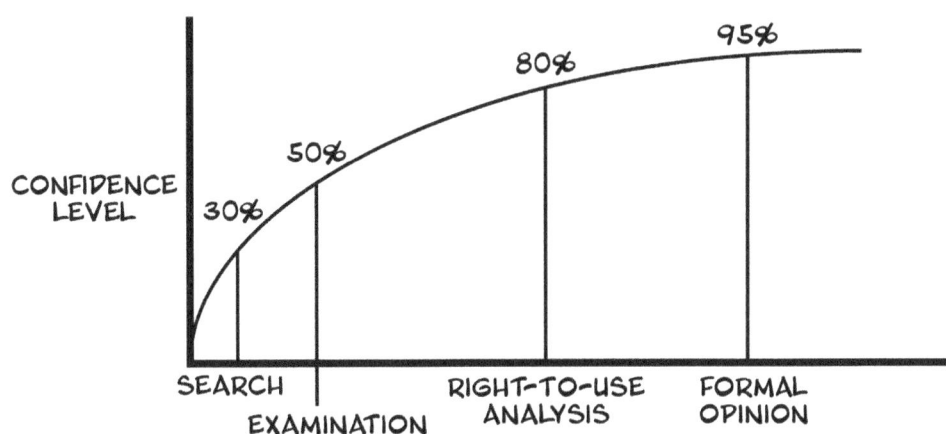

(b) Preparing An Opinion Letter

The first step in preparing an opinion letter is usually to review the patent claims and the file wrapper (i.e. the official correspondence between the applicant and the patent office during prosecution of the patent). If the review of those documents indicates that the client is probably not infringing the claims, then the most cost-effective solution may be for the attorney to merely provide a comfort letter. Such letters run in the lower end of the price range, and merely state that "upon preliminary review" it appears that infringement is unlikely because of one or more listed factors. That provides some level of assurance to the client, but leaves the possibility open for further analysis.

File wrappers can be free with Lexis TotalPatent, or downloaded directly from the patent office for newer patents. Obtaining file wrappers for older patents is $315 from the patent office. One should generally order all U.S. family applications as well (continuations, divisionals, CIPs) because there are often definitions and other important information contained in those other applications. One usually doesn't secure copies of corresponding foreign applications and patents because of the high cost. But it is usually a good idea to download the PCT search report / written opinion because that often has different references from the U.S. prosecution.

(c) Contents Of An Opinion Letter

<table><tr><td>

Non-infringement letters can be helpful, but are not determinative in precluding enhanced damages

</td><td>

A good patent infringement opinion addresses both validity and infringement. The validity issues can be dealt with in an abstract sense, because they have nothing to do with the client's products. The claims are either valid or invalid, depending on the prior art. Nevertheless, the analysis is often quite difficult because the attorney must address each claim (and there can be many claims), and for each of the claims must address anticipation and obviousness, as well as many other aspects including adequate disclosure, enablement, possible fraud on the patent office, and so forth.

</td></tr></table>

The infringement portion of the analysis must apply every element of every claim (at least every independent claim) against the potentially infringing product/method. In some circumstances it is also important to address pending applications, and the likelihood that the patentee will obtain broader coverage in subsequently issued patents.

The quality of the right-to-practice search is obviously of paramount to the validity of the opinion. In that regard, one should extremely careful in reviewing claims. One common mistake is to focus on only the first claim of a patent. In some cases that can be extremely misleading. In U.S. 6192381,[288] for example, claim 1 is directed to using a database management system having a template with data fields having substantially unlimited size.

> 1. A method of entering, storing, displaying, and retrieving data using a data management system having a display device, one or more input devices, and a storage device, said method comprising:
>   (a) loading a document containing data from the storage device;
>   (b) loading a template containing format instructions and at least one data field from the storage device, each data field having a size that is not limited by the data management system;
>   (c) linking the document with the template; and
>   (d) displaying the document and the data within the document responsive
>   to the template on the display device as specified by the format instructions.

If a searcher were to have dismissed this patent upon brief review of claim 1, he would have missed claim 17, which is directed to an entirely different subject matter, namely entering and validating data, and creating "to do" lists from that data.

288 U.S. 6192381 (Feb. 2001) "Single-document active user interface, method and system for implementing same."

17. A method of entering, storing, displaying, and retrieving data using a data management system having a display device, one or more input devices, and a storage device, said method comprising the steps of:

    (1) entering, by the user, a plurality of the data;

    (2) validating, by the computer, that the plurality of the data is in substantial conformance with a predetermined format, as the user enters the plurality of the data;

    (3) when the plurality of the data is not in conformance with the predetermined format, *creating a "to do list"* for review and correction by the user...; and

    (4) repeatedly performing said steps (1)-(3), continuously adding to the "to do list," and allowing the user to continue to enter the plurality of the data,....

Claim 18 is directed to yet another, very different subject matter.

18. A method of entering, storing, displaying, and retrieving data using a data management system having a display device, one or more input devices, and a storage device, said method comprising the steps of:

    (1) entering, by the user, a plurality of the data including multiple groups with multiple entries of data for a substantially same field or substantially same set of fields;

    (2) managing, by the data management system, the plurality of the data including the multiple groups with the multiple entries of data in at least one of a single document, single logical document and file, by maintaining each of the multiple entries directly after each other corresponding with each of the multiple groups; and

    (3) *displaying only the field in the substantially same field or the substantially same set of fields corresponding to the entry selected by the user.*

Nor can one rely upon the abstract to ascertain the focus of the claims. This can happen for many reasons, including circumstances in which a single application has numerous children (divisionals, continuations, CIPs), and the abstract remains the same despite extensive claim changes. U.S. 6653946,[289] for example, is at least a sixth generation application. There, the abstract is addressed to automatic collection of tolls, whereas claim 1 is directed to transmission patterns of antennae.

---

289 .S. 6653946 (Nov. 2003) Electronic vehicle toll collection system and method."

A system for automatic collection of tolls includes an in-vehicle toll processor having memory for storing a toll-money-available quantity purchased by the user, and a toll-facility-identification site that transmits a toll-facility-identifier signal indicating the identity of the upcoming toll facility. As the vehicle approaches the identification site, the in-vehicle processor receives the identifier signal and calculates the toll to be debited. When the vehicle passes through the toll facility, the in-vehicle processor transmits its identity, its net balance and the toll, which it debits from an account balance....

1. An apparatus for locating and identifying a mobile transceiver comprising:
   a plurality of stationary transmitters, each of said transmitters transmitting
      a radio frequency signal carrying identification information, and wherein
      adjacent ones of said transmitters transmit signals...,
   a mobile transceiver having a preassigned identity and including a transmitter,
      a receiver, and a data processor;
   said mobile transceiver identifying a closest one of said plurality of stationary
      transmitters and thereafter transmitting a signal which indicates the
      identity of the closest transmitter.

When construing claims, play devil's advocate. Try to look at claims from a worst case standpoint, not the way you want them to be interpreted. Judges and juries sometimes interpret wording in crazy ways. Be mindful of interpreting claims to narrowly. "A claim interpretation that excludes a preferred embodiment from the scope of the claim is rarely, if ever, correct."[290]

M) Proactive Strategies – From The Patent Holder's Standpoint

(1)   Cease And Desist Letters

Similar considerations exist from the patent holder's perspective. Should a patent holder immediately mail out cease and desist letters to potential infringers? It depends. If the patent holder doesn't have the money to pursue an infringement litigation, and the validity or infringement positions are somewhat questionable, then it might be worthwhile waiting to gain a stronger financial position. But that consideration must be weighed against the possibility that the potential infringer will also become stronger, and in any event will almost certainly become more closely wedded to selling the infringing product. As discussed above, it is much easier for the potential infringer to back down at the early stages than later on. Still, some patent holders prefer to allow someone else to develop the marketplace for them, and then swoop down to enforce their patent(s) months or

---

290 *Accent Packaging v. Leggett & Platt* 2013 U.S. App. LEXIS 2446 (Fed. Cir. 2013); *On-Line Techs., Inc. v. Bodenseewerk Perkin-Elmer GmbH* 386 F.3d 1133, 1138 (Fed. Cir. 2004).

even years into the game. This is an entirely viable strategy. There is no patent statute of limitations per se, and damages go back five years (provided the patent holder was properly marking his product, or can establish that the infringer had actual notice).[291] Thus the effective time period for filing a patent infringement action is the duration of the patent plus six years.

The tone of cease and desist letters can fall anywhere from extremely aggressive to conciliatory. Although there are advantages and disadvantages to each, the best approach is often to advise the recipient of a possible infringement, and to give some indication of willingness to resolve the issue without court intervention.

(a) Aggressive letters

Aggressive letters typically demand that the accused halt all allegedly infringing activity, usually within 10 days or other short period of time. In some cases such letters go on to demand verified destruction of all infringing products, identification of the number of products sold or manufactured, profit margins, listing of customers, and so forth.

The aggressive approach can be successful at instilling fear in inexperienced individuals, but typically does not have that effect on sophisticated companies. In the latter case, the accused party simply forwards the letter on to their counsel, who tends to view infringement accusations in a jaundiced light. Among other things, an aggressive letter places the recipient in imminent apprehension of pending litigation, and thereby opens the door to the recipient suing the sender for declaratory judgment of non-infringement in the locality of the sender. In that instance the sender not only failed to get the effect he wanted, but made matters much worse by allowing the recipient to determine the venue of the litigation, and allowing the recipient to be the plaintiff! Still further, aggressive letters may support Rule 11 sanctions against the sender if the subsequent litigation is deemed frivolous, legally unreasonable, without factual foundation or asserted for an improper purpose.

(b) Conciliatory Letters

These letters state that the recipient's products / methods may fall within the scope of the patent, and that action needs to be taken. The sender usually provides some sort of time demand, but the demand is not set in stone, and is reasonable. In some instances these letters include a claim chart comparing elements of the claims with elements of the accused products / services. But note that claim charts at this stage can also be bad idea because they can lock the patent holder into a position that may be problematic later on in litigation. A format we have following in the past is as follows:

> "This office represents <client> in intellectual property matters. <client> is the owner of US patent no. <patno>, a copy of which is provided for your reference.
>
> It has come to our attention that your product, <product>, falls within the scope of one or more of the claims of the <patno> patent. <client> may be willing to negotiate a mutually advantageous license agreement, and asks that you have your attorney contact the undersigned. In the absence of a suitable license arrangement, <client> will need to redesign <product> so that it falls outside the scope of the patent.
>
> We look forward to hearing back from you on these issues by _____."

Conciliatory letters used to work a lot better than they do now. In 2007 the Federal Circuit found a case or controversy within the meaning of 28 U.S.C. § 2201(a) of the Declaratory Judgment Act where the supposed infringer (plaintiff in the DJ action) advised the defendant patent holder that it had made a studied and determined infringement determination, and asserted the right to a royalty based on this determination.[292] The fact that the patent holder said it would not sue plaintiff failed to eliminate the justiciable controversy. Under this

---

291 35 U.S.C. § 286, Time limitation on damages.
292 *SanDisk Corp. v. STMicroelectronics, Inc.*, 480 F.3d 1372 (Fed. Cir. 2007).

law, even a conciliatory letter seeking to license the patented technology may well provide sufficient threat to support a declaratory judgment action by the patent holder.

Another problem with this approach is that the recipient may read the letter as expressing weakness on the part of the sender. If the letter is too weak, it may even support a defense of estoppel.

Still another problem with being too conciliatory is that the courts might refuse to grant injunctive relief down the road on the grounds that the patent holder had previously offered to license the patent. That issue arose in 2006 as a result of *eBay, Inc. v. MercExchange*,[293] in which the Supreme Court effectively forced the country into the world of compulsory licensing. Among the relevant considerations in refusing to require mandatory injunctive relief was whether the patent holder had offered to license the patent to the infringer. In view of that decision, patent holders may want to merely hint at the possibility of licensing, to preclude a declaratory judgment action, without actually offering to license and without ever engaging in negotiation.

(2)   Offensive Patent Insurance

Patent holders should at least consider purchasing offensive patent infringement insurance. This usually runs about 3% of the face value of the coverage. Thus, the annual cost of securing a $1,000,000 war chest is about $30,000. Having such a war chest can tip the balance of the decision towards send out a cease and desist letter. Best to contact Sandra Walker at IPISC.[294]

Even if the patent holder does have offensive patent insurance, he should be very careful about what is said in cease and desist letters. The availability of declaratory judgment actions means that a potential infringer can sue a patent holder for invalidity and non-infringement where the potential infringer resides. That can greatly increase the cost of litigating the patent for the patent holder. One viable strategy is to file a complaint local to the patent holder, and then send out the cease and desist letter before serving the complaint. That way venue is established local to the patent holder.

(3)   Reissue

Patent holders can bring a reissue proceeding[295] to modify the scope of the claims, to add claims, to correct priority, to revise the specification, or to alter inventorship resulting from a substantive error[296] made during prosecution.

If a reissue petition is filed within two years of the issue date of the patent, the claims can even be broadened. This is, however, a high-risk strategy because reissue requires the patent holder to surrender the patent during the process. The patent may be declared invalid altogether, and may never come back out of the patent office. There is also a heightened written description requirement for reissue patents, dating back to 1893:

> [T]o warrant new and broader claims in a reissue, such claims must not be merely suggested or indicated in the original specification, drawings, or models, but it must further appear from the original patent that they constitute parts or portions of the invention, which were intended or sought to be covered or secured by such original patent.[297]

---

293 *eBay Inc. v. MercExchange, L.L.C.*, 2006 U.S. LEXIS 3872 (U.S. 2006).

294 http://www.patentinsuranceonline.com/; swalker@patentinsurance.com

295 35 U.S.C. § 251.

296 Reissues cannot be filed to remedy procedural errors. *Medrad, Inc. v. Tyco Healthcare Group LP*, 2005 U.S. Dist. LEXIS 40353 (D. Pa. 2005).

297 *Corbin Cabinet Lock Co. v. Eagle Lock Co.*, 150 U.S. 38 (1893).

That standard did not change when the reissue statute was modified in 1952.[298] The America Invents Act, however, did institute a huge change, in that reissue can now be brought even to correct errors of a deceptive intent.

Reissue fees are somewhat complicated, by the size of the application, the number of claims, and so forth. The out of pocket costs, however, are likely in the low thousands.

(4)   Supplemental Examination

Instead of filing for reissue, a patent holder can file a request for supplemental examination[299] of his/its patent under a new section of law implemented by the America Invents Act.

This new section appears to be geared towards providing prior art references to the patent office that were not provided during the original examination process, but without surrendering the patent during the process. The patent holder can provide detailed explanation of the relevance and manner of applying each reference.[300] Following submission of the request, the patent office has three months to decide whether any substantial new issue of patentability has been raised.

If the patent for which supplemental examination is requested is jointly owned by more than one entity, all of those entities must act together as a composite entity in proceedings before the Office. Under rare circumstances, such as in the case of a deceased or legally incapacitated joint owner, the Office may permit less than all of the joint owners to file the request.

Supplemental examination is expensive, and has been only sporadically utilized

One major drawback is that the process is relatively expensive; $4,620/$1,848/$924 (large / small / micro entities) for requesting supplemental examination, and $12,700/$5,080/$2,540) for reexamination following supplemental examination,[301] both of which must be paid when filing the request.[302] If the Patent Office decides that there is no need for reexamination, the reexamination fee is refunded.

For whatever reason, supplemental examination has been very poorly utilized. There were only 28 such cases in FY2021.

The Patent Office has a good list of questions and answers relating to supplemental examination.[303]

(5)   Patent Marking In The U.S.

There is no absolute requirement for patent marking in the U.S. Instead, the marking statute[304] merely provides that a patent holder "may" mark his products with the word "patent" or the abbreviation "pat." together with the relevant patent number(s). The kicker is that for the most part, patent infringement damages are only awarded as of the date of actual or constructive knowledge of the patent. Thus, failure to mark may disqualify the patentee

There is no law requiring patent marking, but failure to mark can reduce damages to zero

298 *Antares Pharma, Inc. v. Medac Pharma Inc.*, 771 F.3d 1354 (Fed. Cir. 2014).

299 35 U.S.C. § 257, rules at 77 Fed. Reg. 48828.

300 37 C.F.R. 1.610.

301 https://www.uspto.gov/learning-and-resources/fees-and-payment/uspto-fee-schedule

302 37 C.F.R. 1.610. https://www.uspto.gov/web/offices/pac/mpep/s2811.html

303 https://www.uspto.gov/patents/laws/america-invents-act-aia/america-invents-act-aia-frequently-asked#type-supplemental-examination

304 35 U.S.C. § 287(a). https://www.law.cornell.edu/uscode/text/35/287

from suing for damages based upon infringing sales that occurred prior to the date of actual notice to the infringer.

Failure to mark is excused in some circumstances. Obviously, there is no need to mark where the patentee (and any licensee) is not practicing the claimed invention, where the patent has both apparatus and method claims but the patentee is only practicing the method(s), and where the patent has only method claims. But if a patent has both method and apparatus claims, and the patentee is making or selling a product to which one of the apparatus claims apply, then the limitation on damages applies.

The questions that arise from patentees usually have to do with what constitutes adequate notice -- what sort of placement is sufficient, and whether previously labeled products have to be re-labeled when a patent issues. Unfortunately, the answer is that there are no bright lines. Patentees are expected to use "reasonable efforts" to apprise the public of the existence of the patent(s), and that includes notification that is consistent and continuous. But patentees are not expected to do the impossible, or even the impractical to provide notice to the public. For example, where the product is too small to mark, the patent identifying information can properly be placed on a label affixed to the product, or to the packaging. Similarly, sales of unmarked products or those marked "patent pending" can usually be sold out without being re-marked with the patent number upon issuance of the patent, especially where such re-marking is impractical. Still further, patentees can properly mark products by referring to "US patents" where listing of all the relevant patents is unrealistic.

Patent marking can now be done on the web

The America Invents Act of 2011 allows for virtual marking. All the patent owner has to do is put the word "patent" or the abbreviation "pat" together with the address of a posting on the Internet that associates the patented article with the number of the patent number(s).

The America Invents Act also came close to eliminating actions for false marking. The new rule is that only the federal government or a competitor may now sue for false marking, and failure to remove an expired patent marking from a product is no longer considered false marking. These are very significant improvements over prior law, under which a handful of law firms were gaming the system by filing hundreds of false marking actions.

Patentees should definitely include a marking requirement in the license agreement. That way, even if the licensee fails to mark properly, the patentee may still be entitled to damages on the theory that the patentee's "reasonable efforts" to force the licensee to mark constituted constructive notice. Of course, a patentee should maintain a paper trail sufficient to demonstrate the "reasonable efforts."

It is illegal to intentionally mislead the public by falsely marking a product as being patented.[305] Although the courts are generally lenient where the product was at one point covered by a patent, the patentee should make good faith and reasonable efforts to keep all patent marking up to date.

(6)   Patent Marking Outside The U.S.

Canada has no statutory requirement for a patentee to mark patented articles, so of course there is no penalty for failure to mark. Marking is, however, still recommended because it arguably provides public notice of the patent rights.

---

305 35 U.S.C. § 292 imposes a $500 fine "for every such offense" of false marking.

In China (PRC), patent marking is compulsory,[306] and must be done in Chinese. Patentees must follow a specific format, which is the Chinese character for patent, followed by the two digits of the year of the patent application, a third digit denoting the type of patent, the patent number, and a parity bit.[307]

In Korea, patent marking is permissible,[308] much as in the United States. Major distinctions are that products made under Korean method patents should also be marked,[309] and there are severe penalties for false marking, including liability of employees for company violations.[310]

In Japan, there is no downside for failure to mark. Marking is done entirely for commercial benefit, and indeed some patent holders intentionally avoid marking so as not to give free advice to competitors.

In Taiwan, patent marking is compulsory,[311] and no damages are allowed unless the infringer knew or should have known of the patent. There is no specific language requirement.

N) Foreign Countries

(1) Enforcement Of Foreign Patent Rights

In addition to major differences among the various countries in prosecution of patent applications, there are also enormous differences in enforcement. Indeed it is the difficulty in enforcement that usually tips the balance in recommendations against foreign filing. The truth is that an ordinary patentee often cannot realistically enforce a patent in Europe, Japan or Korea, let alone Russia, China, India, or Indonesia.

In Europe, a patentee needs to bring separate patent actions in each country for each infringer, even if the patents at issue are essentially equivalent. Determination of invalidity must be made in the courts of each separate country,[312] and patent infringement suits against related companies cannot be combined in a single court even if the defendant companies are acting in accordance with a common policy.[313] It just isn't realistic to bring actions in each of Great Britain, Germany, France, Italy, and Spain, and it is even less realistic to bring actions in the economically smaller countries such as Netherlands, Belgium, Luxembourg, Greece, Switzerland, Portugal, and so forth.

This will be changing soon in Europe. In late Spring 2023, the Unitary Patent (see CHAPTER VI - F) should be implemented, which should obviate the need to register a patent separately in each county. In addition, the enforcement system is supposed to operate through specialized trial courts in Paris, London, and Munich and potentially other locales.

Patent enforcement many become more practical in Europe with a new Unified Patent System

Much has been made about the adoption of tougher enforcement in China, India, Korea, and some other countries. However, the enforcement problems are still legion. It was a huge news item in Korea a few years back when a non-Korean company was the first ever to prevail on patent infringement against a Korean company in a Korean court. Even after that watershed,

---

306 Taiwan Patent Law, Article 79.
307 Chinese Patent Law, Article 15; Implementing Regulation, Articles 4, 83.
308 Korean Patent Statutes, Article 223 et seq.
309 Korean Patent Law Enforcement Regulations, Article 121.
310 Korean Patent Statutes, Articles 227, 230. Prison term up to three years, or a fine up to 20 million won.
311 Taiwan Patent Law, Article 79.
312 *GAT v. LuK*, C-4/03, Article 16(4) (Jul. 2006) (Brussels Conventions).
313 *Roche v. Primus*, C-539/03 (Jul. 2006) (Article 6(1) Brussels Regulation).

the chances of prevailing against one of the chaebol[314] in a Korean court are probably close to zero because of their incredible political strength.

Political considerations are also paramount in China. In 2004 the State Intellectual Property Office of China ("SIPO") revoked Pfizer's patent on the anti-impotence drug, sildenafil citrate (marketed as Viagra™) under pressure of Chinese pharmaceuticals. Although the Chinese companies had argued insufficient detailed description and lack of novelty, SIPO issued the revocation without even giving any basis for the revocation. Chinese pharmaceutical companies also challenged Glaxo Smith Kline's patent on rosiglitazone, one of three patented ingredients in its antidiabetic drug, Avandia.™ Probably knowing that they had no chance of prevailing, Glaxo voluntarily abandoned the patent at the beginning of the oral hearings.

More recently, litigation in China has taken a huge turn for the better. Possibly 90% of infringement actions return a positive verdict for the patent holder, and enforcement of judgments has become much more realistic. Recommended litigation firms include Beijing Gaowo[315], Liu Shen[316] and Scihead[317].

The tactical error in these latter cases may have been failure of the patent holders to run the technology through local companies. In many foreign countries the only realistic strategy for enforcing patents is to license the patent to a home grown company, and have that company enforce the patent.

The picture differs somewhat where the competitors are multinational corporations. Such companies often have the sophistication to appreciate that they must honor competitors' patents if they want their own patents to be honored. Thus, even though a patent may be realistically unenforceable in the courts of a foreign country, multinationals often negotiate cross-licenses.

(2)   International Trade Commission (ITC)

Can a patent holder bring suit through the International Trade Commission (ITC) to stop products from passing through the U.S. borders? The short answer is "yes," but there are several important considerations.

An ITC action under section 337 of the Tariff Act of 1930, 19 U.S.C. § 1337(a)(2) and § 1337(a)(3). generally moves to a conclusion much more rapidly that a district court action, offers a better chance of immediate preliminary relief, and allows for "general exclusion orders" to stop imports industry-wide (i.e., ITC injunctions can cover particular accused infringers as well as other non-parties).

On the downside, the ITC has no power to award damages, and can only be pursued when the imports threaten a US industry for the protected article. (US industry must either exist or be "in the process of being established."[318] This 'domestic industry test' has been interpreted to require that the domestic product also falls within the scope of the asserted patent[319]. Patent licensing activities do satisfy the "domestic industry" requirement, and relief is "available to a party that has a substantial investment in exploitation of a patent through either engineering, research and development, or licensing."[320]

314 Chaebol is a large industrial conglomerate controlled by an individual or family in South Korea.
315 http://www.gaowoip.com/en/
316 http://www.liu-shen.com/
317 http://www.scihead.com/ (in Chinese)
318 19 U.S.C. § 1337(a)(2). https://www.law.cornell.edu/uscode/text/19/1337
319 *Alloc v. ITC*, 342 F.3d 1361 (Fed. Cir. 2003).
320 *Interdigital Communs., LLC v. ITC*, 2013 U.S. App. LEXIS 689 (Fed. Cir. Jan. 10, 2013).

(3) Extraterritorial Reach Of U.S. Patent Law

(a) Apparatus and Composition Claims

For much of its history, the U.S. has had little or no extra-territorial reach with respect to patents. In *Deepsouth Packing*,[321] for example, a 1972 defendant was able to escape liability for patent infringement merely by manufacturing its product in kit form in the U.S. and then assembling it overseas.

In 1984 Congress closed the *Deepsouth* loophole by enactment of 35 U.S.C. § 271 (f)(1) and (2), at least with respect to apparatus and composition claims. Those sections effectively establish liability for directing or encouraging foreign assembly of a product that would be infringing in the U.S., or providing components of such a product from within the U.S.

In 2005 the Federal Circuit issued three decisions that read the statute quite broadly. In *Eolas v Microsoft*,[322] the Federal Circuit held that Microsoft was liable under 271(f) for shipping a master computer readable disk that was further copied abroad, with the copies installed as software on assembled computers. In *AT&T v Microsoft*,[323] the Federal Circuit went one step further, holding Microsoft liable not only for its actions here in the U.S., but for overseas production of copies of the infringing software. In *Union Carbide v Shell*,[324] the Federal Circuit held that Shell was liable for supplying catalyst to its foreign affiliates to perform a chemical process that would have been infringing in the U.S.

> **U.S. courts have only limited extraterritorial reach**

Nevertheless, the Federal Circuit has continued to express reservations about expanding the extra-territorial reach of U.S. intellectual property laws. In a 2011 unfair competition case[325], the Federal Circuit upheld the International Trade Commission's expansive interpretation of extraterritorial reach of 19 U.S.C. § 1337 by distinguishing the " territorial limitations in the patent-granting clause" from the lack of a parallel federal civil statute regulating trade secret protection.

(b) Method Claims

The extraterritorial reach of U.S. patent law is much broader with respect to method claims than with respect to apparatus or composition claims. It turns out that when patented methods are employed abroad, infringement will obtain against the resulting product unless: "(1) [the product] is materially changed by subsequent processes; or (2) it becomes a trivial and nonessential component of another product."[326]

Interestingly, the federal government carved out an even larger exception for itself. The federal government is liable for infringement of a method patent only when it practices every step of the claimed method in the U.S.[327]

(c) Enforceability of Internet Related Patents

If a company has a U.S. patent, can they protect their U.S. markets when a competitor has infringing software operating in a foreign country? It depends. Unless the infringer has a presence in the U.S., the US courts likely cannot get jurisdiction over the infringer. And unless the infringer has assets in the U.S., any damages judgment could be very difficult to enforce.

---

321 *Deepsouth Packing v Laitram Corp*, 406 U.S. 518 (1972).
322 *Eolas v Microsoft*, 399 F. 3rd 1325 (Fed. Cir. 2005).
323 *AT&T v Microsoft*, 414 F, 3d 1366 (Fed. Cir. 2005).
324 *Union Carbide v Shell*, 425 F.3d 1366 (Fed. Cir. 2005).
325 *Tianrui Group Company Limited et al.. v. ITC*, 661 F.3d 1322 (Fed. Cir, 2011).
326 35 U.S.C. § 271(g)(1),(2).
327 28 U.S.C. § 1498; *Zoltek Corp. v. United States*, 442 F.3d 1345, 1347 (Fed. Cir. 2006).

It may be possible to get one or more Internet Service Providers to exclude the infringing websites, but then the infringers would just set up mirrors with different URLs. It may also be possible to go after users of the software, but that the claims would need to be drafted so that someone in the U.S. is infringing.

(d) Transnational Systems

In January 2006 the U.S. Supreme Court denied cert. on review of the Federal Circuit's 2015 decision in the Blackberry case.[328] Among other things, that denial left the door open for patentees to assert their patents against "transnational" systems where the system as a whole is put into service in the U.S. In *NTP, Inc. v. Research in Motion*, the Federal Circuit held that the use of a claimed system under section 35 U.S.C. § 271(a) is the place at which the system as a whole is put into service, i.e., the place where control of the system is exercised and beneficial use of the system is obtained. The Court went on to hold that use of the devices did not constitute infringement under § 271(f), because Research In Motion (RIM) sold its wireless handheld devices in the United States for use in the United States.

(4) Infringement of Foreign Patents

Also expanding the possibility of extraterritorial reach, *Voda v. Cordis*[329] established that where a U.S. court is hearing an infringement claim against an American infringer, the court may exercise its discretion to include supplemental subject matter jurisdiction to hear parallel foreign patent infringement claims stemming from the same patent application. In that case an American manufacturer moved his manufacturing facilities abroad to avoid the jurisdiction of the American court. The manufacturer, however, still had to deal with foreign patent equivalents of the U.S. patent.

---

328 *NTP, supra*, 418 F.3d at 1317.
329 *Voda v. Cordis Corp.*, 122 Fed. Appx. 515 (Fed. Cir. 2005), *granting appeal in Voda v. Cordis Corp.*, 2004 U.S. Dist. LEXIS 28102 (D. Okla. 2004).

Appendix A - Sample Provisional Patent Application

Methods Of Using Apoptosis Committed Cells

Field of The Invention

[0001] The field of the invention is the use of dendritic cells.

Background of The Invention

[0002] Cells can become diseased under a number of different conditions, including nutritional or metabolic insults, viral, bacterial and mycotic infections, and various infestations. In some instances, the cells can also become neoplastic, resulting in cancer. In many instances the diseased cells can be removed from the organism in some manner, inactivated in some manner, or even returned to a healthy state. Often, however, the treatments are quite invasive, and may not even be particularly effective. Thus, there continues to be a need for less invasive and more effective treatments.

[0003] Diseased cells can be treated *ex vivo*, i.e., outside of system in which they became diseased. Typically, the system is a body such as a human or animal body, and diseased cells are removed from the body, treated in some manner, and then reintroduced into the body. There are many methods for treating cells *ex vivo*, including irradiation, interaction with various chemicals, and stimulation by antigens.

[0004] US 5,788,963 to Murphy et al. (Aug. 1998) teaches that prostate cancer can be treated by removing immune system cells from a patient, activating the removed cells via presentation with prostate cancer antigen, expanding the activated cells, and then introducing the expanded cells into the patient. Although Murphy reports significant results using this method, there are significant drawbacks.

[0005] One problem with the Murphy method is selection of antigen to be presented to the immune system cells. Library or "stock" antigen is unavailable for each different type of cancer, let alone other diseases, and even if library antigen were available for every type of disease, such antigens would likely correlate only minimally with the target antigens for the system being treated. Murphy's solution is to remove a population of diseased cells from the system being treated, lyse the cells, and then present the lysate to the immune system cells. That solution undoubtedly does provide some target antigen, but the target antigen is mixed among a large amount of non-target antigen.

[0006] Another problem with the Murphy method is presentation of antigen to the immune system cells. It was already known that free antigen is extremely inefficient at activating T cells and other lymphocytes *ex vivo*, and Murphy attempted to improve the activation efficiency by presenting the antigen to dendritic cells. The dendritic cells become activated in this manner, and are then used to activate T-cells against the antigen. Unfortunately, antigen in lysate is relatively inefficient at activating dendritic cells. Worse still, it is entirely possible that the dendrocytes will become activated against non-target antigen, and that immune system components activated in this manner will provoke an auto-immune reaction in the system upon reintroduction.

[0007] Thus, there is still a need to improve antigen selection and antigen presentation in the *ex vivo* stimulation of immune system components.

Summary of the Invention

[0008] According to the present invention diseased cells are removed from a body or other system, and committed to apoptosis *ex vivo*. During this process the apoptosis committed cells present surface antigen, and that antigen is employed to activate dendrocytes or other APCs. Such antigen is then employed against diseased cell remaining *in vivo*.

[0009] In preferred methods both the selection of antigen and the presentation of antigen is performed by the cells undergoing apoptosis, and in especially preferred methods the apoptosis committed cells present antigen to dendrocytes or other APCs, which then activate NK or other lytic lymphocytes. Such methods are thought to mimic antigen presentation processes normally taking place with a body, and are contemplated to be particularly efficient. In alternative methods, apoptosis selected antigens can be reintroduced directly back into the system.

[0010] Various objects, features, aspects and advantages of the present invention will become more apparent from the following detailed description of preferred embodiments of the invention.

Brief Description of the Drawing

[0011] Figure 1 is a flowchart of a preferred method for treating a patient according to the present invention.

Detailed Description

[0012] In Figure **1** a method for treating a patient generally comprises the following steps: removing a sample of diseased cells from a patient (**10**); committing the removed cells to apoptosis (**20**); and introducing antigen presented by the committed cells to cells of the patient's immune system (**30**).

[0013] The patient is contemplated to be any higher organism having diseased cells present in its body at the time of the treatment. Contemplated patients include vertebrates, especially mammals, and most especially humans. Treatment of livestock and pets, such as cats and dogs, are also of particular interest. Diseased cells are contemplated to be any cells of which the patient wants to eliminate, including cancer, viruses, fungus, toxins, or bacteria. A sample of diseased cells from the patient may be collected by any suitable harvesting procedure, including, for example, scraping, resection, or aspiration. The number of removed cells may therefore vary greatly, and it is contemplated that the number may vary from 10^6 cells or less, to 10^7 cells or more. It is contemplated that diseased cells can be removed from anywhere on the patient's body, including brain, skin, bone marrow, reproductive organs, or other major organs.

[0014] Cells can be committed to apoptosis using any suitable methods and apparatus. A highly preferred method comprises incubating the removed cells in interferon, especially type 1 interferon, for a suitable period of time. Experimentation shows that such time spans are commonly in excess of 24 hours, and possibly up to two weeks or longer. Other methods are also contemplated, including nutrient, toxic, and physical stressors, as well as genetic inhibitors or inducers. For example, it is contemplated that factors which down regulate any of the stress accommodation genes may be used to commit cells to apoptosis.

[0015] Committing the diseased cells to apoptosis caused the committed cells to exhibit surface antigens corresponding to the related disease. It is contemplated that such antigen can be presented to cells of the patient's immune system either *in vivo* or *ex vivo*.

[0016] Thus, specific embodiments and applications of methods of using apoptosis committed cells have been disclosed. It should be apparent, however, to those skilled in the art that many more modifications besides those already described are possible without departing from the inventive concepts herein. The inventive subject matter, therefore, is not to be restricted except in the spirit of the appended claims.

CLAIMS

What is claimed is:

1. A method of treating diseased cells in a system, comprising:
    removing a sample of the diseased cells from the system;
    committing the removed cells to apoptosis ex vivo, whereby the committed cells selectively produce surface antigen; and
    employing the surface antigen to treat diseased cells remaining in the system.

2. The method of claim 1 further comprising harvesting the surface antigen and depositing the harvested antigen back into the system.

3. The method of claim 1 further comprising presenting the surface antigen to a collection of cells of the patient's immune system *ex vivo*.

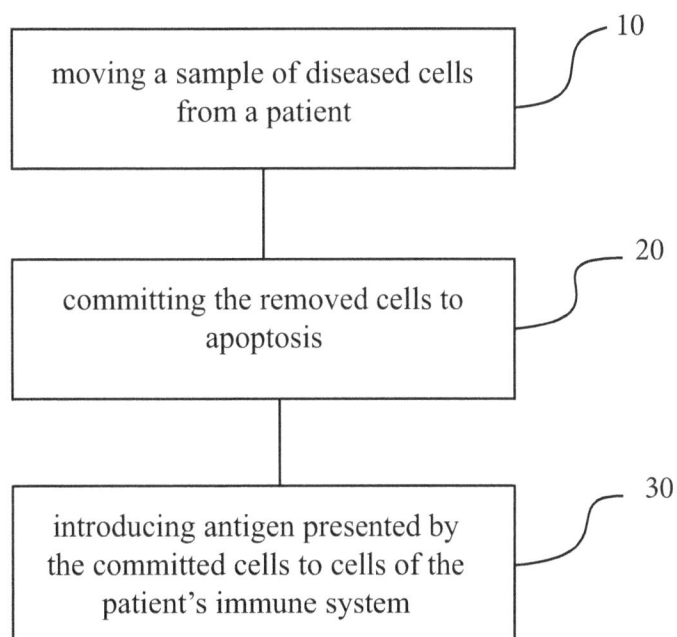

```
     ┌──────────────────────────────────┐   ⌐ 10
     │  moving a sample of diseased cells│
     │           from a patient          │
     └──────────────────────────────────┘


     ┌──────────────────────────────────┐   ⌐ 20
     │   committing the removed cells to │
     │              apoptosis            │
     └──────────────────────────────────┘


     ┌──────────────────────────────────┐   ⌐ 30
     │   introducing antigen presented by│
     │  the committed cells to cells of  │
     │       the patient's immune system │
     └──────────────────────────────────┘
```

Figure 1

Appendix B - Sample Patent Infringement Opinion

CONFIDENTIAL:ATTORNEY-CLIENT

PRIVILEGED COMMUNICATION

Addressee	
_____	
_____	

RE: Infringement Analysis re _____

Your Ref: _____

Our Ref: _____

Dear Mr. Smith:

We understand that _____ is currently developing _____ in the field of _____ . Aspects of that development effort are disclosed in a draft patent application (our docket _____), and summarized as follows:

We also understand that _____ wants to avoid infringement of any patents issued to others, and to that end has asked us to conduct a right to use patent analysis with respect to U.S. patents. This letter responds to that request, and provides a right-to-practice opinion regarding the currently planned software and implementation. To that end we have conducted right-to-practice patent searches using the U.S., WIPO, EU Japanese and Chinese abstract databases through Lexis™ Total Patent™, and analyzed the patents and applications discovered with those searches. Given cost constraints, our search was not comprehensive, and it is entirely possible that we missed one or more relevant documents.

Based on our study and analysis of the facts as we understand them, and in view of the governing law and caveats as set forth below, it is our opinion that the systems, devices, and methods contemplated by _____, could be developed and deployed in a manner that would be found by the federal courts to avoid infringement of any of the claims of any issued U.S. patents. The most significant issues relate to _____. We are concerned that _____. We identified some key patents in this report, but given cost constraints we were not able to conduct a comprehensive analysis of such patents. Further research and analysis may well be advisable.

--- OR ---

You asked us to provide an infringement opinion on whether your <<device>>, as depicted in the attached images, would infringe any of U.S. Patents _____, _____, and _____,. This letter summarizes our analysis.

Our analysis to date indicates that your <<device>> would likely not infringe any of U.S. Patents _____, _____, and _____, as several of the required elements present in the claims of the above referenced patents appear not to be present.

Our opinion reflects an outcome that we would reasonably expect in a properly contested and properly decided patent infringement action, based on the law and facts that we have at our disposal. Of course, the results of any litigation are uncertain and this opinion letter does not represent a guarantee of the outcome of any potential litigation. In setting forth our opinion, we have focused on what we believe are the strongest bases for sustaining a finding of non-infringement. Thus, there may be other grounds or arguments for non-infringement in addition to those discussed herein.

ISSUES

Issue 1 - Whether your <<device>> falls within the scope of any of the claims of U.S. Pat. no. _____.

Issue 1 - Whether your <<device>> falls within the scope of any of the claims of U.S. Pat. no. _____.

Issue 1 - Whether your <<device>> falls within the scope of any of the claims of U.S. Pat. no. _____.

SHORT ANSWERS

1.   Likely no. To the extent that claims 1-4 and 12 can be read to encompass the <<device>>, those claims are anticipated by _____ and should be declared invalid. The <<device>> falls outside the scope of all the other claims.

2.   Likely no. All claims should be declared invalid over _____ and _____.

3.   Likely no. The <<device>> falls outside the scope of all claims.

APPLICABLE LAW

Infringement analysis can be exceedingly complicated, both by patent and procedural legal issues, as well as by technical engineering or scientific issues. We utilized the following principles in our analysis.

Rights In Patent Ownership

"The rights to which one is entitled by ownership of a patent are principally the right to exclude others from making, using, and selling patented subject matter."[330]

Claims Define The Scope Of The Patent Right

The most important concept to understand in evaluating utility patent infringement is that "[i]t is the claims, not the written description, that define the scope of the patent right."[331] "The language of the claims (plus equivalents of the claimed invention) defines the bounds of the patentee's exclusive rights."[332]

Determination Of Infringement Is A Two Step Process

"A determination of infringement requires a two step analysis, 'First, the claim must be properly construed to determine its scope and meaning. Second, the claim as properly construed must be compared to the accused device or process.' "[333]

Independent/Dependent Claims In The Infringement Analysis

---

330 *Kimberly-Clark Corp. v. Procter & Gamble Distributing Co., Inc.*, 973 F.2d 911 (Fed. Cir. 1991).

331 *Laitram Corp. v. NEC Corp.*, 163 F.3d 1342 (Fed. Cir. 1998).

332 *Wiener v. NEC Electronics, Inc.*, 102 F.3d 534 (Fed. Cir. 1996), *citing Bell Communications Research, Inc. v. Vitalink Communications Corp.*, 55 F.3d 615, 619-20 (Fed. Cir. 1995).

333 *Ethicon Endo-Surgery, Inc. v. United States Surgical Corp.*, 149 F.3d 1309 (Fed. Cir. 1998) citing *Carroll Touch, Inc. v. Electro Mechanical Sys., Inc* (Fed. Cir. 1993).

Every independent utility patent claim stands in its own right, and may be held infringed irrespective of infringement with respect to any other claim.[334] The general rule is that if one does not literally infringe an independent claim, a claim dependent on the independent claim also cannot be literally infringed. There are rare circumstances wherein a dependent claim could be infringed under the doctrine of equivalents even though the independent claim was not infringed.[335] Because of this distinction between independent and dependent claims, infringement analysis is directed almost exclusively to the independent claims.

Determination Of The Meaning Of Claims

"Claims should be construed as they would by those skilled in the art."[336] One of the most common mistakes is to infer limitations from the specification into the claims. "Where a Specification does not require a limitation, that limitation should not be read from the Specification into the claims."[337]

"To determine the proper meaning of claims we first consider the so-called intrinsic evidence, i.e., the claims, the written description, and if in evidence, the prosecution history."[338] If the meaning of a term in a claim is unclear, "It is entirely proper to 'use the specification in order to determine what the inventor meant by terms and phrases in the claims.' "[339] "The court may receive extrinsic evidence to educate itself about the invention and the relevant technology, but the court may not use extrinsic evidence to arrive at a claim construction that is clearly at odds with the construction mandated by the intrinsic evidence."[340]

"The court…determines whether there is any estoppel derived from the prosecution history that bars remedy even when there is technologic equivalency, for the patentee is precluded from reaching, under the doctrine of equivalents, subject matter that was disclaimed in order to obtain the patent."[341]

Establishment of Infringement

"[T]he patentee must prove that the accused device embodies every limitation in the claim, either literally or by a substantial equivalent."[342]

> "Intent is not an element of infringement…A patent owner may exclude others from practicing the claimed intention, regardless of whether infringers even know of the patent."[343]

A product or method can infringe directly, or a company or person can infringe under contributory infringement or inducement to infringe. Liability for contributory infringement arises when one "INDEX sells within the United States... a component of a patented machine... knowing the same to be especially made or especially adapted for use in an infringement of such patent, and not a staple article or commodity of commerce suitable for substantial non-infringing use."[344] Liability for inducing infringement arises when one acts in a manner that actually induces infringement,[345] and the actor knew or should have known that his actions would

---

334 *Jones v. Hardy*, 727 F.2d 1524, 1528 (Fed. Cir. 1984).

335 *Wilson Sporting Goods Co. v. David Geoffrey & Associates*, 904 F.2d 677 (Fed. Cir. 1990).

336 *Loctite Corp. v. Ultraseal Ltd.*, 781 F.2d 861 (Fed. Cir. 1985).

337 *Benetton Sportssystem USA, Inc. v. First Team Sports, Inc.*, 38 Fed. Appx. 599 (June 14, 2002); *E. I. Du Pont de Nemours & Co. v. Phillips Petroleum Co., 849 F.2d 1430 (Fed. Cir. 1988).*

338 *Vitronics Corp. v. Conceptronic, Inc.* (Fed. Cir. 1996)." *Digital Biometrics, Inc. v. Identix, Inc.* 149 F.3d 1335 (Fed. Cir. 1998).

339 *Minnesota Mining & Mfg. Co. v. Johnson & Johnson Orthopaedics, Inc.* (Fed. Cir. 1992)." *Laitram Corp v. Morehouse Industries, Inc.* 143 F.3d 1456 (Fed Cir. 1998).

340 *Karlin Technology Inc. v. Surgical Dynamics, Inc.* 177 F.3d 968 (Fed. Cir. 1999).

341 *Multiform Desiccants, Inc. v. Medzam Ltd.* 133 F.3d 1473 (Fed. Cir. 1998), *see also Festo Corp. v. Shoketsu Kinzoku Kogyo Kabushiki Co.* 234 F.3d 558 (Fed. Cir. 2000).

342 *Conroy v. Reebok International, Ltd.*, 14 F.3d 1570 (Fed. Cir. 1994).

343 *Hilton Davis Chemical Co. v. Warner-Johnson Co. Inc.* 62 F.3d 1512 (Fed. Cir. 1995).

344 35 U.S.C. § 271(c) (2000); *Golden Blount, Inc. v. Robert H. Peterson Co.*, 365 F.3d 1054, 1061 (Fed. Cir. 2004).

345 35 U.S.C. § 271(b); *Golden Blount, Inc. v. Robert H. Peterson Co.*, 365 F.3d 1054, 1061 (Fed. Cir. 2004).

induce direct infringement.[346] Both contributory infringement and inducement to infringe are dependent upon the proof of direct infringement by some other party. There can be no indirect infringement without direct infringement.[347]

Infringement Under The Doctrine Of Equivalents

In the absence of literal infringement, there can still be infringement under the doctrine of equivalents if the accused device is substantially similar to that claimed. Courts have recognized various tests over the years to determine whether a patent is infringed under the doctrine of equivalents, but none of those tests are completely satisfactory. As noted in a 1997 Federal Circuit case, "The relationship between infringement and the claims becomes even more tenuous under the doctrine of equivalents, where a product is deemed to infringe the patentee's rights to exclude even though the product does not fall within the scope of the patent's claims."[348] The problem is exacerbated because application of the equivalents tests is ordinarily treated as a question of fact.[349]

For many years the dominant test was the function-way-result test, which focuses on whether "the accused process [performs] substantially the same steps as the patented process, in substantially the same way, to obtain the same result."[350] But the outcome of that test lies with the level of abstraction used by the trier of fact. Is a wood screw equivalent to a nail? On a high level of abstraction one could argue that yes, they are equivalent because they both are physical devices that are forced into two pieces of wood (same steps) by hand or power tools (same way) to keep the two pieces together (same result). On the other hand one could readily argue at a lower level of abstraction that screws and nails are not at all equivalent. A screw relies on rotational insertion using a screw driver, and results in a joint that can only be pulled apart by damaging the pieces. A nail relies upon linear insertion (different steps) using a hammer (different way) and often results in a joint that can be pulled apart without damaging the pieces (different result).

The same flaw results from focusing on interchangeability.[351] In a great many cases one could reasonably argue screws and nails are roughly interchangeable, one could just as readily argue that each has advantages and disadvantages over the other. It all depends upon the granularity of the analysis.

For awhile the Federal Circuit was focusing on the "substantiality" or "insubstantiality" of the differences between the accused device or method and that set forth in the claims. This principle was confirmed in the famous *Hilton Davis* case,[352] holding that "[T]he substantiality of the differences between the claimed and accused products or processes is the ultimate question under the doctrine of equivalents…" and "In either event, the vantage point of one of ordinary skill in the relevant art provides the perspective for assessing the substantiality of the differences."

There is even a special twist in the analysis for claims that define elements using "INDEX means plus function" terms. In those cases the court must compare the accused structure with the structure, materials, and acts expressly disclosed in the body of the patent and must find the equivalent structure as well as identity of claimed function for that structure.[353]

---

346 *Micro Chem. Inc. v. Great Plains Chem. Co.*, 194 F.3d 1250 (Fed. Cir. 1999.

347 *Met-Coil Sys. Corp. v. Korners Unlimited, Inc.*, 803 F.2d 684, 687 (Fed. Cir. 1986).

348 *Hoechst-Roussel Pharmaceuticals, Inc. v. Lehman*, 109 F.3d 756 (Fed. Cir. 1997) *citing Wilson Sporting Goods Co. v. David Geoffrey & Assocs.* 498 U.S. 992; 111 S. Ct. 537 (Supreme Court 1990).

349 *Dawn Equipment Co. v. Kentucky Farms, Inc.*, 140 F.3d 1009 (Fed. Cir. 1998).

350 *Pennwalt Corp. v. Durand-Wayland Inc.*, 833 F.2d 931, 934 (Fed. Cir. 1987); *Fromson v. Anitec Printing Plates, Inc.*, 132 F.3d 1437 (Fed. Cir. 1997).

351 *Multiform Dessicants, Inc. v. Medzam, Ltd.* 133 F.3d 1473 (Fed. Cir. 1998).

352 *Hilton Davis, supra*, 62 F.3d 1512.

353 *Pennwalt Corp. v. Durand-Wayland Inc., supra,* 833 F.2d at 934.

In the *Bicon* case,[354] the Federal Circuit focused on the importance of the amount of detail used in the claims in limiting the scope of equivalents. According to the so-called specific exclusion rule, "A claim that contains a detailed recitation of structure is properly accorded correspondingly limited recourse to the doctrine of equivalents." While some commentators immediately panned the idea as being unworkable, the Court was careful to point out that reliance on amount of detail is not a change in the law, but instead has been used for almost ten years.[355] Indeed, focusing on the amount of detail is a very good way to limit the scope of equivalents. After all, as the Federal Circuit notes:

- the term 'unmounted' is not equivalent to mounted;[356]

- a minority is not equivalent to a majority;[357] and

- a hemispherical shape is not equivalent to a conical outer surface.[358]

To hold otherwise would effectively write those limitations out of the claims. What is really happening here is that patent practitioners don't spend the time to figure out what the invention is. Instead, they blather on with a hundred pages or more of specification, secure allowance by filing dozens or even hundreds of narrow claims, and then rely upon the doctrine of equivalents to provide the needed protection. That practice is destroying the patent system. Patent practitioners should rise or fall according to the skill with which they practice their craft. They need to clearly analyze the prior art, and then draft short claims that clearly delineate how the invention is different from that art.

Defenses To Infringement

Defenses to allegations of patent infringement fall into two broad groups: statutory and equitable.[359] The statutory defenses are set forth in 35 U.S.C. § 282 and include non-infringement, absence of liability for infringement, unenforceability, and invalidity (for failure to meet the conditions of patentability or to comply with any requirement of sections 112 or 251).[360] The equitable defenses include unclean hands, unenforceability of the patent for fraud and inequitable conduct, misuse, and delay in filing suit resulting in latches or estoppel.[361]

ANALYSIS OF THE ISSUES

Critical Claim Language

Three are only four terms in the claims where the meaning is likely to be disputed, "aaa," "bbb" and "ccc." With respect to "aaa" the dictionary definition is _____. There is no express teaching in the specification that would cause one to interpret the term differently, but during prosecution the application expressly disclaimed _____. The patent holder could argue that _____ but that argument would likely fail because _____....

With respect to "aaa."...

---

354 *Bicon, supra*, 2006 U.S. App. LEXIS 6813 at 25-27.

355 See *Tanabe Seiyaku Co. v. United States ITC*, 109 F.3d 726, 732 (Fed. Cir. 1997) ("The sharply restricted nature of the claims has much to do with the scope we accord to the doctrine of equivalents."). *Ethicon Endo-Surgery, Inc. v. U.S. Surgical Corp., supra*, 149 F.3d at 1317 (subject matter is "specifically excluded" from coverage under the doctrine of equivalents if its inclusion is "inconsistent with the language of the claim").

356 *Asyst Techs., Inc. v. Emtrak, Inc.*, 402 F.3d 1188, 1195 (Fed. Cir. 2005).

357 *Moore U.S.A., Inc. v. Standard Register Co.*, 229 F.3d 1091, 1106 (Fed. Cir. 2000).

358 *Tronzo v. Biomet, Inc.*, 156 F.3d 1154, 1160 (Fed. Cir. 1998).

359 *Mylan Pharms., Inc. v. Thompson*, 268 F.3d 1323, 1331 (Fed. Cir. 2001).

360 35 U.S.C. § 282

361 *J.P. Stevens & Co. v. Lex Tex, Ltd.*, 747 F.2d 1553, 1561 (Fed. Cir. 1984).

With respect to "bbb."...

With respect to "ccc."...

U.S. Pat. no. _____.

Claim 1

Claim 1 recites:

<<listing of claim 1 with relevant portions emphasized>>

The <<device>> does not literally infringe claim 1 because _____. There is a potential argument that device would infringe under the doctrine of equivalents because _____. The argument could be further supported by _____. That argument, however, should fail on the grounds that _____.

Claims 2-4

Claims 2-4 recite the following:

<<listing of claims 2-4 with relevant portions emphasized>>

The <<device>> clearly cannot directly infringe claims 2-4 because those are method claims, and the actor of the method would be _____. It is possible, however, that the patent holder could assert infringement of these claims on the grounds of contributory infringement or inducement to infringe. In the case of contributory infringement, the patent holder would have to prove that the only substantial use of the _____ is as a component of the <<device>>. That argument, however, is unlikely to prevail because _____. In the case of inducement to infringe the patent holder would have to show that the company actively induced others to infringe. The only possible argument there would likely be founded on the company's prints advertisements showing .....

<<All remaining claims of each of the patents at issue should be discussed in turn. It is important to weigh all reasonable sides of every issue, and avoid unsupported summary conclusions>>.

Appendix C - Due Diligence Checklist

1) Patents

   a) List all company owned patents and pending patent applications (U.S. and foreign). For each item show application serial number, title, inventors, filing date, patent number (if any), family relationship (e.g. divisional, continuation, CIP), and status.

   b) List all patents in-licensed by the company from others. For each such patent identify licensor, patent number, licensed goods or services, date of license, royalty rate or other consideration, and include a copy of the license.

   c) List all patents out-licensed from the company to others. For each such patent identify licensee, patent number, licensed goods or services, date of license, royalty rate or other consideration, and include a copy of the license.

   d) List all assignments. For each item show assignee/assignor, patent/application number, date, and reel/frame number of recordation. Assignments must be traceable back to the named inventors.

   e) List all prior art references known to the company, its named inventors, and its IP counsel that may render any company patent claim invalid or unenforceable.

   f) List all patent opinions that the company has requested or received.

   g) List all partners, employees, consultants, and other company-related individuals who might be involved as inventors, and identify employment or other agreements establishing company rights in their inventions.

2) Trademark (including service marks)

   a) List all company owned trademarks, whether registered or not (U.S. and foreign). For each mark show int'l class, goods and services, application serial number, filing date, registration serial number (if any), and status.

   b) List all trademarks in-licensed by the company from others. For each such mark identify licensor, goods or services, date of license, royalty rate or other consideration, and include a copy of the license.

   c) List all trademarks out-licensed from the company to others. For each such mark identify licensee, goods or services, date of license, royalty rate or other consideration, and include a copy of the license

   d) List all trademark opinions that the company has requested or received.

3) Copyright

   a) List all company owned copyright protected works, including software, specifications, books, manuals, notebooks, and other documentation. For each item identify the author(s), and dates of creation, publication, date and serial number of copyright registration or application. For company authorship, identify provisions in employment or other agreements that establish the materials as works for hire.

b) List all copyright protected works used by the company in its operations.

   i) For computer software, establish that sufficient licenses have been purchased for each computer. Include standard software (e.g. Windows™, WORD™, etc) and specialty software (e.g. CAD programs, accounting packages).

   ii) Establish that protocols are in place for preventing employees from: (a) using illegal software on their computers; (b) illegally copying books and articles; and (c) illegally downloading and/or playing music.

   iii) List all identifiable public or "open source" materials used by the company in its own software.

   iv) List all company software that was distributed without a license.

c) List all assignments. For each item show assignee/assignor, patent/application number, date, and reel/frame number of recordation. Assignments must be traceable back to the authors.

d) List all copyright opinions that the company has requested or received.

e) List all partners, employees, consultants, and other company-related individuals who might be involved as authors of copyright protected works, and identify employment or other agreements establishing company rights in their inventions.

4) Trade Secret

a) Identify all trade secrets owned by the company.

b) List all procedures used to protect the trade secrets (i.e., limited physical access and egress, restrictions on removing electronic files that contain trade secrets, periodic company meetings to convey and reiterate trade secret policies, deployment, use, and storage of notebooks, and trade secret provisions in employment agreements).

c) List all partners, employees, consultants, and other company-related individuals who might create or gain access to trade secrets, and identify employment or other agreements establishing company rights in such trade secrets.

d) Identify all trade secrets brought to the company by its employees, and establish that the company has rights to use such trade secrets.

5) Counsel

a) List each IP counsel that have provided services to the company over the previous 5 years, and identify the scope of work performed.

b) Provide estimates of attorney charges per patent for searching, drafting, prosecuting patent applications.

c) Provide estimates of average page length of utility patent applications, average number of independent claims, average number of total claims, average time from disclosure to filing, and average time to issuance.

d) Provide justification for provisional / utility patent filing strategies, or absence of same.

e) Provide justification for foreign filing strategies for patent and trademark filings, or absence of same.

f) Provide chart showing: (a) number of issued patents; (b) number of pending patent applications; (c) expenditures for patent drafting, filing, and prosecution; and (d) expenditures for patent maintenance for each of the last 10 years.

g) Provide chart showing: (a) number of registered trademarks; (b) number of pending trademark applications; (c) expenditures for trademark drafting, filing, and prosecution; and (d) expenditures for trademark maintenance for each of the last 10 years.

6) Competition

a) Describe all IP owned or controlled by any competitors that is material to the company's technology or its business

   i) Include all technology needed or used by the company in the conduct of its operations, which is not public domain but may be patented by others.

   ii) Include all marks that are owned by others, and used by the company without license.

   iii) Include all copyright works needed or used by the company in the conduct of its operations, which are owned by others and used by the company without license.

b) List all warning or accusations received by the company from others with respect to possible infringement of their IP rights. Include date of first contact, and date and nature of resolution.

c) List all warning or accusations issued by the company with respect to possible infringement of its IP rights. Include date of first contact, and date and nature of resolution.

7) Agreements.

a) Establish that all partners, employees, consultants, and other company-related individuals who did or might create IP for the company have executed appropriate employment agreements.

b) Demonstrate that procedures are in place for providing accountings, making any royalty or progress payments, and in all other ways complying with terms in license agreements.

c) Specific agreements that need further evaluation....

Appendix D - Sample Assignment Form

WHEREAS, the undersigned, <<assignor>> an individual having its principal place of business at <<business address>>; (referred to hereinafter as "Assignor") have invented a certain invention entitled "<<name of invention>>" for which a utility application for Letters of Patent of the United States of America was filed on <<filing date>>, serial number <<serial number>>;

WHEREAS, <<assignee name>>, having its principal place of business at <<business address>> (referred to hereinafter as "Assignee"), is desirous of acquiring the entire right, title and interest in, to and under said invention, and in, to and under said Letters Patent or similar legal protection to be or having been obtained therefor in the United States of America, its territorial possessions and in any and all countries foreign thereto;

NOW, THEREFORE, for good and valuable consideration, the receipt of which is hereby acknowledged, Assignor hereby sells, assigns, transfers and set over unto the Assignee, its successors and assigns the entire title, right and interest in and to said invention, and to all Letters Patent or similar legal protection, not only in the United States and its territorial possessions, but in all countries foreign thereto to be obtained for said invention by said application or any continuation, division, renewal, substitute, reissue or reexamination thereof or any legal equivalent thereof in a foreign country for the full term or terms for which the same may be granted, including all priority rights under any International Convention, and the right to sue in Assignee's own name for all past, present, and future infringement.

Assignor hereby covenants that no assignment, sale, agreement or encumbrance has been or will be made or entered into which would conflict with this Assignment;

Assignor further covenants that Assignee will, upon its request, be provided promptly with all pertinent facts and documents relating to said invention and said Letters Patent and legal equivalents in foreign countries as may be known and accessible to Assignor and will testify as to the same in any interference or litigation related thereto and will promptly execute and deliver to Assignee or its legal representatives any and all papers, instruments or affidavits required to apply for, obtain, maintain, issue and enforce said invention and said Letters Patent and said equivalents thereof in any foreign country which may be necessary or desirable to carry out the purposes thereof.

WITNESS my hand at _____, _____ this _____ day of , _____,

<<assignor>>

Appendix E - Sample License Agreement

This agreement ("this Agreement") is effective _____ by and between _____ ("Licensor"), and _____ ("Licensee"). Licensor and Licensee may be collectively referred to hereinafter as "The Parties."

RECITALS

WHEREAS Licensor is the owner by assignment of U.S. patent numbers _____ and _____, which together with any additional related trade secrets and know-how is collectively referred to hereinafter as "The Proprietary Rights";

WHEREAS Licensor and Licensee desire to further develop and commercialize The Proprietary Rights;

WHEREAS Licensor and Licensee are desirous of fixing and defining between themselves their respective ongoing interests, rights, responsibilities, and limits in connection therewith;

NOW THEREFORE, in consideration of the mutual covenants and promises herein contained, The Parties agree to be legally bound by the following covenants and they agree and certify as follows:

GRANT OF LICENSE

1.   Licensor hereby grants to Licensee (a) an exclusive, worldwide, license covering all of The Proprietary Rights, including all inventions, improvements, enhancements, modifications to, and embodiments of, The Proprietary Rights made, conceived or owned by Licensor and/or Licensee during the term of this Agreement, all of which automatically become part of the Intellectual Property; (b) all patent applications and patents based on or covering the same which the Licensor now owns or controls or hereafter owns or controls; and (c) an express right to grant sublicenses to Affiliates or Third Parties, to make, have made, further develop, research, improve, use, sell, and distribute products embodying The Proprietary Rights, under terms and conditions determined by License and sub-licensee, provided any sublicense comply with the provisions concerning transferability set forth below.

TERM

2.   This Agreement shall be in effect until the date of the last to expire of any patents or other intellectual property relating to The Proprietary Rights, unless terminated earlier as set forth below.

--- OR ---

2.   This Agreement shall be in effect until _____ unless terminated earlier as set forth below.

3.   Licensee shall have the right to terminate this Agreement upon giving Licensor ninety (90) days prior to written notice to that effect. Upon termination of this Agreement by such notice, all rights granted to Licensee will automatically revert back to Licensor.

4.   In the event that Licensee (a) shall become "Insolvent" (as such term is defined in the Bankruptcy Code of the United States of America, as amended from time-to-time, (b) shall fail to pay its debts general-

ly as they become due, (c) shall voluntarily seek, consent, or acquiesce in the benefits of any bankruptcy or similar debtor-relief laws, (d) shall become a party to or is made the subject of any proceeding provided for by any debtor-relief law that could suspend or otherwise affect Licensee's rights under this Agreement, or (e) ceases to actively pursue prosecution, development and/or commercialization of The Proprietary Rights for a consecutive 12 month period, Licensee shall be considered to be in default of this Agreement.

5.   At any point during which Licensee is in default of this Agreement, Licensor shall have the option to provide Licensee with written NOTICE mailed to Licensee's principal place of business, that Licensor intends to terminate this Agreement, and if Licensee fails to remedy the breach within the thirty day period following receipt of such NOTICE, this Agreement will terminate, and all rights granted to Licensee will automatically revert back to Licensor.

CONSIDERATION

6.   In addition to any other consideration provided for herein:

7.   Licensee shall pay Licensor a one-time license issue fee of $_____ upon execution of this Agreement as an advance against royalties, which license issue fee is non-refundable;

8.   Licensee shall pay Licensor a royalty of _____% of gross revenue realized by or on behalf of the Licensee from commercialization of any of The Proprietary Rights. All monies due the Licensor shall be payable in United States funds collectable at par in _____, California, or as directed from time to time by Licensor. Royalties earned with respect to revenue arising in any country outside the United States shall be reduced by any taxes, fees or other charges imposed by the government of such country on the remittance of the royalty income. The Licensee shall also be responsible for any bank transfer charges; and

9.   Licensee shall pay Licensor a minimum royalty according to the following schedule, with License fees paid under paragraph 6.2 offset against the minimum royalty:

Time Period From Effective Date Hereof	Minimum Quarterly Royalty
1st - 4th quarters	
5th - 8th quarters	
9th - 12th quarters	
13th quarter onwards	

10.   Amounts due to Licensor under this Agreement that are not paid on the due date will incur a simple interest carrying charge of ____% per month, which charge is due and payable immediately upon being incurred, and which must be paid in full in a timely manner along with any underlying royalties to avoid breach of this Agreement.

11.   The Licensee will not sell, license, lease or otherwise commercialize any existing _____ product that competes with any product licensed under this Agreement.

12.   The Licensee will not take any affirmative steps to challenge the validity of any of the Proprietary Rights, or their ownership by Licensor, except as compelled by law.

13.   The Licensee shall keep books and records in accordance with accounting principles that are generally accepted in the United States, accurately reflecting all transactions and other information relevant to the calculation of royalties under this Agreement. Such books and records shall be open to inspection by representatives or agents of Licensor at reasonable times upon reasonable request, and costs for inspection shall be borne

by Licensor. Within 30 days following the end of each calendar quarter, Licensee shall provide a summary to Licensor sufficient to support the license fees accruing during the previous quarter.

14.   Licensee shall take all commercially reasonable steps to ensure that all Licensed Products are designated with proper patent notice under 35 U.S.C. 287(a) "Limitation on damages and other remedies; marking and notice."

15.   Licensee has a duty to, and hereby does, assign to Licensor any improvements and/or modifications to Licensed Products made by Licensee, its employees or agents. Licensee will promptly notify Licensor of the existence of any such improvements and/or modifications, and will fully cooperate in Licensor's pursuit of corresponding intellectual property protection. Licensee will take all reasonable steps to ensure that its employees and agents are bound by, and cooperate in enforcing, the provisions of this paragraph.

RECOVERY OF RIGHTS

16.   Upon termination of this Agreement other than through breach by Licensor, all right, title and interest in the Proprietary rights shall be deemed to have been transferred back to Licensor on the date of the breach, the consideration therefore having been the License fees paid through the date of such breach.

MAINTENANCE OF RIGHTS

17.   The _____ <<Licensee or Licensor>> assumes all responsibility to prosecute and maintain, at its own expense, patent applications relating to The Proprietary Rights and any related future inventions.

INFRINGEMENT

18.   Each of Licensor and Licensee shall promptly inform each other in writing of any alleged infringement of any intellectual property rights which it shall have notice committed by a Third Party regarding any patents within The Proprietary Rights, and each shall provide the other with any available evidence of such infringement. Within thirty (30) days after receipt of the notice of alleged infringement, Licensor and Licensee shall meet and mutually agree on a procedure for resolving the alleged infringement.

19.   If within six (6) months after the notice of alleged infringement specified in paragraph 10 above, Licensee shall have been unsuccessful in resolving the alleged infringement in a manner mutually acceptable to Licensor and Licensee, then Licensor shall have the right, but shall not be obligated, to prosecute at its own expense any infringement of the Patent Rights, and Licensor may, for such purposes, use the name of Licensee as party plaintiff.

20.   In any infringement suit either party may institute to enforce the Patent Rights pursuant to this Agreement, the other party hereto shall, at the request and expense of the party initiating such suit, cooperate in all respects and, to the extent possible, have its employees testify when requested and make available relevant records, papers, information, samples, specimens, and the like. Any damages recovered from an infringing party pursuant to such infringement suit shall be used first to pay costs, and then distributed between Licensee and Licensor in accordance with their respective funding of the infringement suit.

REPRESENTATIONS AND WARRANTIES

21.   Licensor hereby represents to Licensee as follows:

        21.1. Licensor holds good and marketable title to The Proprietary Rights granted to Licensee;

21.2. Licensor has the full right, power, and authority to grant the license set forth herein;

21.3. There are no outstanding agreements, assignments, or encumbrances inconsistent with the provisions of this Agreement which, in the opinion of Licensor, in any manner prohibit the transactions contemplated by this Agreement or impair the ability of Licensor to perform its obligations hereunder;

21.4. Licensor has no knowledge of any infringement or of any pending or threatened claim relating in any manner to The Proprietary Rights; and

21.5. Licensor has no knowledge of or reason to believe that any of The Proprietary Rights are invalid or unenforceable or that their exercise would infringe the patent rights of any Third Party.

21.6. LICENSOR MAKES NO OTHER REPRESENTATION OR WARRANTY, EXPRESS OR IMPLIED, NOR DOES LICENSOR ASSUME ANY OBLIGATIONS WITH RESPECT TO THE INFRINGEMENT OF PATENTS OR OTHER INTELLECTUAL PROPERTY ARISING AS A RESULT OF LICENSEE'S ACTIVITIES UNDER THIS AGREEMENT.

MISCELLANEOUS PROVISIONS

22.   Transferability. This Agreement and the rights and privileges hereof are assignable, licensable or otherwise transferable by either party without the written consent and approval of the other party, subject to the requirement that all the terms and conditions of this Agreement shall be binding upon the respective successors and assigns of The Parties hereto and shall insure to the benefit of and be enforceable by The Parties hereto and their respective successors and assigns.

23.   Notices. All notices required hereunder shall be given in writing and shall be personally delivered or sent by postage prepaid mail, addressed to The Parties at their addresses listed below, or at such other addresses as the respective parties may designate from time to time to the other by written notice. Notice is reputably presumed to have been received five days after the mailing date.

24.   Choice of Law. This Agreement shall be governed by, construed, interpreted and enforced under and according to the laws of the State of _____.

25.   Dispute Resolution. The parties expressly agree to the jurisdiction of the Superior Court of the State of California and to the jurisdiction of the Central District Court of California, with venue in Orange County, California, for the resolution of any dispute concerning the enforcement, breach, interpretation or validity of this Agreement.

--- OR ---

All claims, disputes and other matters in question arising out of, or relating to, this Agreement or the performance hereof shall be submitted to, and determined by, arbitration if good faith negotiations among the parties hereto, if any, does not resolve such claim, dispute or other matter. Such arbitration shall proceed in accordance with the International Dispute Resolution Procedures or the Small Claim Rules for arbitration established by the American Arbitration Association ("AAA"), unless the parties hereto mutually agree otherwise, and pursuant to the following procedures:

25.1. Reasonable discovery shall be allowed in arbitration.

25.2. All proceedings before the arbitrators shall be held in Orange County, California, under the laws of California.

25.3. The award rendered by the arbitrator(s) shall be final and binding, and judgment may be entered in accordance with applicable Law and in any court having jurisdiction thereof.

25.4. The award rendered by the arbitrator(s) shall include (i) a provision that the prevailing party in such arbitration recover its costs relating to the arbitration and reasonable attorneys' fees from the other party, (ii) the amount of such costs and fees, and (iii) an order that the losing party pay the fees and expenses of the arbitrator(s).

25.5. The arbitrator(s) shall by the agreement of the parties expressly be prohibited from awarding punitive damages in connection with any claim being resolved by arbitration hereunder.

26.   Severability. In the event any part or parts of this Agreement are found to be invalid, illegal, or unenforceable in any respect, the remaining provisions shall nevertheless be binding with the same effect as if the invalid, illegal, or unenforceable part or parts were originally deleted.

27.   Successors and Assigns. This Agreement shall be binding upon and inure to the benefit of The Parties to this Agreement and their respective successors, sublicensees, assignees and agents.

28.   Hold Harmless. Each of The Parties hereto shall indemnify and hold the other party, its directors, officers, members, employees, successors, sublicensees, assignees and agents harmless from and against any and all claims arising from acts and omissions of the party, its directors, officers, members, employees, successors, sublicensees, assignees and agents.

29.   Costs and Fees. In the event that any legal proceedings arise as a result of this Agreement, the prevailing party is entitled to receive attorney fees.

30.   Time of the Essence. Time is of the essence in this Agreement.

31.   Failure to Enforce. Failure of any Party herein to enforce any of the terms of this Agreement shall not constitute waiver to enforce that term in the future.

32.   Expected Performance. Each Party herein agrees to perform all acts and execute and deliver all documents as may be necessary or appropriate to carry out the intent and purposes of this Agreement. Licensee agrees that Licensor may not have an adequate remedy at law for money damages in the event that this Agreement has not been performed in accordance with its terms, and therefore agrees that Licensor shall be entitled to specific enforcement of the terms hereof in addition to any other remedy to which it may be entitled, at law or in equity.

33.   Entire Agreement. This Agreement embodies the entire understanding of The Parties and supersedes and replaces any and all pre-existing agreements or understandings between Licensee and Licensor. No amendment or modification of this Agreement shall be valid or binding upon Licensee or Licensor unless made in writing and signed on behalf of each of The Parties by their respective duly authorized representative.

34.   No Construction. No party hereto nor any attorney for any party shall be deemed the attorney of this Agreement for the purpose of interpreting or construing any of the provisions hereof.

35.   Representation by Counsel. Each of The Parties hereto acknowledges that it has had the opportunity to be represented by independent legal counsel of its own choice throughout all of the negotiations that preceded the execution of this Agreement and that each has executed this Agreement with the consent and on the advice of any such independent legal counsel; and further acknowledges that it and any such counsel have had an adequate opportunity to make whatever investigation or inquiry they may deem necessary or desirable in connection with any of the subjects of this Agreement prior to the execution hereof.

36.   Counterparts. This Agreement may be executed in any number of counterparts, each of which shall be

deemed an original but all of which together shall constitute one and the same instrument.

So agreed and executed this ___th day of _____.

_____   _____

Date

                              By: _____

_____   _____

Date

                              By: _____

Appendix F - Commercialization Assistance Agreement

This Agreement is made on _____ ("Effective Date"), by and between Patent Holder, ("Patent Holder") having a principal place of business at _____, and _____, ("Company"), having a principal place of business at _____. Patent Holder and Company are referred to from time to time hereinafter as the Parties.

Recitals

WHEREAS Patent Holder filed a PCT patent application (_____) claiming an invention related to _____, which application, along with any continuations, divisionals, foreign filings, and patents issuing therefrom are collectively referred to hereinafter as "The Technology."

WHEREAS Company wishes to obtain exclusive rights to license and/or sell the Technology to one or more third parties.

WHEREAS Patent Holder is willing to provide to Company such rights in accordance with and subject to the terms and conditions contained in this Agreement.

NOW THEREFORE, in consideration of the mutual covenants and promises herein contained, The Parties agree to be legally bound by the following covenants and they agree and certify as follows:

Grant

1.   Patent Holder hereby grants to Company Technologies the exclusive right to sell or license any or all of Patent Holder's patent rights that may exist in any country or region with respect to the Technology.

Term

2.   The term of this Agreement is three (3) years from the effective date of this agreement.

3.   The Agreement will be automatically renewed a the conclusion of each three year term for successive three (3) year terms unless either Party gives written notice of termination prior to the expiration of the then-current three year term.

Company Duties to Patent Holder

4.   Company shall use its best efforts to: (a) identify one or more suitable third party licensees and/or purchasers for the Technology; (b) negotiate with such third party(ies); and (c) secure suitable licenses and/or sales agreements with such third party(ies).

Patent Holder Duties to Company

5.   Patent Holder shall reasonably support Company's commercialization efforts as requested, including:

6.   Share Patent Holder's technical expertise relating to the Technology, including providing copies of any support material and documentation in the possession, custody or control of Patent Holder.

7.   Make himself reasonably available by telephone to assist Company in negotiations with third parties.

8.   Prosecute the _____ application, and any other U.S. and foreign application(s) that Patent Holder deems to be appropriate in his sole judgment.

Terms of Contracts With Third Parties

9.   Patent Holder has final authority to approve or deny the terms of any license or sale, with the provision

that such approval shall not be unreasonably withheld.

Sharing of Income Or Other Benefits

10.   Company shall pay to Patent Holder 50% of all income or other benefit derived by or on behalf of Company, its officers, and/or directors, from licensing or sale of the Technology, regardless of whether such income or other benefit is/are derived during or after the Term.

11.   In the event that: (a) Company begins substantive negotiations with a third party during the Term with respect to license or sale of the Technology; (b) Company fails to conclude a license or sale agreement with such third party during Term; and (c) Patent Holder does conclude a license or sale agreement with the third party within 24 (twenty-four) months following expiration or termination of this Agreement, then Patent Holder shall pay Company 50% of all income or other benefit derived by or on behalf of Patent Holder from such agreement with the third party.

12.   Offsets

13.   Up to 5% (five percent) of any given quarterly payment due to Patent Holder can be offset up to an accrued total of $5,000 (Five thousand dollars) for out of pocket transportation and lodging expenses actually and reasonably incurred by Company in performing its duties under this Agreement.

14.   Up to an additional 20% (twenty percent) of any given quarterly payment due to Patent Holder can also be offset up to an accrued total of $25,000 (twenty-five thousand dollars)for the fee advance provided in section seven herein.

15.   Fees contemplated in this section six shall be due and payable 30 days after the end of each calendar quarter, for income or benefits derived during the preceding calendar quarter. Late payments shall be increased by 1% interest per month, or portion thereof. Each payment shall include an accounting of income or benefits realized during the relevant calendar quarter.

Fee Advance

16.   Company shall advance Patent Holder $25,000 (twenty-five thousand dollars) upon Company's execution of this agreement, said advance to be applied against future payments due to Patent Holder by Company. The advance is non-refundable, even if the accrued offsets to the fee advance provided in paragraph 6.3.2 herein are ultimately less than $25,000 (twenty-five thousand dollars).

Termination

17.   Company or Patent Holder each have the right to terminate this Agreement at any time, with or without cause, by giving the other party 120 (one-hundred twenty) days written notice.

18.   In addition, either Party may provide a defaulting Party with written Notice by mail, stating that the non-defaulting Party intends to terminate this Agreement, and if the defaulting Party fails to remedy the default within the thirty day period following receipt of such Notice, this Agreement will terminate at the end of the thirty day period.

19.   All of the provisions of sections six and ten herein shall survive expiration or termination of this Agreement.

Warranty.

20.   Patent Holder warrants has the right to convey the licenses or sales contemplated by this Agreement.

21.   PATENT HOLDER MAKES NO OTHER REPRESENTATION OR WARRANTY, EXPRESS OR IMPLIED, NOR DOES PATENT HOLDER ASSUME ANY OBLIGATIONS WITH RESPECT TO THE INFRINGEMENT OF PATENTS OR OTHER INTELLECTUAL PROPERTY ARISING AS A RESULT OF

ANY ACTIVITIES UNDER THIS AGREEMENT.

Miscellaneous

22.   Corporate Authority. Company represents and warrants that:

22.1. It is a corporation that is validly existing and in good standing under the laws of the jurisdiction in which it is organized;

22.2. It has full corporate power to execute, deliver and perform its obligations under this Agreement.

22.3. The person executing this Agreement on its behalf has its full authority to do so; and

22.4. It shall indemnify, defend and hold the other Party harmless from and against any and all claims that may now or hereafter be made against any of them by virtue of any breach of the provisions of this paragraph.

23.   Counterparts. This Agreement may be executed in any number of counterparts, each of which shall be deemed an original but all of which together shall constitute one and the same instrument.

24.   Dispute Resolution. The Parties expressly agree to the jurisdiction of the Superior Court of the State of California and to the jurisdiction of the _____ Court of _____, with venue in Orange County, California, for the resolution of any dispute concerning the enforcement, breach, interpretation or validity of this Agreement.

--- OR ---

All claims, disputes and other matters in question arising out of, or relating to, this Agreement or the performance hereof shall be submitted to, and determined by, arbitration if good faith negotiations among the Parties hereto, if any, does not resolve such claim, dispute or other matter. Such arbitration shall proceed in accordance with the then-current International Dispute Resolution Procedures or the Small Claim Rules for arbitration established by the American Arbitration Association ("AAA"), unless the Parties hereto mutually agree otherwise, and pursuant to the following procedures:

24.1. The tribunal will consist of [one / three] arbitrator(s).

24.2. The language to be used in the arbitral proceedings will be English. Reasonable discovery shall be allowed in arbitration.

24.3. All proceedings before the arbitrators shall be held in _____, California, under the laws of California;

24.4. The arbitrator(s) may in their discretion provide injunctive relief;

24.5. The award rendered by the arbitrator(s) shall be final and binding, except that either Party can appeal the ruling of the arbitrator(s) to the AAA appeals panel. Judgment may be entered in accordance with applicable Law and in any court having jurisdiction thereof;

24.6. The award rendered by the arbitrator(s) shall include

(i) a provision that the prevailing party in such arbitration recover its costs relating to the arbitration and reasonable attorneys' fees from the other party, (ii) the amount of such costs and fees, and (iii) an order that the losing party pay the fees and expenses of the arbitrator(s), wherein --------- is deemed to be the prevailing party in the event that he is awarded any recovery; and

-- OR --

(i) a provision that each Party in such arbitration cover its own costs relating to the arbitration and its own attorneys' fees, and (ii) an order that each Party pay an equal share of the fees and expenses of the arbitrator(s); and

24.7. The arbitrator(s) may by the agreement of the Parties expressly be prohibited from awarding punitive damages in connection with any claim being resolved.

25.   Entire Agreement. This Agreement embodies the entire understanding of The Parties and supersedes and replaces any and all pre-existing agreements or understandings between them. No amendment or modification of this Agreement shall be valid or binding upon either of the Parties unless made in writing and signed on behalf of each of The Parties by their respective duly authorized representative.

26.   Expected Performance. Each Party herein agrees to perform all acts and execute and deliver all documents as may be necessary or appropriate to carry out the intent and purposes of this Agreement. Each of the Parties recognizes that the other Party may not have an adequate remedy at law for money damages in the event that this Agreement has not been performed in accordance with its terms, and therefore agrees that each Party shall be entitled to specific enforcement of the terms hereof in addition to any other remedy to which it may be entitled, at law or in equity.

27.   Failure to Enforce. Failure of any Party herein to enforce any of the terms of this Agreement shall not constitute waiver to enforce that term in the future.

28.   Hold Harmless. Each of The Parties hereto shall indemnify and hold the other party, its directors, officers, members, employees, successors, sublicensees, assignees and agents harmless from and against any and all claims arising from acts and omissions of the acting or omitting party, its directors, officers, members, employees, successors, sublicensees, assignees and agents.

29.   No Construction. No party hereto nor any attorney for any party shall be deemed the attorney of this Agreement for the purpose of interpreting or construing any of the provisions hereof.

30.   Representation by Counsel. Each of The Parties hereto acknowledges that it has had the opportunity to be represented by independent legal counsel of its own choice throughout all of the negotiations that preceded the execution of this Agreement and that each has executed this Agreement with the consent and on the advice of any such independent legal counsel; and further acknowledges that it and any such counsel have had an adequate opportunity to make whatever investigation or inquiry they may deem necessary or desirable in connection with any of the subjects of this Agreement prior to the execution hereof.

31.   Severability. In the event any part or parts of this Agreement are found to be invalid, illegal, or unenforceable in any respect, the remaining provisions shall nevertheless be binding with the same effect as if the invalid, illegal, or unenforceable part or parts were originally deleted.

32.   Successors and Assigns. This Agreement shall be binding upon and inure to the benefit of The Parties to this Agreement and their respective successors, sublicensees, assignees and agents.

33.   Time of the Essence. Time is of the essence in this Agreement.

34.   Transferability. This is a personal service agreement with respect to Company, and Company may not assign any of its rights and privileged to any party unless Patent Holder has given approval to the assignment. Patent Holder may freely assign, license or otherwise transfer his rights and privileges herein without the consent or approval of Company, subject to the requirement that all the terms and conditions of this Agreement shall be binding upon the respective successors and assigns of Patent Holder, and shall insure to the benefit of and be enforceable by Company.

IN WITNESS WHEREOF, the parties hereto have executed this Agreement on the day and year first above written in multiple counterparts, each of which shall be considered an original.

_____   _____

Date   Patent Holder

                              By: _____

_____   _____

Date   Company

                              By: _____

Appendix G - Invention Disclosure Form

Date:	F&A Contact:	Client/Matter No:
Client Name:	Client Contact:	Client Business Unit:
Title of the Invention:		
Briefly describe the invention (include any drawings/schematics or other docs when possible):		
What is the problem the invention is trying to solve?		
How does the invention solve the problem?		
What is the closest prior art that you know of?		
How does the invention differ from the prior art and what are the advantages of your invention?		

Has the invention been disclosed outside of the company? Yes ☐ No ☐	Is the invention related to an earlier filed application? Yes ☐ No ☐	Is any part of the invention funded by the U.S. government or other agency? Yes ☐ No ☐
If so, what is the earliest date of disclosure / publication / sale / offer for sale / use anywhere in the world:	If so, please list all related applications:	If so, please list government contract numbers:

U.S. Patent Type: Prov ☐ US ☐ PCT ☐ Design ☐
International Countries:
Whether subject to secrecy agreement, license agreement, joint development agreement? Yes ☐   No ☐

Inventor Information					
Date	Full Name	Address	Email	Citizenship	Signature

Appendix H - IP Portion Of Employment Agreement

In consideration of my employment by _____, or any of its successors, assigns, affiliates or subsidiary companies (each hereinafter referred to as the "Company"), and as a condition of my employment with the Company, I agree as follows:

I.   TRADE SECRETS AND CONFIDENTIAL INFORMATION.

A.   Confidentiality of Company Information. I agree to regard and preserve as confidential all information obtained by me relating or pertaining to the Company's business, business plans, projects, services, products, processes, past and potential customers, including, but not limited to, any contact information therefor, vendors, trade secrets, marketing strategies, confidential information (including business and financial information) or unpublished know-how, whether patented or unpatented, and to all of my activities for or on behalf of the Company, and not to publish or disclose any part of such information to others or use the same for my own purposes or the purposes of others, during the term of this employment or thereafter. Any information of the Company which is not readily available to the public shall be considered by me to be confidential information and therefore within the scope of this Agreement, unless the Company advises me otherwise in writing.

B.   Prevention of Unauthorized Release of Company Confidential Information.

I agree to advise the Company promptly of any knowledge I may have of any unauthorized release or use of any Company confidential information, and shall take reasonable measures to prevent unauthorized persons or entities from having access to, obtaining or being furnished with any Company confidential information.

C.   Termination of Employment. I agree that, upon termination of my employment with the Company (voluntary or otherwise), I will return to the Company all property belonging to the Company, and that all files, documents, records, notebooks, databases, lists, manuals, and tangible articles, whether originals or copies, containing or embodying confidential information, including information or data stored on computer drives, computer disks, compact disks ("CDs"), tape backups or other forms of information storage, then in my possession, or under my custody or control, whether prepared by me or others, will be left with the Company. I recognize that the unauthorized taking of any of the Company's trade secrets may be prosecuted as a crime under section 499(c) of the California Penal Code. I further recognize that unlawful misappropriation of the Company's trade secrets may also result in civil liability under California Civil Code Section 3426, et seq.

D.   Exit Interview. I agree that, upon termination of my employment with the Company (voluntary or otherwise), I will attend an exit interview and execute a completed Termination Certificate in a form substantially the same as that attached hereto in blank as Exhibit "A."

II.   INVENTIONS.

A.   Disclosure of Inventions. I acknowledge and agree that, among my other duties for the Company, I will be employed by the Company in a position which could provide the opportunity for conceiving and/ or reducing to practice inventions, improvements, developments, ideas or discoveries, whether patentable or unpatentable (collectively hereinafter referred to as "Inventions"). Accordingly, I agree to promptly disclose to the Company in confidence, in writing, all Inventions conceived or reduced to practice by me while in the Company's employ, either solely or jointly with others, and whether or not during regular working hours. I further agree to maintain adequate and current written records of such Inventions.

B.   Company Inventions. The assignment provisions in Paragraph C below shall apply only to "Company Inventions" as defined herein. Company inventions shall mean any invention that 1. relates, at the time of conception or reduction to practice of the Invention to (a) the Company's business, projects or products, or to the manufacture or utilization thereof, or (b) the actual or demonstrably anticipated research or development of the Company; or 2. results from any work performed directly or indirectly by me for the Company; or 3. results, at least in part, from my use of the Company's time, equipment, supplies, facilities or trade secret information;

PROVIDED, HOWEVER, THAT A COMPANY INVENTION SHALL NOT INCLUDE ANY INVENTION WHICH QUALIFIES FULLY UNDER THE PROVISIONS OF CALIFORNIA LABOR CODE SECTION 2870, INCLUDING ANY IDEA OR INVENTION WHICH IS DEVELOPED ENTIRELY ON MY OWN TIME WITHOUT USING THE COMPANY'S EQUIPMENT, SUPPLIES, FACILITIES OR TRADE SECRET INFORMATION, AND WHICH IS NOT RELATED TO THE COMPANY'S BUSINESS (ACTUAL OR DEMONSTRABLY ANTICIPATED), AND WHICH DOES NOT RESULT FROM WORK PERFORMED FOR THE COMPANY.

C.   Assignment of Company Inventions. I agree to assign, and hereby do assign, to the Company all my right, title and interest in and to all Company Inventions. Also, I hereby assign, and agree to assign, to the Company all Inventions conceived or reduced to practice by me within one year following my termination of employment with the Company (voluntary or otherwise), if the Invention is a result of Company information obtained by me during my employment with the Company.

D.   Execution of Necessary Documents. I agree that, upon request and without compensation therefor, but at no expense to me, and whether during the term of my employment or thereafter, I will do all lawful acts, including the execution of papers and lawful oaths and the giving of testimony, that in the opinion of the Company, its successors and assigns, may be necessary or desirable in obtaining, sustaining, reissuing, extending or enforcing United States and foreign Letters Patent, including Design Patents, on all of such Company Inventions, and for perfecting, affirming, maintaining or recording the Company's complete ownership and title thereto, and to otherwise cooperate in all proceedings and matters relating thereto.

E.   Exceptions. I have listed in writing and provided to the Company information sufficient to identify all unpatented, but potentially patentable, ideas and inventions conceived by me before this employment (and which have not been assigned to a former employer) and which are, therefore, excluded from the scope of this Agreement.

III.   COPYRIGHTS.

I agree that all right, title and interest in any and all copyrights, copyright registrations and copyrightable subject matter which occur as a result of my employment with the Company shall be the sole and exclusive property of the Company, and agree that such works comprise works made for hire. I hereby assign, and agree to assign, to the Company all right, title and interest in any and all copyrights (including all rights of reproduction), copyright registrations and copyrightable subject matter which occur as a result of my employment with the Company. I hereby irrevocably appoint the Company as my attorney-in-fact for the purpose of executing any and all documents and performing any and all other acts necessary to give effect and legality to the provisions of this Paragraph.

IV.   CONFLICTING OBLIGATIONS AND RIGHTS.

A.   Former Employment. I agree to inform the Company in writing of any obligations I may have to preserve the confidentiality of proprietary information or materials belonging to any former employer of mine or to any other party. I further agree that I will not make any illegal, proscribed or inappropriate use of any software, hardware, media, printed materials or other tangible materials of any kind from outside sources, including but not limited to my former employer(s).

B.   Existing Rights. I agree to immediately inform the Company in writing of any existing proprietary rights I may claim in any patents, copyrights, works, trade secrets, trademarks, or other inventions or ideas, whethcr patentable or unpatentable. I agree never to bring any claim against the Company based on any pre-existing right not so identified.

Appendix I - Sample Bilateral NDA

NON DISCLOSURE AGREEMENT

This agreement ("this Agreement") is by and between _____, and _____.

The purpose of this Agreement is to protect Confidential Information that may be disclosed between the Discloser and the Recipient (as defined below).

Definitions

1.   "Confidential Information" means all information provided, whether orally, visually, or in written form (irrespective of such information being labeled or identified as "confidential" or "secret"), relating to either party's business plans, financial information and software product(s). Without limiting the generality of the foregoing, "Confidential Information" shall include, whether or not designated or marked as confidential, all trade secrets or information held to be secret by the discloser, computer programs, source code, routines, data information, documentation, know-how, business and financial information, and technology relating to or forming any part of the computer systems or software of the parties hereof.

2.   "Discloser" means the company providing access to the Confidential Information.

3.   "Recipient" means the person or company that receives Confidential Information from the Discloser.

4.   Discloser and Recipient may be referred to herein individually as a Party and collectively as the Parties.

5.   "Effective Date" means the date this Agreement is executed by both parties.

Undertaking

6.   In consideration of the parties providing each other with Confidential Information with a view to entering into possible contractual relations, the parties undertake to keep confidential all Confidential Information and not without the Discloser's prior written consent to disclose the Confidential Information in whole or part to any other person save those of its employees involved in any discussions between the parties and who have a genuine need to know the Confidential Information.

7.   The Recipient shall not during the period of the Agreement (save in the proper exercise of its duties) nor at any time thereafter utilize for its own purposes or divulge, publish or reveal to any person any information whatsoever concerning the business organization, finances, dealings, transactions or affairs of the Discloser, and shall use its best endeavors to prevent the disclosure or publication of any such matters by others, and shall keep with complete secrecy all Confidential Information entrusted to it, and shall not use or attempt to use any such Confidential Information in any manner which may injure or cause loss either directly or indirectly to the Discloser or their businesses or may be likely to do so.

8.   Recipient shall not remove any copyright or proprietary rights notice attached to or included in any Confidential Information disclosed by the other party under this Agreement, and Recipient shall reproduce all such notices on any copies of Confidential Information received from the discloser. Recipient shall not

decompile, disassemble, reverse engineer or otherwise reduce any software code of the Discloser to a human readable form.

9.   Recipient agrees that the Confidential Information disclosed to it shall not be duplicated, copied, or reproduced except as authorized by the Discloser in writing, and that all copies of Confidential Information shall be returned to the Discloser, or destroyed upon request of the Discloser, or upon the termination or expiration of this Agreement. The Recipient undertakes to keep and maintain a full record of any copies of any products (in whatever form) provided to the Recipient and the names of those people to whom the products have been shown.

Purpose and Use

10.   Recipient shall use the Confidential Information solely for the purpose of:

11.   Evaluating or reviewing the Discloser's products to determine its interest in entering into a business relationship with the Discloser.

12.   The potential integration of the Recipient's products with the Discloser's products.

Recipient Responsibilities

13.   The Recipient agrees to take full responsibility for the actions of its employees with respect to the Confidential Information, whether or not such employee was acting within the scope of his or her employment. The Recipient agrees to indemnify the Discloser for any damages, costs or expenses (including court costs and reasonable legal fees) suffered by the Discloser as a result of any breach of this Agreement by the Recipient.

14.   The Recipient shall protect the disclosed Confidential Information by using the same degree of care, but no less than a reasonable degree of care, to prevent the unauthorized, use, dissemination or publication of the Confidential Information as the Recipient uses to protect its own Confidential Information of a like nature.

15.   The Recipient undertakes to make aware all relevant employees, agents and sub-contractors of the confidentiality of the Confidential Information and to take such steps as shall be necessary from time to time to ensure compliance by its employees, agents and sub-contractors of the Agreement.

Extent of Restriction

16.   This Agreement imposes no obligation upon the Recipient with respect to Confidential Information which was (i) in the Recipient's possession before receipt from the Discloser; (ii) is or becomes a matter of public knowledge through no fault of, or breach of the Agreement by, the Recipient; (iii) is rightfully received by the Recipient from a third party without a duty of confidentiality; (iv) is disclosed under operation of applicable law; (v) is disclosed by the Recipient with the Discloser's prior written approval, or c) is independently developed by Recipient where Recipient establishes that such development was accomplished without access to the Confidential Information of the Discloser;.

Non-Enticement

17.   The Recipient undertakes with the Discloser that during the currency of this Agreement and for a period of 12 months following it's termination or expiry it will not directly or by its agents or otherwise and whether for itself or for the benefit of any other person induce or endeavor to induce any officer or employee of the Discloser to leave his or her employment.

Intellectual Property Rights

18.   Neither party acquires any intellectual property rights under this Agreement except the limited right to use set out in section 9 above.

Services

19.   Neither party has an obligation under this Agreement to purchase or otherwise acquire services or item from the other party.

Obligations and Warranties

20.   Neither party has an obligation under this Agreement to commercially offer any products using or incorporating the Confidential Information. The Discloser makes no representation or warranty that any product or business plans disclosed to the Recipient will be marketed or carried out as disclosed, or at all. Any actions taken by the Recipient in response to the disclosure of the Confidential Information shall be solely at its own risk.

Consequential Damages

21.   The Recipient acknowledges and agrees that the information is provided on an as is basis. The Discloser makes no warranties, express or implied, with respect to the Confidential Information and hereby expressly disclaims any and all implied warranties of fitness for a particular purpose. In no event shall the Discloser be liable for any direct, indirect, special, or consequential damages in connection with or arising out of the performance or use of any portion of the Confidential Information.

Termination

22.   The Recipient further undertakes to return to the Discloser upon request all Confidential Information and any copies thereof. The Recipient will destroy or expunge such Confidential Information on any computer, word processor or other device in their possession, custody or control and destroy (or procure the destruction of) any document or data prepared by the parties which contains or is based on Confidential Information. The Recipient will upon request confirm in writing to the Discloser that such destruction and expunction have taken place.

Miscellaneous

23.   Media Releases. All media releases and public announcements or disclosures by either Party relating to this Agreement shall be coordinated with and approved by the other Party in writing prior to the release thereof.

24.   Corporate Authority. Each of the corporate Parties represents and warrants that:

25.   It is a corporation that is validly existing and in good standing under the laws of the jurisdiction in which it is organized;

26.   It has full corporate power to execute, deliver and perform its obligations under this Agreement.

27.   The person executing this Agreement on its behalf has its full authority to do so; and

28.   It shall indemnify, defend and hold the other Party harmless from and against any and all claims that may now or hereafter be made against any of them by virtue of any breach of the provisions of this paragraph.

29.   Transferability. This Agreement and the rights and privileges hereof are assignable, licensable or otherwise transferable by either Party without the written consent and approval of the other Party, subject to the requirement that all the terms and conditions of this Agreement shall be binding upon the respective successors and assigns of the Parties hereto and shall insure to the benefit of and be enforceable by the Parties hereto and their respective successors and assigns.

30.   Headings. The headings in this Agreement are solely for convenience of reference and shall not be given any effect in the construction or interpretation of this Agreement.

31.   Gender. Where appropriate, the singular number set forth in this Agreement shall be interpreted as the

plural number, and the gender shall be interpreted as masculine, feminine or neuter, as the context dictates.

32.   *Force Majeure.* Neither Party to the Agreement shall be responsible for any losses resulting if the fulfillment of any terms or provisions is delayed or prevented by virtue of civil disorders, wars, acts of enemies, strikes, floods, acts of God, or by any other cause which is beyond the control of the Party whose performance is hindered, and which that Party could not have prevented through the exercise of reasonable diligence.

33.   Relationship Of Parties. This Agreement does not constitute or create a joint venture, partnership, agency relationship, or formal business organization of any kind, and the rights and obligations of the Parties shall be those of independent contractors only.

34.   Notices. All notices required hereunder shall be given in writing and shall be personally delivered or sent by postage prepaid mail, addressed to the Parties at their addresses listed below, or at such other addresses as the respective Parties may designate from time to time to the other by written notice. Notice is reputably presumed to have been received five days after the mailing date.

35.   Choice of Law. This Agreement shall be governed by, construed, interpreted and enforced under and according to the laws of the State of _____.

36.   Dispute Resolution. The Parties expressly agree to the jurisdiction of the Superior Court of the State of California and to the jurisdiction of the _____ Court of _____, with venue in Orange County, California, for the resolution of any dispute concerning the enforcement, breach, interpretation or validity of this Agreement.

--- OR ---

All claims, disputes and other matters in question arising out of, or relating to, this Agreement or the performance hereof shall be submitted to, and determined by, arbitration if good faith negotiations among the Parties hereto, if any, does not resolve such claim, dispute or other matter. Such arbitration shall proceed in accordance with the then-current International Dispute Resolution Procedures or the Small Claim Rules for arbitration established by the American Arbitration Association ("AAA"), unless the Parties hereto mutually agree otherwise, and pursuant to the following procedures:

37.   The tribunal will consist of [one / three] arbitrator(s).

38.   The language to be used in the arbitral proceedings will be English. Reasonable discovery shall be allowed in arbitration.

39.   All proceedings before the arbitrators shall be held in _____, California, under the laws of California;

40.   The arbitrator(s) may in their discretion provide injunctive relief;

41.   The award rendered by the arbitrator(s) shall be final and binding, except that either Party can appeal the ruling of the arbitrator(s) to the AAA appeals panel. Judgment may be entered in accordance with applicable Law and in any court having jurisdiction thereof;

42.   The award rendered by the arbitrator(s) shall include (i) a provision that the prevailing party in such arbitration recover its costs relating to the arbitration and reasonable attorneys' fees from the other party, (ii) the amount of such costs and fees, and (iii) an order that the losing party pay the fees and expenses of the arbitrator(s), wherein --------- is deemed to be the prevailing party in the event that he is awarded any recovery; and

-- OR --

(i) a provision that each Party in such arbitration cover its own costs relating to the arbitration and its own attorneys' fees, and (ii) an order that each Party pay an equal share of the fees and expenses of the arbitrator(s); and

43.   The arbitrator(s) may by the agreement of the Parties expressly be prohibited from awarding punitive damages in connection with any claim being resolved.

44.   Severability. In the event any part or parts of this Agreement are found to be invalid, illegal, or unenforceable in any respect, the remaining provisions shall nevertheless be binding with the same effect as if the invalid, illegal, or unenforceable part or parts were originally deleted.

45.   Successors and Assigns. This Agreement shall be binding upon and inure to the benefit of the Parties to this Agreement and their respective successors, sublicensees, assignees and agents.

46.   Hold Harmless. Each of the Parties hereto shall indemnify and hold the other party, its directors, officers, members, employees, successors, sublicensees, assignees and agents harmless from and against any and all claims arising from acts and omissions of the acting or omitting party, its directors, officers, members, employees, successors, sublicensees, assignees and agents.

47.   Costs and Fees. In the event that any legal proceedings arise as a result of this Agreement, the prevailing party is entitled to receive attorney fees.

48.   Time of the Essence. Time is of the essence in this Agreement.

49.   Failure to Enforce. Failure of any Party herein to enforce any of the terms of this Agreement shall not constitute waiver to enforce that term in the future.

50.   Expected Performance. Each Party herein agrees to use best efforts, including performing all acts and executing and delivering all documents, as may be necessary or appropriate to carry out the intent and purposes of this Agreement. Each of the Parties agrees that the other Party may not have an adequate remedy at law for money damages in the event that this Agreement has not been performed in accordance with its terms, and therefore agrees that such other Party shall be entitled to specific enforcement of the terms hereof in addition to any other remedy to which it may be entitled, at law or in equity.

51.   Entire Agreement. This Agreement embodies the entire understanding of the Parties and supersedes and replaces any and all pre-existing agreements or understandings between them. No amendment or modification of this Agreement shall be valid or binding upon each of the Parties unless made in writing and signed on behalf of each of them, or by their respective duly authorized representative.

52.   No Construction. No Party hereto nor any attorney for any Party shall be deemed the drafter of this Agreement for the purpose of interpreting or construing any of the provisions hereof. In resolving any dispute or construing any provision in the Agreement, there shall be no presumption made or inference drawn (i) because the attorneys for one of the parties drafted the Agreement, (ii) because of the drafting history of the Agreement, or (iii) because of the inclusion of a provision not contained in a prior draft of the deletion of a provision contained in the prior draft.

53.   Representation by Counsel. Each of the Parties hereto acknowledges that it has had the opportunity to be represented by independent legal counsel of its own choice throughout all of the negotiations that preceded the execution of this Agreement and that each has executed this Agreement with the consent and on the advice of any such independent legal counsel; and further acknowledges that it and any such counsel have had an adequate opportunity to make whatever investigation or inquiry they may deem necessary or desirable in connection with any of the subjects of this Agreement prior to the execution hereof.

54.   Counterparts And Facsimiles. This Agreement may be executed in any number of counterparts, in-

cluding facsimile counterparts, all of which, taken together, shall constitute one and the same agreement, and any Party to this Agreement may enter into this Agreement by executing a counterpart. This Agreement shall become binding and enforceable between and among each signatory Party as of the date of execution by that Party without regard to the number of other parties that may elect to become Parties hereto. Signature by a Party's attorney shall be a representation by that attorney that they are authorized to enter into this Agreement on behalf of their client(s).

So agreed and executed this ___th day of _____, 2011.

_____   _____

Date   By: -------

_____   _____

Date

                                 By: -------

Glossary

Abandoned Application	An application that is no longer pending. Applications can go abandoned because the applicant expressly abandons them, or because the applicant failed to respond to a final rejection. A parent application of often, but not always, abandoned when a child application is filed.
Active Patent	A patent that is still in force; i.e., it has not lapsed or gone abandoned.
Allowable Claims	A claim that is deemed allowable by the patent office. Each claim of a patent application can be allowed or rejected independently of all other claims.
Angel Investor	An affluent individual who provides capital for a business start-up, usually in exchange for convertible debt or ownership equity.
Apparatus Claim	A claim to a physical thing, such as a machine or a chemical composition. This contrasts with method claims, which are drawn to steps in a process.
Application	A filing for a patent. A utility application can have a status of pending or abandoned. A formal patent application has a specification, usually at least one claim, and usually at least one page of drawing. The specification usually has a title and the following sections: field of the art, background, short description of the drawing, detailed description, and examples. A provisional application can be very short, having perhaps only a few paragraphs and a drawing.
Application Filing	The date on which an application is filed. Filed applications are pending.
Assignee	A person, company or other entity to which title (i.e., ownership) in a patent application or a patent has been transferred.
Best Mode	The best way that an inventor knows how to practice his invention.
Boutique Law Firm	A small (usually then than 20 attorneys) law firm that specializes in a particular area of law.
Child Application	An application that claims priority to one or more parent applications.

CIP Application	A child application that contains additional disclosure relative to the parent. CIP applications have multiple priority dates, one to the filing date of the parent with respect to subject matter disclosed in the parent, and another to the filing date of the CIP with respect to the additional disclosure (termed "new matter").
Claim Drafting	The writing of patent claims, especially with an eye to broadly protecting a patentable invention.
Claims	Numbered sentences following the patent specification, which define the scope of the claimed invention(s). Each claim covers a slightly different but overlapping scope.
Co-Inventor	An inventor that shares inventorship with another person. Intentional failure to list a co-inventor on a patent application may render any ensuing patent unenforceable.
Commercialize	Placing something into the stream of commerce. Patent and patent applications can be commercialized in many different ways, including selling the patent or application, licensing the underlying technology, or selling products or services that utilize the technology.
Commercially Viable Solution	An embodiment of an invention that is commercially significant. There are almost always many embodiments that are technically feasible, but commercially unimportant. One of the goals of patent drafting is to secure for the applicant patent rights to as many of the commercially viable embodiments as possible.
Continuation Application	The term is strictly construed to mean a child application that supersedes the parent application. The USPTO used to refer to these continuations as FWC (file wrapper continuations) and used to issue a new serial number. The office then changed the name to RCE (Request for Continuing Application) and continued prosecution without changing the serial number. The latest incarnation is called a CPA (Continuing Patent Application), which also uses the same serial number as the parent, but now there is no pretense that the continuing application is anything other than a reincarnation of the parent. The term "continuing application" somewhat confusingly includes continuations, divisionals, and continuations-in-part.
Daughter Application	A spin-off from an existing application. Possible daughter applications are divisionals, continuations, and continuations-in-part.

Dependent Claims	A claim that is dependent on at least one other claim. The limitations of a dependent claim are those contained within the dependent claim, as well as all limitations contained within any claims upon which the dependent claim is directly or indirectly dependent. Thus, if claim 3 is dependent on claim 2, and claim 2 is dependent on claim 1, then claim 3 contains all the limitations of claims 1, 2, and 3.
Disclosure	This term usually refers to information that an inventor provides to a patent attorney or agent to assist in writing a patent application. The term can also refer to information in a patent or other document that is used as prior art against a later filed patent application.
Divisional Application	A child application having the same specification as, and claiming priority to, a parent application. A divisional is usually employed to prosecute claims that were withdrawn or canceled from the parent.
Drafting Charges	Amount charged for writing the text of a patent application. The term is also sometimes used to mean costs associated with preparation of the drawing.
Drawing	The figures of a patent. Technically there is only one drawing, even though the drawing may extend over several pages.
Elements	Words or phrases of a patent claim that refer to a portion of the subject matter being claimed. Thus, in a claim to a chair, the elements may be the legs, seat, arms, back, coverings, connectors, and so forth.
Embodiment	Implementation of an idea. Embodiments can be actual (in which case the technology is used in the physical world), or constructive (in which case the law deems an embodiment to have been made by virtue of one having filed a patent application with an adequately detailed disclosure).
Enforceability	The ability to prevail against an infringer in a court of law on a claim of patent infringement.
Examiner	The person at the patent office who reviews the prior art, and makes determinations as to patentability. Examiners are not concerned with enforceability.
Expired Patent	A patent that is past the end of its life span. In the United States, patents issuing from applications filed after June 7, 1995, have a life span extending for 20 years from their earliest claimed priority date, plus whatever extensions may apply.

Family	A group of at least two patents and/or patent applications that are linked by virtue of priority claims to one another. A patent family often has three or more "generations".
Filing Costs	Filings fees plus charges for completion and submission of the various papers that accompany a patent application.
Filing Date	The date that a patent application is considered to have been received by the patent office. The filing date is the same as the priority date if there is no priority claim
Filing Fee	The fee charged by the patent office to accept a patent application for processing.
Foreign Application	An application that is filed outside of the country having original filing. Thus, if a patent is originally filed in the United States and later in Japan, the Japanese application is a foreign application.
Formal Application	An application other than a provisional application. This usually means a utility or PCT application. Formal applications must have at least one claim, whereas a provisional application need not have any claims.
Grandchild Application	An application that claims priority to both a parent application, and a parent of the parent.
Green Fields Patenting^{SM}	A patenting strategy that focus not on what the inventor thinks he invented, but on what the inventor (or assignee) wants to stop others from doing. Used synonymously with Blue Sky Patenting ^{SM}.
"In Force" Patent	A patent that has not been invalidated, by expiration (reached the end of its life span), by lapsing (failure to pay a maintenance fee), or invalidated by a court or the patent office.
Improvement	An embodiment of an invention that was not disclosed in a prior application.
Independent Claims	A claim that is not dependent on any other claim. All of the limitations of the claim are therefore contained within the independent claim.
Informal Application	A provisional application. Such applications are informal in that, among other things, they do not need to include any patent claims.
Invalidated Patent	A patent that can no longer be used as a basis for bringing a patent infringement action. In many cases some, but not all, claims in a patent are invalidated.

Invention	An idea that is new, useful, and non-obvious over the prior art. Years ago the patent office required a working model or other evidence that the idea was actually reduced to practice before a patent would issue. Currently, mere ideas can be patented as long as the patent application can describe to one of ordinary skill in the art (the technology field) how to make and use the claimed invention.
Invention-Centered Approach	A strategy that focuses on claiming an invention by its technical merits, rather than a market-centered approach.
Inventor	A person who conceived or helped conceive of an invention. A patent application can name multiple inventors. The head of a department, or other person who might well be listed on a journal article, is only an inventor for patent purposes if he/she actually contributed to the conception of the invention. Similarly, a person who helped build a prototype is not necessarily an inventor, despite the fact that he/she may have contributed far more physical effort and time than an inventor. Inventors can be listed on a patent application in any order.
IP	Intellectual Property, which is generally considered to include patent, trademark, copyright, and trade secret rights.
Issuance Of A Rejection	During the course of a patent prosecution, the patent office sends out official notices regarding claims that are being argued. Sometimes the claims are allowed, and sometime they are rejected. It is very common to get rejections, and simply means that more work needs to be done to either amend the claims, or convince the patent office that the claims are allowable.
Lapsed Patent Application	A patent application that has gone abandoned for failure to timely pay respond to take a required action, such as respond to an office action or pay a fee.
Lapsed Patent	A patent that has gone abandoned for failure to timely pay issue fees.
Large Entity	In the United States, an assignee that has at least 500 employees. Many countries do not distinguish between large and small entities.

License   A license is a contract or other legal arrangement that gives a
                                 licensee (a person, company, government or other entity) a right
                                 to do something. In the case of patents, a license provides a right
                                 under a particular patent or set of patents. A license under one patent
                                 does not necessarily mean that the licensee can legally practice the
                                 claimed invention. The reason is that the licensee might also be
                                 infringing a claim of a different patent.

Limitations   Patent claims are typically parsed into phrases covering the different
                                 recited elements. If a claim recites "a computer having a power
                                 circuit, a processor, and a memory", that portion of the claim has
                                 three limitations on the computer, namely that it has (1) a power
                                 circuit, (2) a processor, and (3) a memory".

Market-Centered   A patenting strategy that focuses on claiming the commercially
Approach   viable embodiments that preclude competition, rather than on the
                                 technical merits of the invention. Compare with invention-centered
                                 approach.

Means-Plus-   A claim that includes at least one element that is defined by its
Function Claims   function rather than a physical limitation (e.g., "means for opening
                                 a door" rather than "a door knob"). Means-plus-function claims do
                                 not necessarily have to include the term "means for".

Method Claims   A claim drawn to steps in a process rather than a physical thing *per
                                 se*. Method claims usually begin each phrase with a word ending in
                                 "ing", such as "enclosing", or "providing" or "connecting".

Method Of Use   A type of method claim in which the applicant focuses on the manner
Claim   in which some¬thing (often a pharmaceutical or machine) is used.

Monopoly   A monopoly is a situation where one entity controls the rights to
                                 do something. For example, if a pharmaceutical company has a
                                 monopoly on selling a drug, then that company is the only one that
                                 can sell the drug. There are laws against monopolies in the United
                                 States, but patents are an exception to those laws.

Multiple   A claim that is alternatively dependent upon more than one claim.
Dependent Claims   A typical format would be "A device according to any of claims 1,
                                 3, 4, or 7, in which ...."

Office Action   A formal communication from the patent office. Some office actions
                                 are favorable, some are unfavorable (rejections and objections), and
                                 some are informational only.

One Year Deadline	There are two one-year deadlines. A PCT application can only claim priority to an earlier filed application if the PCT application is filed within one year of the earlier filed application. Also, a provisional application will go abandoned unless a formal application is filed within one year of the provisional's filing date, and claims priority to the provisional.
Owned Patents	Patents are initially owned by the inventor(s). The ownership rights, however, are usually assigned to a company, university or government agency for commercialization purposes. Patent rights can be split in many ways, according to market, geography, time span, or in myriad other ways.
Parent Claim	Patents and patent applications have both independent and dependent claims. Independent claims stand alone, while dependent claims include all the limitations of a parent claim from which they depend. Thus, if claim 2 recites "The device of claim 1, wherein ...", then claim 2 is dependent on claim 1 and includes all of the limitations of claim 1. In that instance claim 1 is the parent of claim 2.
Parent Application	An application which a daughter application is spun off.
Patent	A patent is basically a right to sue others for making, using, selling, importing or exporting something that falls within the scope of claimed subject matter. In the most basic sense, a patent is a deal struck with the government. An inventor discloses the details an invention, and the government grants a limited monopoly to that invention.
Patent Agent	A person who has passed the patent bar with the U.S. patent office, but has not passed the attorney bar of any state or District of Columbia, and very likely did not go to law school. Patent agents have all the same rights and responsibilities as patent attorneys with respect to dealings with the patent office.
Patent Application	An application for a patent. Patent applications are "pending" until they are either abandoned, or they mature into a patent.
Patent Attorney	A person who has passed the patent bar, as well as the attorney bar of one of the states or District of Columbia.
Patent Drafter	The person or persons who draft the patent application. Even though the inventor may assist in the process, the task of correctly drafting a patent application ultimately falls to the responsible patent attorney or agent.

Patent Mill	An office that files a large number of patent applications, with an emphasis on quantity rather than quality. Patent mills can make millions of dollars per year, while providing almost universally bad results for their unsuspecting victims.
Patentability Search	A search undertaken to determine whether, or how broadly, an idea can be patented. Documents relevant to patentability are called "references". Patentability searches should usually be undertaken by inventors and their patent attorneys or agents before patent applications are even drafted, and in any event patentability searches are always undertaken by the patent office in determining patentability. Patentability searches are entirely different from right-to-practice searches.
Patentable Idea	An idea that is new, useful and non-obvious over the prior art (i.e., over what is already known), and that is sufficiently definite in the mind of the inventor(s) that it can be enabled (i., described in an adequate level of detail) in a patent application. Years ago the patent office required a working model or other evidence that the idea was actually reduced to practice before a patent would issue. Currently, however, mere ideas can be patented.
Patentable Invention	Same thing as patentable idea.
Patent Office	The national or regional authority charged with receiving and processing patent applications. In the United States the patent office is the USPTO.
Patent Prosecution	The back and forth arguing between the patent applicant (or practitioner) and the patent office prior to an application being issued or abandoned. Unless an application is speeded up in some way, patent prosecution can often take three or more years. Current statistics can be found at http://www.uspto.gov/ dashboards/ patents/ main.dashxml.
Patent Rights	A U.S. patent provides the owner with the right to stop others from making, using, selling, importing and exporting with respect to the claimed area of technology. Interestingly, having a patent does not necessarily mean that the owner can practice the technology. It simply means that the owner has a right to sue others for doing so.

PCT	Patent Cooperation Treaty; an international treaty signed by the United States, and administered by WIPO. The PCT receiving office for the United States is the United States Patent and Trademark Office (USPTO). Patent applications are examined through the PCT procedures, but the PCT never issues any patents.
Petition To Make Special	A formal petition before the USPTO to speed up processing of a patent application based upon satisfaction of particular requirements.
POSITA Or PHOSITA	A Person of Ordinary Skill In The Art. Generally speaking, this is a hypothetical person who knows everything that is known in the field of an invention, anywhere in the world, at any time prior to the filing or other priority date of an application, and who has only an ordinary level of creativity. Ideas that would have been obvious to such a hypothetical person should be rejected by the patent office on the grounds of obviousness.
Preferred Embodiment	A preferred implementation of the subject matter of a patent or patent application. Patent applicants in the United States are required to satisfy the "best mode" requirement, which means that they must describe whatever implementation of the claimed invention(s) that they consider to be "best" at the time that the application is filed.
Primary Application	The oldest formal application in a family of patent applications. Subsequent (secondary) applications in the family usually focus on various subsets of the disclosure of the primary application.
Prior Art	Knowledge that is sufficiently close to the claimed subject matter that it is considered to be relevant to patentability. Prior art can be US or foreign patents, newspaper, journal or other publicly accessible documents, web pages, advertisements, and so forth. Prior art is defined by statute (35 U.S.C. § 102) for purposes of determining anticipation, but is slightly different for purposes of determining obviousness.
Priority; Priority Date	A legal fiction by which something is treated as if it had occurred earlier in time. The claims of a divisional patent application, for example, have a filing date of the divisional application, but for purposes of determining patentability are treated as if that filing date were the filing date of the parent application.
Prototype	A sample or model built to test a concept or process. A working prototype of an invention is not needed to file a patent application on the inventive concepts underlying the invention.

Provisional Application	An informal patent application. Provisional applications are never examined. Unless they are used as a parent in a formal application, they are microfilmed and placed into storage at the on-year anniversary. In the latter case the provisional is then considered to be "dead" (expired).
RCE	See Request For Continued Examination.
Reductionistic Thinking	A process of reducing a complex idea, system, etc., to simpler parts or components that contain the essence of the idea or system.
Rejected Claims	Claims that the examiner considers to be unpatentable over the prior art, either because the claims are anticipated, obvious, and/or for some other reason. Claims that are merely objected to, rather than rejected, contain a technical defect that can usually be overcome relatively easily.
Request For Continued Examination	During patent prosecution, the patent office typically issues a non-final office action, and then a final office action. To get another two bites at the apple, an inventor, attorney or agent can simply file a Request For Continued Examination, and pay additional fees.
Restriction Requirement	A statement by the patent office that the pending claims are deemed to address more than one invention. Restriction requirements are very commonly issued where an applicant has some claims directed to a method and some claims directed to an apparatus.
Retained Patents	Patents are usually assigned to a company, university or government for commercialization. An inventor can, of course, keep ownership of a patent, and try to commercialize it himself. Such patents are "retained" by the inventor.
Right-To-Practice Search	A search undertaken to determine whether practice of a given technology will likely infringe the patent rights of another.
Royalty	Money or other value, usually paid to a patent holder in exchange for a license to a patent. Royalties are typically paid monthly or quarterly, and can be fixed fee, scheduled fee, or dependent on sales or other conditions.
Scope Of Equivalents	A patent claim covers both that which is literally encompassed by the language of the claim, and also that which is equivalent. The idea behind the doctrine of equivalents is that an infringer should not be able to circumvent a patent claim by making an insubstantial modification.

Small Entity	In the United States, an assignee that has less than 500 employees. Many countries do not distinguish between large and small entities with respect to fees.
Tautological Claiming	A claiming strategy in which an independent claim recites a broad subject matter, and dependent claims recite successively narrower subsets of that subject matter.
USPTO	United States Patent and Trademark Office
Utility Application	A patent application that claims a useful invention. Contrasts with a design application, which claims the ornamental appearance of something.
Venn Diagram	A diagram that uses circles and ovals to represent applications of set theory.
White Space	The conceptual space around an idea, which is not already known by others.
White Space Patenting	A patenting strategy that seeks to claim all the commercially viable white space around an inventor's idea.
WIPO	World International Property Organization.

Index

About The Author

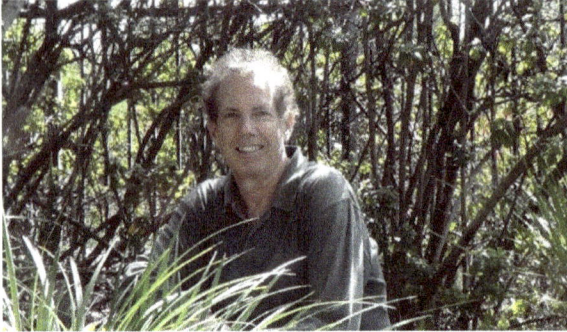

Robert D. Fish, Esq. has been a patent attorney for more than 30 years, practicing White Space and Green Fields Patenting℠. He is currently head of Fish IP Law, LLP, in Orange County California.

Mr. Fish and his team at Fish IP have secured over 15,000 patents, and over 6000 trademark registrations. Together they have attracted a world-class clientele in a diverse array of technologies, including pharmaceuticals, stem cell and other non-pharmaceutical treatment modalities, medical devices, chemical extractions and assaying technologies, human-machine interfaces, augmented reality software and devices, business methods, cryptography, plasmas and other high energy technologies, and oil and gas processing.

Fish IP has worked with over 150 law firms in foreign countries, with several firms in China, S. Korea, UK, EP, and Australia / New Zealand relying on Fish IP for their US prosecution.

Mr. Fish has been involved in several patent enforcement programs, which include in-bound and out-bound licensing, arbitration, and litigation. Mr. Fish has litigated in several state and federal courts, including California, Pennsylvania, Massachusetts, Nevada, and Delaware) and has overseen cases in several European countries

Other Titles in the Series

Cost-Effective Patenting (2002)

Strategic Patenting (2007)
  Building Strong Patent Portfolios

White Space Patenting (2011)
  Patenting Ideas, Not Just Inventions

Patent Magic (2011)
  Prosecution Strategies and Practice Tips

Internet Websites

www.FishIPLaw.com

www.PatentBeast.com

www.ingramcontent.com/pod-product-compliance
Lightning Source LLC
Chambersburg PA
CBHW081502200326
41518CB00015B/2354